MAGICAL PROGENY, MODERN TECHNOLOGY

MAGICAL PROGENY, MODERN TECHNOLOGY

A Hindu Bioethics of Assisted Reproductive Technology

Swasti Bhattacharyya

STATE UNIVERSITY OF NEW YORK PRESS

Published by
STATE UNIVERSITY OF NEW YORK PRESS,
ALBANY

Printed in the United States of America

For information, address
State University of New York Press
194 Washington Avenue, Suite 305, Albany, NY 12210-2384

Production, Laurie Searl
Marketing, Michael Campochiaro

Library of Congress Cataloging-in-Publication Data

Bhattacharyya, Swasti, 1963–
Magical progeny, modern technology : a Hindu bioethics of assisted reproductive technology / Swasti Bhattacharyya.
p. cm.
Includes bibliographical references and index.
ISBN 0-7914-6791-0 (hardcover : alk. paper) -- ISBN 0-7914-6792-9 (pbk. : alk. paper)
1. Bioethics--Religious aspects--Hinduism. 2. Hinduism--Doctrines. 3. Reproductive technology--Moral and ethical aspects. I. Title.
[DNLM: 1. Reproductive techniques--ethics. 2. Religion and Medicine. 3. Hinduism. 4. Bioethical Issues. WQ 208 B575m 2005]
BL1215.B55B43 2006
174′.957--dc22

2005020544

ISBN-13: 978-0-7914-6791-6 (hardcover : alk. paper)
ISBN-13: 978-0-7914-6792-3 (pbk. : alk. paper)

10 9 8 7 6 5 4 3 2 1

For Nancey

Thank you!

Contents

Acknowledgments

Ideas for this book began in a discussion over coffee, developed into a dissertation, and now fill the pages that follow. This project would not have proceeded without the critique, support, and encouragement of a great number of people—to all of them I am most thankful. Professors William May, Christopher Key Chapple, John Crossley, and Elize Sanasarian shepherded me through the dissertation process; their questions and comments were most helpful. Chris, your belief in me and my various projects empowers me to move forward. Chris and Maureen, thank you for your ever continuing mentoring and friendship. I would like to thank my current colleagues and students at Buena Vista University, specifically Dean Jeanne Tinsley and Dr. Jacqueline Johnson VPAA/ Dean of faculty. Their support made it possible to write *during* the academic year! Thanks also to Amy Foster, Adam Strater and Jessica Peiffer for their assistance.

A much earlier version of the material in chapter two was presented at the International Conference on the *Mahābhārata* and was published in *The Mahābhārata: What is Not Here is Nowhere.* This book was edited by T. S. Rukmani and published by Munshiram Manoharlal in 2005. Additionally, earlier condensed versions of some of the ideas presented here appeared in a volume edited by Timothy Shanahan and Robin Wang, *Reason and Insight: Western and Eastern Perspectives on the Pursuit of Moral Wisdom,* published by Wadsworth in 2002. While Dr. Wang's invitation to contribute to this volume got me writing, my participation in the International Conference on the *Mahābhārata* at Concordia University provided me with the opportunity to share and further develop my ideas with South Asian specialists. I thank Dr. Wang and all those involved for their helpful feedback. I appreciate the ease that I experienced working with editor Nancy Ellegate of the State University of New York Press. Thank you.

Writing, much to the dismay of a number of students, is indeed a laborious process. I have been blessed with a friend who once told me I did not know how to write and then proceeded to spend the next twelve years teaching me:

Glenn Hartelius, thank you. My parents laid the foundations from which this work springs; thank you for encouraging me through your questions and for supporting me every step of the way. My friends are irreplaceable; thank you for walking with me!

Finally, I am grateful to the first professor I ever had, Dr. Nancey C. Murphy, who not only listened to but also heard my questions. She opened a door in my mind and instilled in me the confidence to not only walk through, but to fly. Since then, I have always said my first book was going to be dedicated to her—and so it is.

Introduction

People throughout history have struggled with the challenges of infertility and with the issues that naturally arise when considering the implementation of means to circumvent it. New and sophisticated techniques designed to overcome human infertility are at the cutting edge of modern medical science, bringing with them a host of controversial bioethical issues. North American debates concerning such issues have, until quite recently, been primarily shaped by concepts and values that are grounded in traditional Jewish and Christian perspectives. More recently, however, other voices have begun to be heard. Cultural, religious, and philosophical pluralism is no longer an abstract, academic notion, but is rather being increasingly recognized as a social and political reality.

The diversity of alternative worldviews presents distinct challenges for the field of bioethics. While the general principle of inclusiveness may be regarded as a noble ideal, attempts to consider variant religious traditions within the scope of specific bioethical dialogues often lead to one of two ultimately unsatisfactory outcomes. Some conclude that religious traditions are so dissimilar that there exists no common ground on which to base a discussion. Others present these diverse traditions in such simplistic terms that a rather superficial unity is espoused—a unity which subsequently collapses under closer scrutiny.

The aim of this work is to steer a middle path between these two extremes. While acknowledging that there are differences within and between "Asian" and "Western" perspectives that cannot and should not be superficially glossed over or explained away, it is my firm conviction that cross-cultural dialogues concerning bioethical issues can and should be mounted. Differences in axiomatic assumptions and distinctive modes of discourse can certainly present dialogical challenges and difficulties. However, this very contrast has the potential to bring many of the core issues involved into clear focus and to provide a basis for developing more creative and innovative solutions to complex bioethical issues. Armed with this conviction, we examine how key elements of Hindu thought can contribute to contemporary society's viewing, reframing, and dealing with the complex issues relating to infertility and assisted reproductive technology.

The purpose of this book is both to inform and to enrich the ongoing bioethical dialogue concerning assisted reproductive technology and to increase the cultural/religious awareness and sensitivity of the healthcare delivery team. Pursuant to this goal, an example of an applied Hindu bioethics will emerge from this discussion and application of Hindu thought. The significance of this study is practical. Whether living in Los Angeles, Atlanta, or Ames, one need not travel the world to encounter global perspectives; they exist and thrive within nearly every North American geographical setting. People ascribing to Hindu ideology are not simply an "exotic other;" they are individuals and families that live and work under the same roof, next door, down the street, and across town.

As modern society increases its familiarity with different worldviews, there are significant challenges as well as benefits.[1] Individuals exposed to different cultural and religious beliefs and practices have the opportunity to broaden their own perspectives, thus enriching their stock of conceptual and axiological resources from which to draw when making difficult decisions for themselves. Also, having examined and engaged a number of worldviews, these individuals may become better equipped to assist, understand, and interact with family members, neighbors, colleagues, patients, healthcare professionals, and fellow citizens when dealing with complex bioethical issues.

By its very nature the field of bioethics[2] is interdisciplinary, drawing inquires from any number of disciplines: anthropology, law, medicine, philosophy, religion, and sociology, to name several. There are a variety of approaches and methods utilized by those engaged in bioethical discussions. As Shannon says, "Bioethics is teaching us the necessity of genuine interdisciplinary thinking and working [. . .]. Reality—which is interdisciplinary—has taught us to be interdisciplinary in our thinking."[3] Theologians, lawyers, historians, and medical professionals all share a common interest in the normative, meta-ethical, and descriptive questions posed by various aspects of healthcare, and each discipline utilizes different methods in examining bioethics and approaches the field from different perspectives.

In keeping with the nature of the field of bioethics and the traditions within Hinduism, the methodology we employ in this inquiry is necessarily interdisciplinary and "organic." It is interdisciplinary in that it draws together elements from the diverse fields of South Asian studies, literature, religion, bioethics, nursing and some insights offered by a few contemporary voices from a Hindu community in Southern California. Owing to its inherent internal complexities, several different ethical models are utilized in the construction of a Hindu ethic. The very mercurial nature of Hinduism demands the utilization of narrative ethics in order to be able to locate the discussion and to actually say anything of substance. The multivalent nature of these traditions use Beauchamp and Childress' principlism alongside a casuistic approach to applied ethics. From these varied, select strands of ways to do ethics, we weave a tapestry of a Hindu ethic that, while not being exhaustive, incorporates many of the relevant ethical elements drawn from Hindu philosophy, religion, culture, history, and experience.

In addition to its interdisciplinary scope, the methodology we employ in this work may also be regarded as organic in character. Rather than construct a "Hindu ethic" out of abstract principles, in isolation or without context, we weave an ethic from strands of Hindu philosophy, religion, and culture, preserved within the narratives of the *Mahābhārata,* a formative Hindu epic. A pervasive feature of Hinduism, and many other traditions, is its oral mode of transmission. This orality[4] implies a reliance on myths and narrative, and these forms of communication favor open-ended modes of conceptualization. In these traditions, narratives are not utilized to find "*the* answer," or to eliminate options. Rather, myths are used because of their very pliability, their tendency to invite alternative options and applications. Furthermore, Hindu sacred teachings tend to work well in and through an oral textual mode. Do not we all enjoy learning from a good story?

By utilizing this ancient epic as a source for ethics and exploring how it deals with issues relating to the challenges of having children, we obtain a unique and relevant entry point into the central sacred teachings of the Hindu traditions. By cultivating a dynamic conversation among many voices, we both demonstrate and emphasize some of the defining elements of these traditions, most noticeably, plurality and open-endedness. Finally, by working from within this epic narrative, we participate in, and contribute to articulating, an ever evolving, dynamic "Hindu" dialogue.

Ethnic and religious diversity is an ever-expanding reality in Los Angeles and throughout the United States of America.[5] Though religious pluralism has been a part of this land from its inception, Diana Eck speaks of a "New America;" one in which the immigrants of the past thirty years have dramatically and exponentially expanded the religious diversity of this country. For example, "We the people of the United States of America" now includes Buddhists originating from all over Asia; Hindus from India, South Africa, and Trinidad; Muslims from Indonesia, the Middle East, and Africa. Contemporary communities in the United States are comprised not only of individuals espousing religious traditions indigenous to the countries from which they came, these communities also contain various ethnic and cultural expressions of the long established traditions such as Catholicism and those within Protestantism. "We the people" includes the Filipino Catholic, Korean Presbyterian, Shiite Pakistani, Japanese Rinzai Buddhist, Sri Lankan and North American Theravadan Buddhist, South Asian Vedanta Hindus, and second generation American-born Hara Krishnas.[6]

Religions, as eloquently described by Eck, "are not like stones passed from hand to hand through the ages. They are dynamic movements, more like rivers—flowing, raging, creative, splitting, converging."[7] As religions once foreign to the United States flow through this country, they continue to influence what was before and create new American expressions of themselves. Eck's Pluralism Project is an example of a study that examines the flow of these new voices of religion within the United States.

The diversity of voices comes not only from the variety of different religious traditions, but also from the different generations speaking from within and between these religious traditions. Religions indigenous to India, such as Buddhism, Hinduism, and Jainism, have been in North America long enough to have established their own American expression. Second, third, and fourth generation American-born Hindus, Buddhists, and others may speak in their own voice, distinct from both the voices of their parents and grandparents, who may have immigrated to the United States decades ago, and the voices of their fellow American friends and colleagues. Intermarriage between religious and ethnic groups, such as American-born Japanese-Indians, Pakistani-Latinas, and Korean-African Americans, produce yet other voices, voices that when articulated and heard can deeply enrich the lives of all those involved in the discussion.

Diversity alone, according to Eck, "does not constitute pluralism [. . .]. Whether we are able to work together across the lines of religious difference to create a society in which we actually know one another remains to be seen."[8] Eck laments that though "We the people of the United States of America" now stands for the most religiously diverse nation on earth, "We," the people, are quite uninformed and operate out of sketchy and stereotypical views of one another. In order to create a truly pluralistic society in the United States, a society where our great diversity is not just tolerated but is the very source of our strength, Eck indicates that we must know more about one another and must listen to the multitude of voices as they articulate the "we" and contribute to what is "America."

When a multitude of voices are allowed to speak, everyone can benefit. In listening to others and in speaking ourselves, we can gain understanding, new insights, and perspectives. Though born and raised in the United States of America, my family combined South Asian and Japanese ancestry with Hindu, Buddhist, and Christian religious traditions. This diverse family environment placed me at the nexus of several worldviews and allowed me the freedom to question and probe the presuppositions that underlie our philosophical paradigms. However, it was not until a professor, the one to whom this book is dedicated, opened my ears to hear my own voice that I began to understand myself and those around me. In this work, we seek to articulate another voice, one that combines creative insights of traditional Hinduism, as found embedded within the *Mahābhārata,* with the contemporary context in North America. We seek to engage in and contribute to bioethical dialogues regarding assisted reproductive technology.

Chapter 1, "Medicine, Bioethics, and Religious Voices," begins with an exploration of the role of religion in the practice of medicine and bioethics as it is discussed in the academy, the clinical setting, and the public sphere. After establishing the importance of religion within these realms, we turn to a discussion of "Cultural Competency." This is a term utilized by healthcare professionals that acknowledges the need to be understanding as well as sensitive to the different cultures, socioeconomic backgrounds, and belief systems of their patients. Religious beliefs often play a major role in how people make decisions regarding medical care and how they think about bioethical issues.[9] To be truly culturally competent, healthcare providers need to guard against assumptions and stereotypes and engage the actual patient before them. A competent care provider examines her patients with great skill and care, observes the family dynamics, and listens. Ultimately, one should not distinguish between culturally competency and competent care. In order to provide optimal care, it is imperative for those working within the medical field to be good clinicians and to be informed of, and sensitive to, their own religious and cultural perspectives, as well as those of their patients.[10]

Though cultural competency does not require full knowledge of every world religion and culture, being exposed to other worldviews may provide avenues through which clinicians can broaden their own perspectives. To this end, we focus on Hinduism. The term "Hindu" is in many ways artificial and superficial. Although it gives the impression of referring to a single entity, it is a foreign label for a rough collection of related, yet quite diverse, social, religious, cultural, and philosophical traditions originating from within India. Just as great diversity exists within Jewish and Christian traditions, such that one cannot speak of "*the* Jewish" or "*the* Christian" perspective on any topic, it is even more so the case when attempting to discuss "*the* Hindu" perspective on specific issues. The conglomeration of Hinduism has no Pope or Magisterium,[11] no central, overarching authority figure or governing body. Nevertheless, out of the many important systems of thought available within Hinduism, this study is strongly influenced by *Advaita-Vedānta,* a dominant and fairly pervasive school of thought. This focus in no way underestimates the plurality inherent within the Hindu traditions. The aim here is not to construct the definitive Hindu ethic, for that is obviously an impossible task. Rather, the goal is to emphasize selected strands within Hinduism's multivalent traditions to discuss various ethical issues regarding assisted reproductive technology. Its acceptance of differing beliefs, practices, and truths provides a good model for how clinicians, patients, theologians, and philosophers might communicate within this pluralistic, contemporary world.

Chapter 2, "Voices from Hinduism's Past," begins with a discussion of what the *Mahābhārata* is. Then there is a brief synopsis of the *Mahābhārata* and we establish its role and importance in Indian and Hindu society and culture. We then shift our focus to the specific stories of how three queens, Kuntī, Mādrī, and Gāndhārī, overcome challenges of infertility and not only provide heirs for their husbands, but also the descendants upon which this ancient epic revolves. Finally, we extrapolate elements within these paradigmatic narratives that are relevant to modern discussions on assisted reproductive technology.

In these epic narratives, Kuntī and Mādrī circumvent a curse placed upon their husband Pāṇḍu by utilizing a mantra that allows them to call upon the gods of their choice to impregnate them. To ensure Dhṛtarāṣṭra has progeny, Gāndhārī manipulates the product of her conception to bring about the births of her one hundred sons and one daughter. The creative ingenuity reflected in this ancient myth provides fertile ground upon which to discuss ethical issues related to the use of assisted reproductive technologies such as fertility medications, sperm banks, donor artificial insemination (DAI), in vitro fertilization (IVF), embryonic transfers, and surrogacy.

Working from within the *Mahābhārata* narratives, the third chapter, "Narrative as a Source of Ethics," begins with an exploration of three topics extrapolated from the above stories: 1) the priority placed on having children; 2) an acceptance of a variety of creative means to produce children; and 3) the active role some women take in controlling their reproductive choices. The implications of these ancient narratives are intriguing and insightful when brought into contemporary, comparative discussions. To demonstrate points of comparison, a few of these Hindu perspectives are juxtaposed with those present in the Hebrew Bible, New Testament, and Roman Catholic teachings.

Prior to analyzing particular Hindu bioethical perspectives on assisted reproductive technology, it is important to have an underlying understanding of the traditions within Hinduism. Therefore chapter 4, "Characteristics of Hindu Thought," presents a careful exploration of the selected *Mahābhārata* narratives discussed in the second chapter of this work. We draw out six key characteristics that are primary elements within Hindu worldviews. The stories of Kuntī, Gāndhārī, and others within this epic demonstrate a commitment to a variety of beliefs and presuppositions. Dominant and central to most are the following: 1) the centrality of society; 2) the belief in an underlying unity of all life; 3) the responsibilities and flexibility of *dharma*; 4) the multivalent nature of Hinduism; 5) a theory of *karma*; and 6) the teachings of *ahiṃsā.*

Chapter 5 is an "Application of Hindu Thought." Most, if not all, the writing on Hindu ethics in general, and bioethics in particular, is based in interpretations of primary texts and remains very theoretical. Sources regarding applied Hindu ethics are scarce.[12] Our task in this chapter begins by directly applying the six elements of Hindu thought to a particular case, namely that of Jaycee Buzzanca. Her case highlights many of the legal and ethical challenges associated with assisted reproductive technology. In this chapter we examine the ethical complexities through the lens of a Hindu perspective as found embedded with specific *Mahābhārata* narratives.

CHAPTER ONE

Medicine, Bioethics, and Religious Voices

In recent years, the demographics of the population of the United States have been changing throughout the entire country. Though diversity is not new to the United States, the change is in the degree of the diversity, both in terms of numbers of people and variety of traditions, cultures, and religions. The increase in diversity comes from immigrants who establish themselves in this country and then bring their families. Additional factors that exponentially increase the cultural, religious, and ethnic diversity come from the fact that people from Africa, Asia, Latin America, and other areas have been established in the United States long enough to have the second, third, and fourth generations of their families born and reared in this country. As these American-born generations mature, they often develop their own expression of their religious and cultural backgrounds. Furthermore, as individuals from these various groups interact, form relationships, and establish partnerships, there is a blending of perspectives, leading to the development of yet other worldviews. This diversity of religions and cultures, and their multiple expressions, has had a profound impact on healthcare, on the concept and delivery of quality care, and on how bioethical issues are understood.

In this chapter, after demonstrating the influential role of religion in the clinical setting and its subsequent influence in the academy and in public policy, I argue that bioethical discussions need to be broadened to include religious traditions beyond those grounded in Christianity and Judaism. If doctors, nurses, and other healthcare professionals desire to administer quality, culturally competent care, they must take both their own and their patients' religious perspectives and commitments into serious consideration. In this pluralistic world, where countless ideas and worldviews are continually coming into contact, Hinduism, with its multitude of traditions and numerous gods, provides an exemplary model for how individuals can function, communicate, and make difficult moral decisions in and amongst the chaos of life.

Bioethical discussions have been occurring in at least three different arenas: the academy, the clinical setting, and in public policy forums. At its genesis in the early 1960s, theologians played formative roles in the field of bioethics. However, as time passed, these primarily biblical religious perspectives were surpassed by secular, universal, philosophical voices in leading textbooks and at leading bioethics centers. This marginalization of religious voices (primarily Christian) dominated academic discussions, and in turn, this development influenced clinical and public policy settings. Although the deemphasis of religion in the academy has had some influence in the clinical and policy arenas, the significance of religious beliefs for patients and practitioners as they face difficult decisions is evident. Religion may have been downplayed in the academy, but in clinical settings and public policy arenas, it indirectly and explicitly continues to permeate the experiences of those actually engaged in bioethical struggles at the bedside. The power and influence of these clinical experiences in turn affects the position of religious voices within the academy and public policy arena.

Though calls for consistency, rationality, and universal applicability influence and are important for the clinical setting, they are often not its primary focus. The questions and experiences of those in the clinical environment became a powerful influence and may have played a role in a shift that occurred within both the academic field of bioethics and the realm of public policy. In the 1990s, the same scholars who argued for the marginalization of religion within bioethics began acknowledging the cost of excluding religious voices and reevaluating the contributions of religion. When struggling with issues of birth, life, and death, many often turn to some form of religious or spiritual counsel and support.

THE RELATIONSHIP BETWEEN RELIGION, MEDICINE, AND BIOETHICS

There is a well-established relationship between the practice of medicine, medical ethics, and religion. In their essay "What is Bioethics? A Historical Introduction," Kuhse and Singer indicate that for many cultures the religious leader and healer was one and the same individual. For example, the shaman was often both doctor and priest, simultaneously utilizing herbs, exorcisms, and prayers to heal the members of the community.[1] The ancient Indian *Ayurvedic* tradition provides another excellent example of an inextricable connection between the medicine of the Vedic Indians and their religion. This Hindu medicine never became divorced from the rest of life's pursuits, especially not from the religious life.[2] According to the father of medicine in China, Sun Ssu-miao, medicine "is an art which is difficult to master. If one does not receive a divine guidance from God, he will not be able to understand the mysterious points [. . .]."[3] Martin Marty reminds us that Judaism, Christianity, and most of the world's religions began, developed, and continue as healing cults. Relationships between the practice of medicine and various Western religious perspectives, primarily Protestant, Catholic, and one Jewish tradition, are the focus of the book *Caring and Curing: Health and Medicine in the Western Religious Traditions.*[4]

This association between religion and medical ethics extends back to antiquity. Kuhse and Singer trace a connection that includes eras that predate the Oath of Hippocrates. In the sanctuary of Asclepias there is a monument that instructs doctors to be like God, to treat, heal, and be a savior of slaves, of paupers, of rich men, and of princes.[5] In the same vein, Sun Ssu-maio calls on a physician to have mercy on all those who suffer and are sick. Being guided by god, the doctor should "pledge himself [sic.] to relieve suffering among all classes. Aristocrat or commoner, poor or rich, aged or young, beautiful or ugly, enemy or friend, native or foreigner, and educated or uneducated, all are to be treated equally."[6] According to the Indian *Caraka-Saṃhitā,* a physician-in-training first devotes himself to the guru. After he is instructed in the sacred fire ceremonies, he is taught the healing arts and charged to serve and heal everyone equally "without arrogance, with care and attention and with undistracted mind, [and] humility [. . .]."[7] Concerning how physicians are to conduct themselves, these ancient texts reflect fluidity between the practice of medicine, religion, and their code of ethics.

Religion played a pivotal role in the development of the field of bioethics. Discussing the relationship between the field of bioethics and religion, Albert Jonsen argues that there is "a moral tradition that runs wide and deep, although in our days, quite silently, through American culture."[8] He calls that tradition "American moralism." By this term, he means "the deep source in which a certain way of thinking and feeling about the moral life is engendered and nourished."[9] The roots of American moralism are firmly grounded in Christianity, particularly Calvinism. After presenting his argument regarding the tie between American moralism and Calvinism, Jonsen maintains that the North American interest in bioethical issues grew out of this "American moralism."

The 1970 publication of Paul Ramsey's *Patient as Person* was one of the defining events in the development of the field of bioethics. According to Jonsen, Ramsey's desire to bring order and clarity to the confusion accompanying the advances in medical science was grounded in the theology of Calvin and Edwards.

As new medical technology developed in the early 1960s and 1970s, the federal government established committees to consider the ethical and moral implications of the technologies and their use. Jonsen was a member of one of the first ethical panels established by the federal government in 1972, namely, the Totally Artificial Heart Assessment Panel. He was also a commissioner of the National Commission for the Protection of Human Subjects of Biomedical and Behavioral Research. Looking back, Jonsen is skeptical of the work of this Commission's "status as a serious ethical analysis." He suspects that the desire of members of Congress and the public "to see the chaotic world of bioethical research reduced to order by clear and unambiguous principles" is in part a product of Calvinistic thinking.[10] According to Jonsen, Calvinist perspectives influenced moral thinking in a variety of religious traditions within America, Protestant and Catholic alike, and underlie American moralism in general.

Jonsen's thesis provides a particular example of how religious voices were present at the revival of the field of bioethics in North America. Though Calvinism represents only one of the many Christian voices, those perspectives, with a few Jewish voices interspersed, were the primary contributors to the early discussions in bioethics. Along with the dominant voice of Ramsey representing a Calvinist tradition were the Roman Catholic voices of Curran, McCormick, and others. While the teachings of the Magisterium regarding sexual and reproductive ethics can make it appear as if there is unanimity within Roman Catholicism, this is in fact not the case. There are a variety of perspectives that exist within Roman Catholicism, among both the laity and theological scholars.

Many ethical issues arose as a result of the social, cultural, and political changes of the time. Significant advances in biomedical science and their clinical applications, such as heart transplantation and dialysis, became a driving force that brought about a revival in medical ethics. Advancements in such fields as recombinant DNA and gene therapy contributed to the development of what is now called bioethics. As discussed, by the end of the 1960s and 1970s, medical technology extended the possibilities of human life in both directions. On the one hand, dialysis machines, mechanical ventilators, and organ transplant technology prolonged the lives of those who would have otherwise died. On the other hand, assisted reproductive technologies enabled women to give birth to children in ways never before imagined in modernity.

Developments in assisted reproductive technologies bring up challenging new issues surrounding the beginning of human life. For example, 15 July 1978 marks the birth of Louise Brown, the first baby born as a result of IVF. This in vitro technology allowed one woman to donate her oocytes and embryos to another. The development of embryo cryopreservation and thawing techniques led to the first live birth from these techniques in 1984. Further developments in gamete intrafallopian transfers (GIFT) and zygote intrafallopian transfers (ZIFT) became available in 1985 and 1986, respectively.[11] These technologies lead to questions, ethical issues, and choices between options that perhaps were previously known only within the imagination, but unknown in the realities of daily life.

Questions and issues raised by the challenges of, and advances in, biomedical technology are not simply medical; they are moral and ethical as well. For example, a majority of the debates regarding the creation and utilization of human embryos, embryonic stem cells, and cloning revolves around the question: what is the moral status of the embryo or fetus? These debates are often contentious because they highlight issues regarding what it means to be a unique individual, what it means to be a human being. These technological advances raise the moral question of when human life begins. When is the fetus considered a human person, entitled to rights and protection afforded other human beings? Another example of how these medical advances relate to moral issues becomes evident when one considers questions of distributive justice: How just is it to spend one million dollars to save one twenty-five-week premature baby, while the health of children in the same city, in the same neighborhood, is threatened by malnutrition and lack of immunization? All of these questions and moral dilemmas inevitably involve the significance of life, suffering, and death.[12] Throughout history, birth, life, and death are often draped and cradled in the garments of religious rituals and religious beliefs.

Just as religion played a role in the practice of medicine and in the development of medical ethics, so too religion was present and played a formative role at the genesis of the bioethics revival. Protestants such as Joseph Fletcher, Paul Ramsey, and James M. Gustafson, Roman Catholic moral theologians Richard McCormick, Charles Curran, and Germain Grisez, along with Jewish theologians such as David Feldman and Immanuel Jakobovits, were all participants in this revival. Callahan describes a situation where, through the mid-1960s, the *only* resources for bioethics were in some way or other based in religion.[13]

Along with being founders in the field of bioethics, these religious thinkers served as members of formative committees such as The National Commission of the Protection of Human Subjects of Biomedical and Behavior Research (1974), and The President's Commission for Study of Ethical Problems in Medicine and Biomedical and Behavior Research (1979).[14] The Institute of Religion, founded in 1954 at the Texas Medical Center, sponsored one of the first major bioethics conferences in the United States in the late 1960s. Joseph Fletcher, Paul Ramsey, and other Christian thinkers presented major addresses at this conference. Additionally, Christian theologians and philosophers played a role in the formation of the field by helping to create various bioethics institutes such as the Kennedy Institute of Ethics at Georgetown University and the Institute for the Study of Society, Ethics, and the Life Sciences, now known as the Hastings Center in New York. Many Christian theologians and philosophers were also the primary contributors to the first edition of the *Encyclopedia of Bioethics*.[15]

These religiously informed thinkers were so influential in the formation of the field of bioethics because they were able to clearly articulate important insights.[16] Cahill argues that these individuals "were particularly well equipped to advance medical ethics because religious communities had cultivated long-standing traditions of reflection on life, death, and suffering, and had given more guidance on the specifics of moral conduct than had moral philosophy at the time."[17] Citing Weber, Campbell remarks that the religious perspectives provide an interpretation of reality that responds to the "'metaphysical needs of the human mind' to seek order, coherence, and meaning in our lives, to understand ultimate questions about our nature, purpose, and destiny."[18]

MARGINALIZATION OF RELIGION IN THE ACADEMY

Despite the contributions of religion to the origins of modern bioethics, there are those who argue that the field, as it developed in the public sphere in the United States, effectively excluded religious voices. As the field of bioethics came of age in the 1960s, secularism reached its peak as a social movement in the United States. In his essay "Religion, Theology, Church, and Bioethics," Martin Marty argues that this marginalization was grounded in "liberal culture" and "late Enlightenment rationality."[19]

This intellectual movement set up a dichotomy between reason and faith, secular and religious realms of existence. The secular, scientific, public realm was understood as grounded in the rational and universal. Good academic judgments were said to be grounded in empirical evidence and confirmable by any person who has the ability to reason. On the other hand, religion and the private realm were based on faith, on the emotional and the irrational. Stephen Lammers argues that the marginalization of religion occurred within bioethics. He names three specific realms of discourse where bioethics strove to overcome various fractious and lethal religious divisions: the academy, public policy, and the clinical setting.[20]

In this environment, there was neither room nor a perceived need for the particular voice of religion in academic bioethical discussions. An examination of the table of contents of standard bioethics textbooks, such as Beauchamp and Childress's *Principles of Biomedical Ethics,* Shannon's *Introduction to Bioethics,* and Mappes and DeGrazia's *Biomedical Ethics,* seems to support this notion. Although some of the writers of these texts were theologians, one finds *no direct* mention of religion.

Another example of this shift away from religion is evident in Callahan's portrayal of his own adjustment in orientation. Throughout much of the 1960s, he describes himself as a "religious person" who "had no trouble bringing that [religious] perspective to bear on the newly emergent issues of bioethics." By the end of the 1960s his religiosity had declined and all but disappeared. His academic training as an analytic philosopher convinced him that "moral philosophy, with its historical dedication to finding a rational foundation for ethics, was well suited to biomedical ethics." Since religion had become unnecessary in his personal life, Callahan questioned its relevance to bioethics and the "collective moral life."[21]

With the emphasis on secularism and the rise of religious pluralism, many shared Callahan's attitude and argued that ethical and moral discussions in the academic public square ought not to include God or religion. According to this argument, pluralism precludes the possibility of there being "any infallible way" of concluding debates where a single religious system is the clear winner. According to many, morality must be based on observed consequences, not beliefs or superstitions; if an action is wrong, it is wrong because it harms someone or violates their rights. Richard Holloway maintains that religious language, calling up the authority of God, is problematic, even worthless, in moral debates. Human reason, not "divinely clinching arguments," should provide the grounds for our discussions. Holloway believes that one can construct a rational, neutral, and universally acceptable morality. He and other scholars acknowledge that while, at the beginning of the modern revival of bioethics, religion may have played a formative role, its influence has rapidly declined and philosophical categories "more acceptable to the majority of persons" became prominent.[22]

There are various analyses that support the argument that religious voices have been marginalized in the public sphere and particularly in bioethical discussions. A standard work discussing the notion that religion was marginalized in the public arena is Stephen L. Carter's *The Culture of Disbelief: How American Law and Politics Trivialize Religious Devotion.* Carter does not specifically address the issue of marginalization in bioethics; nonetheless, his comments are applicable to our discussion. According to Carter, though millions of individual North Americans in the United States take their religious commitments very seriously, the culture in which they live does not. He describes the many ways modern culture in the United States trivializes religious devotion and often discourages religion as a serious activity.[23]

Cahill and others demonstrate how, as a result of the secularization of this society, even when religious communities choose to enter academic and public policy discussions, the conditions under which they participate in effect marginalizes them. They argue that religious discourse in bioethics is limited because, when in the public square, religions are required to utilize a "public language," as opposed to the religious language of their particular communities. Religious scholars started operating more like philosophers, attempting to rely more on moral principles that they felt could plausibly claim to be universal, rational, and "secular." Additionally, they worked toward developing policy and decision-making resolutions that would coincide with the legal traditions of the United States and command public support. This hindered and distorted the religious message, thereby marginalizing it.[24]

In addition to the milieu of secularism and pluralism, Callahan and others argue that there are issues internal to the religious traditions that contributed to their being marginalized in the academy, public policy, and clinical settings. Callahan suggests that during the 1970s, the theological seminaries and university departments of religion were drawn more to issues of urban poverty and race, and to questions of world peace in the nuclear age, not bioethics. Consequently, since these traditions were focused on other issues, religious voices faded in bioethics. Another internal contributing factor was attributed to confusion concerning the role of religion. According to this argument, leaders in some religious traditions could not decide if it was their responsibility to stand over against culture, transform it, or speak for it.

Thus, scholars have argued that because of religion's own uncertainty, the influence of the secular movement, the pluralistic character of the day, and the way in which the field itself was moving, religious voices were marginalized in academic bioethical discussions. Furthermore, as bioethical arguments entered more into public awareness, interests commanding the attention of the courts, legal system, medical professions, and other professional societies, there was increased pressure to utilize secular language and models to frame and discuss the issues. Callahan points to the 1975 case of Karen Ann Quinlan as an indication that the secular legal system would take the lead in bioethics. Henceforth, the cases in this field would provide the courts with challenging legal cases for which no precedents had been set.[25]

RELIGIOUS VOICES AND THE CLINICAL ARENA

Marty, Callahan, and others present convincing arguments indicating that religious voices have, at least to some extent, been marginalized within the academy and public policy arenas. Lammers acknowledges that this marginalization of religion in these realms has influenced the clinical setting. On the one hand, the emphasis on secularism influenced the dialogues within the practice of medicine. The language of the consumer market dominated, leading to an emphasis on autonomy and a market model of medicine. This new model addressed neither the limits of what medicine could do nor issues of human finitude. Furthermore, Lammers comments on how there seemed to be a decrease in the service orientation of the medical profession. On the other hand, he indicates that clinicians he worked with took the religious beliefs of their patients seriously. They also saw it as part of their job, as healers, to address their patients' religious commitments and concerns. To the extent that religious voices have been marginalized, healthcare providers, patients, and their families have lost a valuable resource for reflection and critical analysis.

However accurate the argument for the marginalization of religion may be in the academy, this is not the case for the clinical setting. Ultimately, in the midst of actual hospital experiences, where individuals are struggling with life and death issues, patients and clinicians alike find it difficult, if not impossible, to discuss their situations without reference to religious beliefs. While working as a registered nurse in labor and delivery, I had a patient who was pregnant after a third GIFT (gamete intra-fallopian transfer) attempt. After three zygotes were implanted in her uterus, the doctors offered to selectively reduce (abort) one of the developing embryos, thereby increasing the chances for a healthier birth of the remaining two fetuses and decreasing some of the risks associated with multiple gestational pregnancies. Even months later, as she retold her story to me, she was shaking her head in disbelief saying, "I couldn't do that. I couldn't let them kill one of my babies. God gave me these three precious gifts and I have to take care of them." She named each fetus, and as they developed one was diagnosed with anencephaly. She cried. Though she was well aware that "Joey," the anencephalic baby, "didn't have a brain" and would not live long after birth, she again refused the offer of selective reduction. She argued that God gave this baby life, however short, and she could not end it. Throughout the pregnancy, she continued to talk to and about all three of her babies as equals. When the triplets were born, she and her husband held Joey until he died.

For this patient and her family, constructing rational, universally acceptable responses to the issues and questions of assisted reproductive technology, abortion, and personhood were not foremost in their minds. On the one hand, she seemed to have no problem utilizing medical technology in order to conceive; moreover, she attributed its success to God. On the other hand, she refused to utilize this technology to selectively reduce one fetus, even if it might enhance her health and the health of the remaining fetuses, arguing that it would be going against God's plan. She was not concerned about this apparent inconsistency. Neither was she concerned about questions and definitions of personhood. Joey, as a developing fetus with anencephaly, did not have the potential to become an adult human being. He most likely was not self-aware and would die witin twenty-four hours of birth. He would never know his mother, yet she treated him and referred to him in the same manner as she did her other babies. Her religious beliefs not only guided her actions, they brought her comfort in the end.

Cahill eloquently identifies how and why religion is so inextricably related to bioethics and the clinical setting. She writes:

> Because they deal in the elemental human experiences of birth, life, death, and suffering, the biomedical arts provide an opening for larger questions of meaning and even of transcendence. Religious themes and imagery can be helpful in articulating these concerns and addressing them in an imaginative, provocative, and perhaps ultimately transformative way. Religious symbolism may be grounded in particular communities and their experiences of God and community, but perhaps it can also mediate a sensibility of transcendence and ultimacy that is achingly latent in the ethical conflicts, tragedies and triumphs that are unavoidable in biomedicine.

She continues, "[. . .] ethics opens onto the transcendence that human persons and communities encounter most fulfilling in the limit experiences of life, suffering, and death, and that compassionate and just solidarity in these experiences defines personal and social virtue in the medical context."[26] Though modern medical technology can assist us in healing, in bringing forth new life, and in extending life, it does not enable us to answer challenging questions such as: What does it mean to be human? When, if at all, does ensoulment occur? What is personhood? What happens when, or after, I die? The practice of medicine often intersects with our definitions and our understanding of what it means to be human. It brings to the forefront questions of mortality and meaning. These questions and issues are raised and are the focus of many religious discussions.

For many clinicians, arguing that religious voices are marginalized is odd. Such attitudes do not coincide with the practical experiences of many patients and healthcare professionals who are *living* the bioethical dilemmas. Lammers writes:

> [. . .] the reality of finitude takes on an immediacy that can be hidden from us in other settings. Academicians and public policy persons can operate as if finitude were an illusion or a bother; nurses and physicians do not have that luxury.[27]

The practice of medicine often engages human experiences at moments of intense fear, joy, and unspeakable sorrow. In these moments, for many, religion is not some theoretical, abstract, academic concept. Religion is the space in which these individuals can both express their joys and struggle with the realities of suffering and death. It is the place people often turn to for meaning and sustenance. Religion is also a thread of connection, to tradition, to the past, to others, and to the future; it is often the thread of hope, and the thread that binds individuals together and helps them move forward in joy or sorrow.[28]

REEMERGENCE OF RELIGIOUS VOICES IN THE ACADEMY AND PUBLIC POLICY FORUMS

The influence of religion has remained a compelling force within the clinical setting, in part because patients and clinicians alike, engaged in the struggle of bioethical situations, call upon, address their concerns to, and find comfort in their various religious convictions. The continuance of religious voices in the clinical setting has perhaps in some way affected the academy. In the early 1990s, many of the same scholars who once argued for the marginalization of religion began acknowledging the cost of excluding religious voices and began reevaluating its contributions. Campbell states it well when he writes: "If it was premature to pronounce 'the death of God' in the 1960s, it seems equally mistaken to begin doing post-mortems on the demise of theological and religious perspectives in bioethics."[29]

As previously mentioned, Callahan, a philosopher who claims to have shed his unnecessary Christian identity, acknowledges that "whatever the ultimate truth status of religious perspectives, they have provided a way of looking at the world and understanding one's own life that has a fecundity and uniqueness not matched by philosophy, law, or political theory."[30] He goes on to question if unbelief and intellectual honesty demand a rejection of religious insights and perspectives, regardless of how valuable. Callahan's statements and questions most likely reflect influences from both enlightenment ideology and Christianity. They also reflect some remorse at his inability, or at least hesitancy, to utilize the resources of his religious tradition.

He and others identify a number of problems and limitations when religion is not included in bioethical discussions. First, in rejecting religion, one is closing one's eyes to and making unavailable all the accumulated wisdom and knowledge of long-established religious traditions. One need not be a Hindu, Jew, or Christian to benefit from the wisdom and experiences of others from the past. Eliminating religion often leads to an unwarranted dependence upon law as a source of morality. Legality is not equivalent to morality; an action may be legal but not necessarily moral or correct. Additionally, an emphasis on secularism can also be oppressive in that it can require individuals to pretend that their private lives and beliefs do not spill over into the public realm.

There are problems with an academic search for universal, neutral, and environmental influence-free solutions. Rather than providing satisfying, purely rational, universal answers, secularism forces individuals to pretend they are not simultaneously members of both particular communities and a general society at large. Wind correctly argues that individuals, be they policymakers, healthcare professionals, or patients, "do not park their beliefs at the bioethical door. Instead they smuggle them in—in plain wrappers—beneath the surface of much of our technical secular discourse."[31] Reich concurs when he argues that it is better and more beneficial if bioethics "were to acknowledge fully and integrate into its dialogues the voices of the people answering the questions, experiencing the suffering, living and dying."[32] The trend toward attempting to converse in universal, religious free language leads to an unnatural and unrepresentative situation, which widens the gap between those in the academic ivory towers and the patient and healthcare professional in the "trenches."[33] Here Reich and others are directly calling attention to the events occurring within the clinical setting and arguing that the voices heard there ought to be included within the discussion. So often the voices of patients and clinicians are interlaced with their religious convictions.

While the academic emphasis on marginalizing religious voices may have been influential in the public arena for a time, it appears that time has passed. Again, perhaps in part because of the influence of the experiences of those in the clinical setting, religious voices are present and are very influential in public discussions on bioethical issues. Of the many religious voices heard in the public sphere, we focus on Hinduism. However, to clearly demonstrate how perspectives grounded in Hindu traditions can have radically different implications, we will juxtapose our Hindu perspectives with those of the Roman Catholic Church. The primary reason for choosing to focus on the voices within the Catholic Church is that its position of power and influence is unmatched, both in the United States and internationally. Its authority and control extends far beyond its own members. The teachings of the Magisterium are heard and shape discussions in the halls of Congress, the White House, around the country, and around the world. Second, though the Catholic Church is not monolithic, the Vatican does set forth an official, authoritative teaching, particularly concerning reproductive issues. This provides good points of comparison, particularly when we examine elements of Hindu traditions.

The Vatican is the only religious group that has an observer status at the United Nations. Because of its independent state status conceded by the Lateran Pacts of 1929, it is granted this privilege and thus has a voice in the UN. There are many examples of the Church's international influence. From the first international meetings regarding world population, beginning in the 1950s, the Vatican's firm opposition to contraception and abortion put it at odds with a majority of international development and population organizations. The voice of the Vatican was heard louder than ever before at the 1994 International Conference on Population and Development held in Cairo. The Church's objections to the wording in the conference documents delayed the entire conference for over four days.[34]

A domestic example of the influence of the Catholic Church is evident in how the American Fertility Society, a professional medical organization, went about developing its perspectives on the new reproductive technologies. In 1986, in its professional journal, *Fertility and Sterility,* the 1984–85 Ethics Committee of the American Fertility Society published "Ethical Considerations of New Reproductive Technologies." This document set forth the Society's then-held ethical positions on a variety of new assisted reproductive technologies.[35] Soon after the publication of this Committee's deliberations, the Vatican's Congregation for the Doctrine of the Faith published the *Instruction on Respect for Human Life in Its Origin and on the Dignity of Procreation* (hitherto referred to as the *Instruction*).[36] The *Instruction* did more than articulate the Roman Catholic Church's opposition to the utilization of assisted reproductive technologies. In its final section, under the title "The Values and Moral Obligations That Civil Legislation Must Respect and Sanction in this Matter," the Church calls for legislative intervention:

> When the state does not place its power at the service of the rights of each citizen, and in particular of the more vulnerable, the very foundations of a state based on law are undermined. The political authority consequently *cannot give approval* to the calling of human beings into existence through procedures which would expose them to those very grave risks [. . .]. Civil law *cannot grant approval* to techniques of artificial procreation, [. . .]. Legislation *must also prohibit* [. . .] embryo banks, post mortem insemination and "surrogate motherhood."[37]

The Vatican's call for the public, legislative prohibition of these technologies went beyond providing moral instructions for its congregants. The Church urged political leaders to take legislative action to disallow the availability of various assisted reproductive technologies.

The Vatican's *Instruction* prompted the 1986–87 American Fertility Society's Ethics Committee to reconvene. After reviewing the *Instruction,* the Committee located a number of differences and reevaluated and reasserted their positions on a variety of issues. Following the Society's Board of Directors approval, these proceedings resulted in a publication of a second report in 1988.

The foreword to this document acknowledges the publication of the *Instruction* and reads as follows: "Because of the conflicting conclusion of the two documents, the present Ethics Committee (1986–87) of The American Fertility Society was convened and considered the Fertility Society guidelines in the light of the *Instruction*."[38] Though the Committee did not actually change its position regarding the utilization of assisted reproductive technologies, the Committee did restate its positions in light of the issues raised by the Vatican. The Committee also responded to the arguments and reasoning of the Church.

The influence of Roman Catholicism continues. The ethical discussions over stem cell research and cloning demonstrate the continuing importance of religion in the public debate. In mid-July 2001, *Los Angeles Times* headlines read: "Pope Urges Bush to Reject Human Embryo Cell Research,"[39] "Bible Guides Senate on Stem Cell Studies,"[40] "Religion Divided on Stem Cell Issue."[41] *Newsweek* ran a story titled, "Battle for Bush's Soul." The lead line states: "The president is trapped between religion and science over stem cells. Lives—and votes—are at stake."[42] In a meeting between Pope John Paul II and President Bush, the Pope declared that the utilization of "human embryos for medical research is an 'evil' akin to abortion and infanticide." Bush responded by promising to "take that point of view into consideration" as he deliberated over the issue of federal funding for embryonic stem cell research.[43]

The role and influence of religion in the development and continuation of the field of bioethics is well established. With increased globalization and multiculturalism, the challenge facing contemporary discussions within bioethics is how to productively include the multitude of religious voices.

RELIGIOUS DIVERSITY

According to Margaret Farley, individual experience "plays an important role in moral discernment. It [individual experience] is a source of moral insight, a factor in moral judgment, a test of the rightness, goodness, and wisdom of a moral decision." Regarding the significance of the role of experience, she continues by saying: "It is central for finding and establishing an overall framework for moral discernment; it is important for formulating and applying general ethical principles and specific ethical rules; and it plays a key role in developing theories of moral disposition."[44] Globalization, pluralism, and multiculturalism all increase, not negate, the need for all to pay closer attention to the cultural and religious perspectives and experiences of patients, families, and healthcare providers.

Over the past decade, religious voices have experienced a resurgence in the academy's bioethical discussions. Prominent bioethical textbooks contain the undercurrents of religious influences. Now there are entire texts that take up the issues of various religious perspectives and bioethics. Wolfe and Gudorf's *Ethics & World Religions: Cross-Cultural Case Studies* (1999), focuses on various religious perspectives on a variety of ethical issues. Part V of this book is titled

"Religion, Medicine, and Public Health." Each chapter of Wolfe and Gudorf's book begins with a particular case study, which is followed by essays providing various world religions' views on the case and the issues that arise.[45]

Hindu Ethics (1989) by Coward, Lipner, and Young contains three chapters presenting Hindu views on purity, abortion, and euthanasia. Crawford's *Dilemmas of Life and Death* (1995) discusses Hindu ethics regarding abortion, suicide, and euthanasia, and his *Hindu Bioethics for the Twenty-first Century* (2003) addresses specific issues such as cloning and the Human Genome Project. Keown commits an entire book to *Buddhism and Bioethics* (2001). Dorff and Newman's *Contemporary Jewish Ethics and Morality: A Reader* (1995), contains two chapters specifically related to bioethics. *Sacred Choices* by Daniel C. Maguire (2001), focuses on contraception and abortion in ten world religions. Though this list is far from exhaustive, it is sufficient to indicate how current books are explicitly focusing on a multitude of religious voices in the field of bioethics. These books provide examples of religious voices in the public sphere and in the academy.

As a result of the increase in globalization, multiculturalism, and pluralism, the once dominant religious voices, particularly ones influenced by Christianity, are no longer the only religious voices present.[46] By expanding bioethical discussions to include "nonwestern" religions in the United States, we enhance our understanding of the issues. More importantly, we engage, not leave behind, the ivory towers of theory and philosophy with the actual struggles, questions, and concerns of those confronting genuine bioethical situations. For patients and healthcare providers, discussions and answers regarding bioethical issues are the grounds upon which concrete actions are taken. These discussions lead to decisions regarding birth, the quality of life, and death.

CULTURAL COMPETENCY

Cultural, religious, and social traditions reveal and celebrate the uniqueness of each individual person, her family and community. As indicated above, the practice of medicine engages human beings in the ordinary events of giving birth, living, suffering, dying, and of caring for those giving birth, living, suffering, or dying. It is in the midst of these ordinary events that worldviews and religious beliefs surface and have a strong hold. Consequently, the growing multicultural, multireligious aspects of society have not gone unnoticed by U.S. governmental agencies responsible for health concerns.

In the 1980s, the U.S. Department of Health and Human Services established the Office of Minority Health (OMH). This office operated under the conviction that the administration of quality healthcare was dependent upon the abilities of medical personal to understand how their own and their patients' religious, sociocultural, and economic backgrounds affect beliefs and behaviors regarding health. Recognizing the increasing diversity of the patient populations and the necessities of addressing the resulting cultural, religious, and social issues, the OMH, along with other medical associations such as American Nurses' Association (ANA), American Medical Association (AMA), and Association of American Medical Colleges, called for national standards of "Cultural Competency."[47]

According to the OMH, cultural competency is defined as:

> Cultural and linguistic competence is a set of congruent behaviors, attitudes, and policies that come together in a system, agency, or among professionals that enables effective work in cross-cultural situations. 'Culture' refers to integrated patterns of human behavior that include the language, thoughts, communications, actions, customs, beliefs, values, and institutions of racial, ethnic, religious, or social groups. 'Competence' implies having the capacity to function effectively as an individual and an organization within the context of the cultural beliefs, behaviors, and needs presented by consumers and their communities.[48]

A briefer definition indicates that competent care is "providing care to patients and their families that is compatible with their values and the traditions of their faiths. This requires awareness of one's own values and those of the healthcare system."[49] In her article "Cultural Competence: A Priority for Performance Improvement Action," Salimbene discusses ten basic components of cultural competency. They are:

1. An awareness of, sensitivity to, and tolerance of differences in culture and language;

2. An ability to refrain from making assumptions (or judgments) about the beliefs, behaviors, needs, and expectations of patients or colleagues of a different cultural background from oneself;

3. An understanding of the role culture plays in formatting the health/illness prevention beliefs and practices of patients;

4. The ability to recognize the role that one's own culture and background plays in determining one's attitudes and beliefs not only about health and wellness but also beliefs about such things as what constitutes acceptable behavior, cleanliness, a healthy lifestyle, the roles of family and friends, and so forth;

5. Enough knowledge about the cultures that one serves to avoid breaching the patient's taboos, healthcare beliefs, or rules of interaction;

6. Enough knowledge about the cultures that one serves to anticipate possible barriers to access to or compliance with care;

7. The skill to deliver culturally and linguistically appropriate patient advice and education;

8. The skill to utilize interpreters effectively so that language barriers do not impact the extent or quality of care;

9. The knowledge and flexibility to modify both one's mode of interaction and one's manner of delivering care so that it is culturally and linguistically appropriate to the patient while it meets the hospital's or clinic's standards of quality patient care; and
10. Confidence in one's ability to offer quality care to patients of other cultures.[50]

This is a recognition that patients' worldviews as well as their religious and cultural beliefs influence, and are tightly interwoven with, their attitudes towards health and medical care. Thus, to ensure delivery of the best healthcare possible, those engaged in the medical professions need not only be well trained in order to provide safe and effective care, they also need to be aware of and sensitive to the various populations their institutions serve.[51]

Having the knowledge and understanding of various cultural and religious influences, a healthcare provider can be sensitive to the particular needs of a patient; she may avert conflicts and be prepared to facilitate the delivery of timely quality care. Conversely, if ignored in the context of health and medicine, religious and cultural issues can be barriers to the promotion and implementation of good competent healthcare. Unfortunate and even horrific events have occurred because healthcare providers have failed to hear the concerns of their patients and have failed to consider the impact of the patients' culture and religion on their interpretations of what is occurring. Anne Fadiman's book, *The Spirit Catches You and You Fall Down,* documents the story of Lia Lee, an epileptic Hmong infant, and the unfortunate events that occurred between the medically competent but culturally incompetent healthcare providers and the Lee family.

At three months, Lia experienced her first seizure after someone entered the room allowing the door to slam. Her parents recognized her symptoms and diagnosed their youngest child with *quag dab peg,* "Spirit catches you and you fall down." In Hmong-English dictionaries *quag dab peg* is translated as "epilepsy." According to her parents, the noise of the slamming door disturbed her soul, caused it to flee from her body and become lost. In the above phrase, the *dab* is a soul-stealing spirit. They understood both the seriousness of her condition for her health, and at the same time they recognized it as a sign of one who is particularly fit for divine office: many epileptics become shamans. Lia's parents were simultaneously proud and concerned; without a physician's diagnosis, they knew she had epilepsy. The problem was that they were not aware of the English term "epilepsy," and their healthcare providers did not know that "Spirit catches you and you fall down" was the Hmong way of describing epilepsy.[52]

By not hearing and understanding the Lee family's cultural and religious interpretations of Lia's condition, the emergency room doctors did not have the full picture of her illness. Consequently, on two consecutive emergency room visits they misdiagnosed her and subjected her to a variety of invasive tests. Six months later, during her third emergency room visit, Dr. Murphy correctly diagnosed Lia and began the necessary treatments. Unfortunately, the healthcare professionals involved in the first two visits were unable to provide competent care because they lacked an ability to communicate adequately and to understand the religious and cultural explanations of Lia's symptoms.[53]

The emergency room doctors and nurses were frustrated when Lia's parents were "not compliant" with their prescribed treatments. However, these medical personnel sent the parents home with written instructions that they could not read. Competent care includes ensuring one is communicating with the patient and family members. It is disingenuous to accuse a patient of noncompliance when little effort is made to ensure that the patient actually understands the instructions. Unfortunately, these types of misunderstandings are not unique to immigrant communities.

There are countless examples where communication, or lack thereof, determines the competence or incompetence of care. A young six- or seven-year-old patient of mine had to be rescheduled for a head MRI because of his inability to lay still enough during the procedure. The plan was to conduct the procedure under conscious sedation, a light anesthetic, so the patient would be able to relax and sleep through the claustrophobic experience. While I was out of the room, the neurosurgery resident explained the plan to the patient and his mother. When it came time to take my young patient to his procedure, he began, uncharacteristically, to cry and resist. His mother and I tried to console him, but he was literally beside himself and would not allow himself to be removed from his bed. The resident requested assistance and at one point the boy was fighting off four male adults. I stopped everything, went to the head of the bed, looked at the boy, and quietly asked him what the problem was. With eyes full of fear and disbelief, he look at his mother and said, "How can you let them take me; he [the resident] said they were going to put me to sleep." He knew dogs and cats were put to sleep and did not return home.

Communication and misunderstandings can also be at the root of issues causing "noncompliance" on the part of the patient. While working as a homecare nurse in rural Virginia, I was assigned to an elderly "noncompliant" patient, one who refuses to take his medications. Upon arrival at his home, I sat down with the patient and reviewed the various medications he was taking. I carefully explained how I was going to fill a large pillbox, one with four time slots for each day of the week, with the appropriate medications for the appropriate time of day. As we discussed what each medication was for, he continued to express concern and resistance to taking his medications. After reviewing his medications with him for a second and third time, two and a half hours later, the patient's underlying concerns became apparent as he blurted out: "I don't wanna die!" He had been hospitalized because he had taken the wrong dose of a medication. His fear of repeating the same mistake was preventing him from realizing that the method we were employing would help him avoid the same mistake. I looked at him and in my best, newly acquired, southern accent, I responded: "Honey, you ain't gonna die, you only gotta remember about what time of day it is." The familiar accent and my words finally put his fears at ease and he expressed understanding for the first time.

All three of these examples, Lia, the young boy, and the elderly gentleman, highlight the importance of hearing and understanding the particular situation. Obviously misunderstandings are not exclusive to cross-cultural, cross-religious situations; many argue that "culturally competent care" is somewhat of a misnomer. Canales and Bowers, in their study of Latina nursing faculty, found that "culturally competent care" was not a salient element for their participants. However, what was "salient for these participants was the perception that *competent care includes cultural competence.*" According to this study, competent care requires that:

> the healthcare professional care for those perceived as different from self; that they learn to care as connected members of a community and the larger society; and that [. . .] [they] care with a commitment towards changing existing social, health and economic structures that are exclusionary."[54]

Competent care indeed encompasses culturally competent care. Healthcare providers need to have the ability to hear, understand, and address the variety of patients that come before them. Particular religious or cultural traditions will be heard, if the doctor, nurse, or other medical personal are adept at hearing the voices of their patients.

Providing quality medical care necessitates cultural competency. Though actual knowledge regarding various cultures is important, comprehensive knowledge of all of the religious and cultural forces influencing individuals is impractical, even impossible, and ought to be neither the primary goal nor focus of cultural competency. Rather, the ultimate goal is to encourage already clinically competent physicians, nurses, and other healthcare providers to be open and willing to learn about, respect, and work with persons from different backgrounds. Being able to recognize and work within and between different cultural and religious perspectives is imperative for clinical care to be competent in this century.[55] To this end, Canales, Bowers, Carrillo, Green, Betancourt, and others caution against categorizing and stereotyping patients.[56] Rather than developing "recipes" for healthcare professionals to follow when treating patients of various ethnic backgrounds, they propose an individual patient approach.

Appearing "different" does not necessarily imply one *is* different. Conversely, similarities in appearance do not necessarily reveal similarities in perspectives or worldviews. One cannot know, simply by looking at an individual, where he was born or raised. After meeting me, people have remarked on how well I speak English. They took note of me, assumed I was "foreign," and were surprised to hear me speak in unaccented, comprehendible English. The patient may look Asian, but having been raised in Iowa, she may have more in common with Caucasian Iowans than Asians from Laos or Los Angeles. The nurse, physician, and others need to engage the patient and "learn-through-connecting" with them; learn through listening. Each patient's situation is unique, influenced by personal background, culture, and religion. Thus, by interacting directly and discovering the core issues for that particular patient, healthcare providers can avoid cultural pitfalls and competently treat the individual.

Competent healthcare professionals will acknowledge that religious ideology may play a role in how patients interpret their illness and treatment. The United States is not only home to many of the religions that exist in the world, it is also home to the diverse expressions of these religious traditions.[57] In this multicultural pluralistic context, giving heed to religious voices demands an ability to hear a myriad of tones. Not only are there individuals who were raised in Catholic and Protestant homes, or Orthodox and Reform Jewish families, there are those from Buddhist, Hindu, Jain, and Muslim families. Each of these religious traditions have different denominations and different generations speaking from within them. Furthermore, there are the voices of those who come from a combination of any one or more of the above.

Again, Canales and others argue that, ultimately, there is no distinction between competent care and culturally competent care. Competence necessarily includes cultural competence. Beyond sensitivity and cultural knowledge, the healthcare providers need practical strategies for communicating with patients and individualizing care so that it is appropriate for each patient.[58] The focus here lies with the individual patient's worldviews, his or her hopes, fears, and understanding of life, suffering, and death. The process of actually engaging worldviews other than one's own has the potential to be both threatening and therapeutic. It can be threatening because the healthcare professional's original presuppositions may be challenged, and therapeutic because once the individual gains a better understanding of how the patient is viewing and experiencing the situation, the healthcare provider may be better able to address the fears and concerns of the patient. This understanding can lead to a dialogue and competent care. Thus, successful cross-cultural care, competent care, involves a triad of attributes: empathy, curiosity, and respect.

COMPLEXITY OF HINDU VOICES

Having discussed the influence of religion in the practice of medicine and bioethics, and having emphasized the need for and importance of cultural competency, let us now focus our attention on one particular world religion, namely Hinduism. Hindus constitute a population in the U.S. of nearly one million people, in addition to the over eight hundred million Hindus who live in India and elsewhere. The editors of the *Journal of the American Academy of Religion* (*JAAR*) dedicated the December 2000 issue to the question, "who speaks for Hinduism?" This is inherently a difficult and controversial question to answer, though not unique to Hinduism. The articles in this *JAAR* present an array of arguments representing various voices from within and without the tradition, from "confessional" and "objective" perspectives, from both Indian and North American scholars, and from different "native" voices. Together the essays emphasize the importance of listening to and engaging in the wide variety of voices present within Hinduism.

In his essay "On Hindu, Hindustān, Hinduism and Hindutva," Arvind Sharma discusses the origin and complexity associated with the term itself. In antiquity, "Hindu" was both a geographical and religious indicator. The term is derived from the Sanskrit term for river, *sindhu,* and gets applied to the Indus river; a river that served as a natural northwest boundary for the subcontinent. Sharma concludes that "Hindu," and derivatives of it, "contain a series of semantic bivalences characterized by unresolved tensions, and further that these tensions help account for the complexities generated by the induction of the world." The word, like the traditions, reveals fluid boundaries between various categories and internal diversity among official, unofficial, orthodox, and popular expressions of Hinduism, such that it defies simple, unequivocal characterization.[59]

Lipner likens Hinduism to a huge "banyan tree that has lost every trace of the original trunk." From the branches of this tree cascade huge aerial roots; they burrow into the earth below and appear as if each were a separate banyan trunk. Lipner's metaphor of the widespread, interlinked tree captures the diversity and multifaceted nature of Hindu traditions. The tree of Hinduism encompasses tribal people, with vastly different belief systems, and orthodox brahminical traditions, preserved in the *Laws of Manu,* the *Mahābhārata,* and other texts.[60] As there is not one trunk, one source, or one foundation for these traditions, so there is not one voice. The complex, polycentric center allows for a multitude of voices to emerge from within the traditions of Hinduism.

According to Radhakrishnan, Hinduism is a conglomeration of movements, not a position; processes, not a result; growing traditions, not a fixed revelation.[61] The traditions themselves do not acknowledge a single authoritative body or voice; they celebrate diversity. According to a passage in the *Mahābhārata,* "The Vedas are varied and the traditions are varied: one is not a sage if his view is not varied."[62] According to Hindu traditions, having the ability to hold a variety of perspectives is a sign of a sage! Consequently, when examining a particular Hindu view, one should always bear in mind that another legitimate, even conflicting, "Hindu" perspective is around the corner. It is true that many Hindus are not bothered by this pluralism. Rather, for a Hindu "it was no less provocative of anxiety to be asked to choose between two incompatible alternatives than it is for us ["Westerners"] to tolerate our own inconsistency."[63]

A defining characteristic of traditions within Hinduism is their multivalent natures. Inevitably, when Hinduism, or Hindu views, are being discussed, one often encounters expressions such as: "Some Hindus believe . . .," "the common people describe these things . . ., the educated Hindus do not share these opinions," "some Hindus say . . ., others have told me . . . ."[64] When asked how

Hindus might respond to a particular question or issue, my responses usually begin with, "It depends . . ."

In conjunction with not having clear "doctrinal" boundaries and definitions, Hindu daily life is not separated from religious life. While this may lead some, such as John Stratton Hawley, to argue that "Hinduism is not a religion; it is a way of life,"[65] it leads others, such as Radhakrishnan, to say: "Religion is not the acceptance of academic abstractions or the celebration of ceremonies, but a kind of life or experience. It is insight into the nature of reality [. . .], or experience of reality."[66] The daily practice of eating provides a perfect example of this. For many within Hinduism, eating is an activity highly regulated by the religion. The food actually eaten, who cooks it, when and with whom it is eaten are all a part of Hindu ritual activity. Desai also points out how many activities that fall under the category of "hygiene" are often religious for many Hindus.[67]

For many Hindus, religion, philosophy, and the conduct of daily life are all tightly interwoven. There is no formal discipline that presents "an internally consistent rational system in which patterns of human conduct are justified with reference to ultimate norms and values."[68] Nevertheless, this does not mean that Hindus do not know about ethics or that they are immoral. It simply indicates that there is neither a discipline within Indian thought that separates ethics from the activities of daily life nor one that focuses exclusively on it.[69] It is within these mercurial, pluralistic, symbiotic[70] Hindu traditions that we find strands of thought that will benefit contemporary North American conversations regarding assisted reproductive technology. This study engages in an examination of how key elements of Hindu thought might relate, frame, and deal with aspects of bioethics, particularly assisted reproductive medical care.

CHAPTER TWO

Voices from Hinduism's Past

Setting a context for a dialogue on infertility and assisted reproductive technology, the previous chapter demonstrated the relevance, benefits, and necessity of examining diverse religious positions concerning bioethical issues. We now turn our attention to voices from Hinduism's past by focusing on the narratives within the *Mahābhārata.* We begin with a brief synopsis of the epic as a whole and establish the significance of this text. Then, to ensure that we are all familiar with the specific narratives being examined, or simply to refresh our memories, we recount the stories of how three queens, Kuntī, Mādrī, and Gāndhārī, overcome challenges of infertility. The *Mahābhārata* does not make direct references to modern forms of assisted reproductive technology; however, the stories of how these three women overcome the challenges of infertility reflect very creative attitudes towards procreation. Their legendary ingenuity can inform our contemporary discussions as we struggle with the implications of modern medicine. As we closely examine the narratives, we can begin to see how questions and issues within the *Mahābhārata* can make relevant contributions to the ethical dilemmas we face when utilizing assisted reproductive technology.

WHAT IS THE *MAHĀBHĀRATA*?

There are two primary categories of Hindu sacred literature: revealed (*Śruti*) and traditional (*Smṛti*). "Revelation," according to ancient, orthodox brahmins, was *śruti,* literally "that which is heard," "knowledge by hearing." Included in this knowledge, orally passed on from guru to student, are works such as *Ṛg-veda, Sāma-veda, Yajur-veda, Atharva-veda,* and the various *Upaniṣads.* Through the hearing of this literature, *Brahman,* the essence of the universe, was "heard." The words of these texts are believed to be without beginning; they were a part of creation, the "sole source of knowledge about matters lying beyond the senses."[1] *Śruti* literature has neither beginning nor author. It is self-validating; it is knowledge that enables one who desires *mokṣa*[2] (liberation) to obtain it.

Of secondary authority is *smṛti* literature. *Smṛti* literally means "recollection," but is used practically to signify "tradition." This traditional literature "is the set of rules for acts of *dharma* that are not explicitly declared by *śruti,* but are implicitly derivable from it." Being grounded in *śruti, smṛti* is authoritative as long as it does not conflict with the authority of the former.[3] *Smṛti* literature includes such works as the *Law Book of Manu, Purānas,* and the epic literature of the *Rāmāyana and the Mahābhārata,* including its most famous eighth book containing the *Bhagavad Gītā.*

Though the *Mahābhārata* itself is not technically considered revealed scripture (*śruti*), it is nonetheless one of the most popular and influential texts originating from India.[4] This epic is regarded as, and indeed the text itself claims to be, India's Fifth (*Pañcama*) *Veda.*[5] Historically, the text is situated between the ancient scriptures of the *Vedas* and *Upaniṣads* and the *Dharmaśāstras.* The *Mahābhārata* stands in a liminal space: embracing its Vedic heritage, all the while evolving and anticipating new socioreligious realities. Occupying such a special place within Hindu *traditions,* this text preserves past ideology, records teachings and insights of its own time, and provides guidance for the future.

BRIEF SYNOPSIS OF THE *MAHĀBHĀRATA*

The central plot of the *Mahābhārata* revolves around the sons of two brothers, Dhṛtarāṣṭra and Pāṇḍu. The relationship among Dhṛtarāṣṭra's one hundred sons, known as the Kaurava brothers, and their five Pāṇḍava cousins is defined by an intense rivalry. Duryodhana, the eldest of the Kauravas, is consumed with jealousy over the successes of his half divine cousins and a desire for a throne he believes is rightfully his. Yudhiṣṭhira, eldest of the Pāṇḍavas and heir to the throne, is often caught between a desire to follow righteousness and renounce the world and the prodding of his brothers, mother, and wife to take his stand and claim what is legitimately his.

As the cousins grow into men, the conflicts escalate. Duryodhana conspires to eliminate his Pāṇḍava cousins. His hatred intensifies as various schemes to thwart his cousins fail and Yudhiṣṭhira and his brothers prosper. Yudhiṣṭhira accepts worthless swamplands as their portion of the kingdom and the brothers transform it into a splendid realm with a spectacular crystal palace. In spite of losing everything in a rigged dice match and being exiled for thirteen years, the Pāṇḍavas return to claim their place in society, offering to take only five small villages in exchange for peace. Duryodhana refuses to abide by this simple request. After all efforts for a peaceful resolution are exhausted, the cousins, each with their array of allies, converge on the battlefield.

Just prior to the commencement of this war, Kṛṣṇa and Arjuna engage in their famous discussion that is captured in the *Bhagavad Gītā.* After struggling with what his proper course of action ought to be, Arjuna and his brothers participate in the devastating battle. Though the Pāṇḍavas win the war in the end, everyone on both sides dies—everyone, save one embryo, a grandson of the third eldest Pāṇḍava, Arjuna. In the concluding book of the epic, Yudhiṣṭhira is surprised to find Duryodhana in heaven while his own brothers and their wife, Draupadī, end up in hell. It is explained that the one hundred Kaurava brothers fought according to the rules of war, whereas the five Pāṇḍavas, under Kṛṣṇa's advice, fought treacherously. After a period of purification in hell, the Pāṇḍava brothers also attain *mokṣa.*

The complex plots of the *Mahābhārata* weave together stories of gods, goddesses, animals and humans, kings and low class women, men with multiple wives and a wife with five husbands. van Buitenen has "little doubt that the story was in part designed as a riddle." This riddle has captured the heart of India and Hinduism. In doing so, this text continues to be a source of intrigue and insight. The birth narratives of the Pāṇḍavas and Kaurava, found in the first book, "*The Book of Beginnings*" (*Adi Parvan*), are the parts of the riddle that are of particular interest for our present purposes.

WHY THE *MAHĀBHĀRATA*?

The story of the *Mahābhārata* is known from circa 500 B.C.E. Unlike the *Vedas,* which once written down required "letter-perfect" transmission, the *Mahābhārata* is a very fluid, dynamic, and popular text that attained its current form sometime around 200–400 C.E. van Buitenen describes it as a "library of opera" where one can "say that 400 B.C. was the founding date of that library, and that A.D. 400 was the approximate date after which no more substantial additions were made to the text."[6] Through its eighteen books (*parvans*) and traditional 100,000 couplets, this epic unveils the stories of the Bhārata descendants, namely the five Pāṇḍava brothers and their one hundred Kaurava cousins. In Sanskrit, "*Mahā*" means "great/complete" and "*Bhārata*" is the name of the central clan upon which the story line is based. "*Bhārata*" can also mean "Hindu," "Indian," or more generally "man/humans;" therefore, in many ways the paradigmatic narratives are telling the great history of humankind.

The *Mahābhārata* encapsulates the whole of Indian life and enjoys a formative role within it. The text itself claims to be all encompassing, "whatever is here, on Law, on Profit, on Pleasure, and on Salvation, that is found elsewhere. But what is not here is nowhere else."[7] Elsewhere the text says of itself:

> A man who knows it and makes others listen to it, and also folk who listen to it, attain to the realm of Brahmā and become the equals of the Gods. For it is a supreme means of sanctification equal to the *Vedas,* this ancient Lore, praised by the seers, the greatest of the stories that are worth hearing. In it the Law is set forth in its entirety, and so is Profit; and in this most sacred History lies the spirit of salvation.[8]

According to the text itself and tradition, reading the narratives of the *Mahābhārata* can ultimately bring one to salvation. Radhakrishnan, India's former president and well-known modern philosopher, includes the studying of this epic, along with meditation, fasting, and worshipping God, in his discussion regarding ways to "attain the Supreme."[9]

In his book *Dilemmas of Life and Death: Hindu Ethics in a North American Context,* Crawford states that the great works of Indian epic literature, *Mahābhārata* and *Rāmāyaṇa,* "are not just works of antiquity but embody the social sinew which connects past with present and makes the epics dateless, deathless treasuries of true dilemmas."[10] There is a universal quality to the dilemmas faced by the heroes and heroines of the *Mahābhārata.* Through their actions they have become role models for how individuals ought to live and how society ought to function.[11]

Vinoba Bhave, friend, colleague, and coleader with Gandhi of India's independence movement, says the following:

> *Mahabharata* is a comprehensive treatise on the science of society. Vyasa has in his hundred thousand slokas given us innumerable portraits, customs and heroic actions that are as beautiful as they are real. The *Mahabharata* tells us clearly that none but God is wholly free from blemish; that none too is an embodiment of absolute evil. On the one hand, faults are pointed out even in Bhishma and Yudhishthira, and, on the other, light outsheds on the good points of Karna and Duryodhana. The *Mahabharata* describes human life as a fabric woven out of both black and white threads. Himself standing aloof, Bhagavan Vyasa projects on the screen of the world a picture, made up of both light and shade of the universal movement. Because of this perfect detachment and the big literary skill of Vyasa, the *Mahabharata* has turned out to be a huge mine containing pure gold.[12]

The paradigmatic narratives within the *Mahābhārata* are indeed mines that upon excavation will reveal the jewels that reflect India's past, its present, and Hinduism's ethical ideology.

Hindu tradition ascribes at least a superficial unity to the text by claiming that it is the product of a single author—the sage Kṛṣṇa Dvaipāyana Vyāsa.[13] Sullivan and others have argued that when Hindus attribute authorship to Vyāsa, they are implying that the status and authority of the *Mahābhārata* as religious text is to some extent dependent on the status and authority of Vyāsa. According to this traditional view, religious authority is personal and embodied in the guru. Thus, the claim that the epic is the Fifth *Veda,* endowed with religious authority, is validated by the conventional belief that its author is Vyāsa, one who not only stands at the head of a chain of great teachers, but is also the progenitor of the Bhārata family.[14]

This epic occupies a place of great importance in the collective psyche of the Indian people. It sustains their beliefs and governs their conduct to this day.[15] James Fitzgerald and Joseph Dahlmann both argue that the epic is a conscious "tutor of the people for higher religious and moral ideas," playing a major role in educating Indian peoples by "structuring and informing their imagination and sensibilities in fundamental ways for over the past 1,500 years."[16] From generation to generation, Indian and Hindu parents utilize the *Mahābhārata's* colorful narratives to teach and reinforce the feelings of continuity and cohesions of the traditions to their children.

The impact of this epic is enormous, not only throughout Indian and Hindu societies, but in the international arena as well. Scholars analyze and utilize the *Mahābhārata* as a primary source for establishing and examining Hindu perspectives on a variety of topics, both of antiquity and modernity.[17]

The *Bhagavad Gītā,* literally the "Song of God," records a conversation between the warrior Arjuna and Kṛṣṇa, an avatar of the god Vishnu, on the eve of the great battle. Encapsulated within their colloquy are three primary paths for living on this earth and finding liberation: (i) the path of knowledge (jñāna-yoga); (ii) the path of action (*karma*-yoga); and (iii) the path of devotion (*bhakti*-yoga). Opinions differ regarding the *Bhagavad Gītā's* place within *Mahābhārata.* While some argue that it is an integral part of the great epic,[18] others see it as a later insertion into the climax of the epic.[19] Regardless of its original position within the narrative, great philosophers of India for centuries have treated the *Bhagavad Gītā* as not just *smṛti,* but as near-*śruti,* sacred scripture. It has been, and continues to be, a primary source of inspiration for philosophers and practicitoners alike. Śankara, the great eighth century C.E. *Vedānta* philosopher, argued that the *Gītā* contains the very quintessence of the *Vedas* and that knowledge of this story leads one to freedom.[20] The eleventh century C.E. Bhakti theologian, Rāmānuja, interpreted the *Gītā* as a basis for the salvific relationship between an individual and loving God.[21] On a political front, both Bal Gangadhar Tilak, a national leader of the modern Hindu resistance, and M. K. Gandhi utilized this text as a revolutionary manifesto, calling on Indians to contest British rule.[22] Additionally, contemporary scholars throughout the world refer to the *Mahābhārata* and the *Bhagavad-Gītā* as exemplary Hindu texts.

Beyond the world of academia, innumerable artists capture the narratives of the *Mahābhārata* in paintings, marionette theatre, dance, sculptures,[23] comic books,[24] and plays.[25] Artists in Indonesia reenact the adventures of Arjuna and Kṛṣṇa in their *wayang* puppet tradition.[26] In 1975, French playwright Jean-Claude Carriére and filmmaker Peter Brook began a collaboration that resulted in a play, then a three-hour movie, and finally a six-hour video series that traces the central plot line of this great epic. Through their carefully chosen international cast, Brook and Carriére emphasize the universal appeal and relevance of this ancient epic.[27]

Another contemporary utilization of the *Bhagavad Gītā* portion of the *Mahābhārata* is found in Steven Pressfield's, *The Legend of Bagger Vance: A Novel of Golf and the Game of Life*—now a major motion picture produced by Robert Redford. Pressfield begins his book with a citation from the *Bhagavad Gītā.* Then, through the relationship of his characters, Rannulph Junah and Bagger Vance, he creates a narrative that mirrors the discussion between

Arjuna and Kṛṣṇa.[28] Steven J. Rosen, in his book *Gita on the Green: The Mystical Tradition Behind Bagger Vance,* explicitly points out the connections between Pressfield's novel and the *Bhagavad Gītā.*[29] These popular works, along with the timeless writings of influential authors such as Ralph Waldo Emerson and Henry David Thoreau, is evidence of how this epic inspired those within and beyond the Asian continent.[30]

The *Mahābhārata* has had a profound impact on Indian and Hindu culture, philosophy, religion, and society. Along with preserving the teachings of the past, it continues to provide entertainment and guidance for those living in the present. Hindu ethics, along with its principles, morals, and values, is present within the traditions and is tightly interwoven with the practical aspects of life. The narratives within the *Mahābhārata* provide more than thrilling stories, profound crises, and discussions on cosmology, philosophy, theology, and ethics; they also legitimize and inculcate ethical and political patterns fundamentally important to Hindu civilization.[31] Thus, through a careful examination of selected stories from this formative text, it is possible to lay the foundation for an ethical discussion that identifies key Hindu principles and applies them to a discussion of assisted reproductive technology.

Though we utilize this ancient epic, we make no attempt to demythologize the narratives of the *Mahābhārata.* When characters within the text call upon and interact with gods/goddesses, the characters are interpreted as interacting with the realm of the divine. The purpose of our study is to examine these ancient narratives, and to discover and to apply the principles, insights, and questions that are applicable to modernity. Of the *Mahābhārata,* M. K. Gandhi says, "I do not regard the *Mahābhārata* as a historical work in the accepted sense [. . .]. The persons therein described may be historical, but the author of the *Mahābhārata* has used them merely to drive home his religious theme."[32] In a similar attitude, we focus on the religious, ethical, and moral teachings of the text as they relate to issues regarding assisted reproductive technology.

THE BIRTH NARRATIVES

The multifaceted stories of two related royal families, the Pāṇḍavas and Kauravas, form the warp upon which the tapestry of the *Mahābhārata* is woven. With a text such as the *Mahābhārata,* where layers of themes and story lines are intricately interwoven, it is difficult to decide where to begin one's retelling of the particular narratives being examined. Though this chapter focuses on the accounts of how Kuntī, Mādrī and Gāndhārī produce heirs, their particular stories are preceded by events that lead up to, and influence, their situations and the decisions they make. Thus, to highlight a few crucial issues, as well as to provide a larger context for them, a brief summary of the main events, which are relevant to these specific stories, follows.

According to van Buitenen, the original narrative most likely begins with King Śaṃtanu.[33] Through his first wife, the goddess Gangā, Śaṃtanu has one son who survives into adulthood. His name is Bhīṣma and he is the undisputed heir apparent.[34] Years after Gangā returns to heaven, leaving behind the grown prince Bhīṣma, King Śaṃtanu falls in love with a fisherman's daughter, Satyavatī. In order to marry Satyavatī, Śaṃtanu is required to promise her father that the succession of kingship will pass through her sons. In order to fulfill the demands of Satyavatī's father and to ensure his own father's future happiness, Bhīṣma not only renounces all claims to the throne, he also takes a vow of celibacy to insure his promise.[35] King Śaṃtanu and Satyavatī marry and have two sons: Citrāṇgada, who dies unmarried and childless, and Vicitravīrya, who dies leaving two childless widows, Ambikā and Ambālikā.[36]

Long before meeting King Śaṃtanu, Satyavatī had a mysterious sexual encounter with a brahmin that resulted in the birth of a son, Vyāsa. He was born on an island, remained there as a hermit, and set his mind on asceticism. Vyāsa tells his mother that whenever she thinks of him, he will appear and do her bidding.[37] Thus, upon the death of Vicitravīrya, and due to Bhīṣhma's vow of celibacy, Satyavatī calls upon her hermit son. She asks him to provide heirs for her and her husband through *niyoga* (levirate marriage),[38] a traditional practice that allows a woman to have sexual intercourse with a man other than her husband for this express purpose.

Responding to his mother's call, Vyāsa appears and agrees to comply with her request. When Vyāsa shows up to have sexual intercourse with the Ambikā, she averts her eyes because of his homely, wild appearance—he has matted orange hair, fiery eyes, reddish beard. Out of fear she cannot bring herself even to look at him. Because of her reaction, her son Dhṛtarāṣṭra is born blind. Though aware of what happened with her co-wife, the second widow, Ambālikā, turns pale at the sight of Vyāsa: the result is that Pāṇḍu is born pale but is nonetheless endowed with marks of excellence.[39] A third son, Vidura, is born to Ambikā's maid, Ambā. Though without physical defect, wise, and far-sighted as his name indicates, Vidura is not eligible to rule, as he is the son of a servant. After the birth of the two princes, Dhṛtarāṣṭra and Pāṇḍu, the land of the Kurus and its people prosper.

Vyāsa, having ensured the continuation of the royal line, returns to his life of asceticism, while Bhīṣma is present to protect and rule the land while Dhṛtarāṣṭra and Pāṇḍu are growing up. At the appropriate time, they each get married. Gāndhārī, known for her devotion and beauty, becomes Dhṛtarāṣṭra's bride. When she hears of Dhṛtarāṣṭra's blindness and that both her father and mother desire that she marry him, she covers her eyes with a blindfold resolving that she will not experience more than her husband.[40] Kuntī, "one wise in the Law and exceedingly beautiful," chooses Pāṇḍu to be her husband. Later, Mādrī, the daughter of the king of Madras, is brought to Pāṇḍu as his second wife.[41]

Each of these matriarchs experiences difficulties in producing sons. Obviously, the challenge of providing heirs for the throne did not begin with these queens. As is evident from the brief summary provided above, the problem of sustaining suitable heirs for the throne goes back several generations. This issue feeds into an important theme that runs throughout the entire text, that is, the question of who is the legitimate ruler. Śaṃtanu is the established king. Bhīṣma would be his unquestioned heir; however, because of his vow to renounce all claims to the throne and his vow of celibacy, he removes himself from the line of succession. Though Satyavatī and Śaṃtanu's sons, Citrāṅgada and Vicitravīrya, both die prior to producing heirs, Vyāsa agrees to provide sons for Vicitravīrya through his two widows. Even though he is the first born, due to Dhṛtarāṣṭra's blindness, the kingship is not passed on to him. Thus, through this complicated and tenuous line of succession, Pāṇḍu, though the younger of the two brothers, rules over the land of the Kurus. He rules for some time and increases the kingdom, both in land and reputation. Though peace prevails in the land, questions concerning the legitimacy of Pāṇḍu's reign do not come to an end.[42]

KUNTĪ AND PĀṆḌU

Sometime soon after Kuntī and Mādrī marry Pāṇḍu,[43] the king goes on a hunting expedition and kills a buck mating with its doe. Unknown to him, the buck is a powerful ascetic, who, along with his wife, had taken on the forms of these animals. As the ascetic lies dying, he places a curse on king Pāṇḍu: Since Pāṇḍu thoughtlessly aimed to kill the buck while it was engaged in the most sacred of activities, Pāṇḍu will suffer a similar fate. If ever Pāṇḍu is engulfed by love and has sexual relations, he will die instantly. After cursing him the ascetic dies and Pāṇḍu is overwhelmed with grief.[44]

Prior to this curse, Pāṇḍu and his two wives had no children, thus the curse hangs heavy over them. Though he is married to two wise and beautiful women, now he cannot produce children and therefore has no heirs for the throne. After consulting together, the three decide that Pāṇḍu should forfeit his rule to Dhṛtarāṣṭra. Thenceforth, Pāṇḍu and his two wives renounce the world and wander in the forests and mountains. The mountain *siddhas,* great seers, and other ascetics watch over Pāṇḍu. After years of living like hermits and practicing austerity, he becomes like a brother and friend to some of these renunciants while others watch over him like a son. At some point, Pāṇḍu is troubled by the idea that for him, a childless man, there is no door to heaven.[45] The group of ascetics with whom he is associated foresee that he will indeed have sons and they encourage him not to despair.[46] He discusses his concerns with Kuntī and implores her to have children for him through the traditional practice of *niyoga.*

Kuntī, unable to bear the thought of being with any other man, yet wanting to please her husband, chooses this time to inform Pāṇḍu of a boon she received many years before. As a child she was charged with the responsibility of honoring the guests that came to her home. On one occasion, she greatly pleased Durvāsas, a powerfully divine sage. He chose to reward her efforts by granting her a boon: he bestowed upon her a special mantra that, when used, would result in a son engendered by whichever god she chose to call upon. Now, for the first time, Kuntī tells Pāṇḍu about this boon.[47]

Pāṇḍu is thrilled by this news that Kuntī has the ability to provide him with sons and together they carefully decide which god she should call upon first. They desire a son who will be righteous and good, so after much deliberation they select Dharma, the god of justice and order.[48] Kuntī invokes Dharma and in time she gives birth to a son, Yudhiṣṭhira.[49] Following the birth of their first son, they again consider which attributes they desire for a second and third son. After much deliberation, Kuntī summons Vāyu, the god of wind, and then Indra, the king of gods. These divine unions result in the births of Bhīma and Arjuna, respectively.[50]

When Pāṇḍu approaches Kuntī for a fourth time, she chastises him for his greediness and reminds him that the law of *niyoga* does not provide for a fourth son: "They do not speak of a fourth son, even in times of distress. After three she is loose, after four she is a harlot. Here you stand, knowing this Law, which stands to reason: then why do you transgress it [. . .]?"[51] According to the *Mahābhārata,* this law permits a woman to sleep with up to two males to provide heirs. It identifies a woman as "loose" if she sleeps with a third male and "a harlot" if she has sexual intercourse with a fourth. Not willing to take on the label of "harlot," Kuntī refuses to call upon a fourth god.[52]

It is at this point that Pāṇḍu's second wife, Mādrī, implores him to speak to Kuntī on her behalf so that she too may have children.[53] Upon his request, Kuntī agrees to allow Mādrī a one-time use of her boon. Thinking carefully and cunningly, Mādrī calls upon the twin gods, the Aśvins. From them she gives birth to her twin sons, Nakula and Sahadeva. Kuntī, furious and feeling deceived by Mādrī, refuses Pāṇḍu's second request on behalf of Mādrī.[54] Thus, through Kuntī's boon, she and Mādrī are able to circumvent the curse put upon Pāṇḍu and provide him with five sons, henceforth known as the Pāṇḍava brothers—the heroes of the *Mahābhārata.*

GĀNDHĀRĪ AND DHṚTARĀṢṬRA

Prior to marrying Dhṛtarāṣṭra, Gāndhārī comforts and attends to Vyāsa, legendary author of the *Mahābhārata* and her future father-in-law. Vyāsa had been traveling and arrives exhausted with hunger and fatigue. She cares for him, and, due to her kindness, he grants her a boon: She will have one hundred sons that will be of equal station to her husband and herself.[55] After some time, Gāndhārī marries Dhṛtarāṣṭra and becomes pregnant. By the time her sister-in-law, Kuntī, calls upon the god Dharma, Gāndhārī has already been pregnant for about a year. For two long years she carries the pregnancy without giving birth. Not surprisingly, she is beset with misery. Upon hearing of the birth of Yudhiṣṭhira, she feels the hardness of her belly and becomes exceedingly frustrated, terribly miserable, and inconsolably worried.

Up until this point, she had patiently endured the physical and mental challenges of her extended pregnancy. But now she has lost the opportunity to give birth to the first son of the next generation of her husband's clan, and now more than ever she desires the birth of her baby. Chaitanya describes her as entertaining a hope that if she had had her son before Kuntī, then perhaps the line of succession would have reverted to Dhṛtarāṣṭra's progeny, as opposed to Pāṇḍu's.[56] With great effort and the help of her maid, she successfully expels the product of conception. She delivers a dark, solid mass of flesh—a dense ball of clotted blood. She is totally distraught. After two years of being pregnant, how is it that all she has produced is a clotted mass? What has happened to the promise of her one hundred sons? She can think of nothing else to do but to dispose of the fleshy mess she has delivered.[57]

With his divine sight, Vyāsa sees what has just taken place and comes swiftly to her aid. Upon his questioning, Gāndhārī admits she was about to throw out the mass of flesh. She reminds him of his promise of one hundred sons and questions the veracity of his boon. Vyāsa reassures her that his words are never for naught. From the issue of her womb she can have her desired children.[58] However, he foresees the death and destruction that will come about through these sons, and encourages her to allow this pregnancy to be fruitless. But Gāndhārī refuses. She has endured pregnancy for two years and Kuntī has already given birth to a son. Now Gāndhārī wants the one hundred sons that were promised to her.[59]

Vyāsa dictates various orders and Gāndhārī follows his instructions. She collects one hundred clay pots and fills them with *ghee* (clarified butter). Then she sprinkles the ball with cold water. Upon doing this, the ball of flesh falls apart into one hundred pieces—each an embryo the size of a thumb joint.[60] Realizing her desire for her sons will come to pass, Gāndhārī now allows herself to express her wish also to have one daughter. She thinks of all the ascetic austerities she has practiced, all the charitable donations she has made, all the other actions that she has performed to gratify her superiors, and argues that she ought to be granted a daughter as well. As Vyāsa finishes placing the embryos in their clay pots, he informs her that there is one extra piece—the piece that will become her daughter.[61] After each embryo is placed in the *ghee* filled pots, they are incubated in a warm, well-guarded place. After some time, the first of Gāndhārī's sons, Duryodhana, is born. His birth is soon followed by the births of ninety-nine other sons and one daughter, Duḥśālā. Thus, through extraordinary means, the 101 Kaurava children, the future rivals of the Pāṇḍava brothers, are born to Gāndhārī and Dhṛtarāṣṭra.[62]

MINING THE NARRATIVES FOR GEMS

What is to be gained by examining this ancient Indian text when discussing modern assisted reproductive technology? What benefits and insights might the situations of Kuntī, Mādrī, and Gāndhārī bring to bioethical debates on these new technologies? Though speaking from antiquity, these rich narratives are worthy of close examination, specifically in light of modern medical advances. The magical means utilized to obtain children in the *Mahābhārata* are not analogous to actual modern technology; the text is not describing actual precursors to assisted reproductive technology. However, the epic does reflect a shared experience in the struggle against infertility and a shared attitude of openness and creativity towards procreation. Trying to fulfill their desires to have children, the narrative depicts how the three queens overcome major obstacles by utilizing creative and magical means. Today the creativity is expressed through various forms of reproductive technology. While these matriarchs from antiquity sought aid from the gods, contemporary couples seek aid from fertility specialists. While the queens succeed through hierogamy, couples today can succeed through assisted reproductive technology. What the *Mahābhārata* depicts as occurring through divine agency is today brought about through the agency of modern medicine. By highlighting specific aspects of the stories of Kuntī, Mādrī, and Gāndhārī, insights from antiquity can be applied to modern situations. These similar attitudes and situations provide the basis for applying relevant themes found in the *Mahābhārata* to the issues being raised in the context of contemporary bioethical discussions.

PATERNAL SURROGACY

In the initial discussion between Kuntī and Pāṇḍu regarding his desire to have children, the two discuss the legality and appropriateness of "acquiring" children for themselves that are not biologically related to both parents. Pāṇḍu reminds his wife that there are many legal and acceptable ways through which one may obtain sons and heirs. He indicates that in the Law "there are these six sons who are of the blood and heirs. They are the son fathered by oneself, the son presented, the son purchased, the son born by one's widow, the son born by one's wife before her marriage, and the son born by a loose woman." Additionally, Pāṇḍu lists other means of acquiring sons; however, these are neither heirs nor of the blood. They are as follows: "the son gifted, the son bartered, the son by artifice, the son who comes by himself, the son come with marriage, the son of unknown seed, and the son fathered on a lowly womb."[63]

Though one may obtain a son through one of the means included in the second list, that son is not qualified to be an heir. This was the fate of Vidura, Pāṇḍu and Dhṛtarāṣṭra's younger half-brother. Unlike his brothers, Vidura had no physical defects and the text speaks clearly of his wisdom and farsightedness. However, since his mother was Ambikā's servant, he was ineligible to take the throne. The first list presents a variety of options for one desiring an heir. Though the "son fathered by oneself" assumes a genetic relationship between the father and son, this genetic connection is, of itself, neither a necessary nor a sufficient condition for producing a legitimate heir.

One of the traditionally sanctioned means of producing a legitimate heir that is particularly relevant to the present narrative is the controversial practice of *niyoga*. The *Laws of Manu* 9.33-55 utilizes a metaphor likening the woman's womb to a field. The husband is the owner of the field and the "sperm donor" merely the sower of seed. According to this passage, the husband, "owner of the field," is the rightful owner of the child, the "fruit of the field."[64] Also in *Manu* 9.145, "the son born in an appointed woman should take (his share) in the estate just like a natural son, for according to the law, that seed and the offspring belong to the owner of the field." A child, specifically a son, born through *niyoga* belongs to the woman's legal husband.

Niyoga is clearly not a license for illicit sex. *Manu* places limits on the number of partners a woman may have:

> When the line of descendants dies out, a woman who has been properly appointed should get the desired children from a brother-in-law or co-feeding relative. The appointed man, silent and smeared with clarified butter, should beget one son upon the widow in the night, but never a second. Some people who know about this approve of a second begetting on (such) a woman, for they consider the purpose of the appointment of that couple incomplete in terms of duty [. . .].[65]

Though the text reflects some debate as to whether it is acceptable for a woman to have one or two sons via *niyoga,* there is clearly a limit. It is to be used only as a means of providing heirs for a family.

Niyoga is intended to be a practice devoid of lust—one that is solely intended to fulfill the practical function of producing a necessary heir for a woman and/or her husband. According to *Manu,* a son fathered by a woman's brother-in-law, when she already has a son, does not deserve a share in the inheritance because this second son is a "child of lust."[66] Again, the text reads, "If a woman who is appointed gets a son born of lust from some other man, or indeed from her brother-in-law, they say that that son is not fit to inherit the estate, and begotten in vain."[67] This same child, resulting from "lust," is also unqualified to perform the funeral rites for the husband.[68]

Several generations of the Bhārata clan participated in this traditional, though clearly disputed, practice of *niyoga.* Satyavatī is the first to advocate its use when she requested that Vyāsa serve as a surrogate, to father her grandsons, Pāṇḍu and Dhṛtarāṣṭra. Sutherland notes interesting moral and legal parallels between *niyoga* and contemporary surrogate motherhood. "The question which exercised the ancient Indian lawmakers, namely, who the real father was, is being asked with respect to mothers in our society. In both contexts, it is a complex consideration."[69] Manu records the dilemma of trying to determine paternity. "They say that a son belongs to the husband, but the revealed canon is divided in two about who the 'husband' is: some say that he is the begetter, others that he is the one who owns the field."[70] As will be discussed in chapter 5, the debates regarding paternity, and now maternity, continue with increasing complexity.

Outside of *niyoga,* the text records other forms of paternal surrogacy. While Vyāsa was the genetic father to Pāṇḍu and Dhṛtarāṣṭra, Bhīṣma, Śaṃtanu's eldest surviving son, was for a time the clan's functional parent, acting as surrogate father and leader. Upon Śaṃtanu's death, Bhīṣma becomes the patriarch of the family and guides it through several generations. Out of necessity, he acts as a regent, ruling the country until his half-brother, Vicitravīrya, and other heirs to the throne grow to maturity. Though true to his vow of celibacy, Bhīṣma is the surrogate father and grandfather to both the Pāṇḍavas and Kauravas. Additionally, until his death, Pāṇḍu is the surrogate father to the five half-divine sons of Kuntī and Mādrī. From these strategies of paternal surrogacy, we find an acceptance of a variety of means to obtain offspring.

SPERM DONATION AND GENE SELECTION

Pāṇḍu's request that Kuntī conceive a son for him through *niyoga* is not unique to his family. Kuntī, however, rejects Pāṇḍu's suggestion that she participate in *niyoga,* a form of sperm donation, and instead informs him of her secret boon. By utilizing Kuntī's mantra to call upon the various gods, she and Mādrī are able to overcome Pāṇḍu's infertility by accessing a "divine sperm bank," so to speak. While Kuntī and Mādrī obtained their sperm samples from gods, today individuals visit medical doctors specializing in infertility, fertility clinics, and sperm banks.

In their utilization of this heavenly sperm bank, these queens participate in a form of genetic selection. Consider Pāṇḍu's wishes for his first-born. He wants a son who "shall become the standard of Law for the Kurus;" thus he implores Kuntī first to summon Dharma for "having been given by Dharma, his mind will not rejoice in lawlessness [. . .]."[71] Dharma is not only the one who personifies cosmic order and keeps it going, he represents the principle of cognition of this order.[72] Thus, Pāṇḍu assumes a son fathered by Dharma will be one who will set the "standard of Law" for the clan and who will "not rejoice in lawlessness." Indeed, at the birth of Yudhiṣṭhira, a disembodied voice declares: "He shall of a certainty be the greatest of the upholders of the Law, Pāṇḍu's firstborn son [. . .]. He shall be a celebrated king, widely renowned in all three worlds, [. . .]."[73]

As the *Mahābhārata* unfolds, Yudhiṣṭhira does indeed set the legal standard; furthermore, friend and foe alike respect him for his truthfulness and lawfulness.[74] According to the citizens of the land, Yudhiṣṭhira "is a truthful man who knows the value of compassion. For he, as he knows the Laws, will surely honor Bhīṣma Śaṃtanava and Dhṛtarāṣṭra and his sons, and provide them with various privileges."[75] It is due to this reputation, and not necessarily to an objective right to rule, that a young Yudhiṣṭhira is installed on the throne as king following the death of his father. Thus, Pāṇḍu's selection of Dharma to father his first child is based on a calculated decision. He desires particular attributes in his son; consequently, he chooses the god most likely to bestow those attributes.

The same careful selection process is utilized for choosing the gods who will father Kuntī's second and third sons. Having obtained a son who is law-minded, Pāṇḍu then says to Kuntī: "They declare that the baronage (*kṣatriya* or warrior class) triumphs through strength; thus, for a second son, choose one of triumphant strength!"[76] Thus, upon his urging, Kuntī summons Vāyu and, through this union, gives birth to Bhīma—the strong-armed one whose powers are terrifying to all. At his birth a voice states, "He is born to be strong over all that is strong!"[77]

For his third son, Pāṇḍu wonders how he can "obtain a superior son who will be supreme in the world." He then thinks of Indra, the king and ruler of the gods. Indra's power and enterprise are boundless; from him Pāṇḍu is sure to secure the most powerful son possible.[78] To ensure success with the one who is sovereign over all other gods, Pāṇḍu does more than simply ask Kuntī to call upon Indra. The two of them undertake a year-long vow of practicing various austerities. Only after receiving the following promise from Indra does Kuntī call upon him to impregnate her: "I shall give you a son to be famous in the three worlds, who shall accomplish the goals of the gods, the brahmins, and his friends. I shall give you a superb son who shall destroy all his enemies."[79] Indra responds to Kuntī's summons and their union results in the birth of Arjuna—the greatest warrior and hero of the *Mahābhārata*.[80] It is through this "most superior" son of Indra that, in the end of the *Mahābhārata,* the Pāṇḍava line survives.[81]

Mādrī also selects her divine "donors" with great care. She is well aware that Kuntī's generosity has limits because Kuntī had said: "Think, for this once, of a deity, and of a certainty you shall have a child by him."[82] Desiring to maximize her one-time opportunity, Mādrī deliberately calls upon the Aśvins, who are twin gods. Consequently, her use of the mantra results in her having twins—Nakula and Sahadeva.[83] Although Mādrī's choice of deities is not necessarily related to particular attributes she desires *in* her sons, it is directly related to her wishes to increase her chances of having more than one son. Neither Mādrī nor Kuntī make random choices when calling upon specific gods to father their sons. Each deity is carefully selected because of the particular attribute, or result, he will bestow upon the promised sons.

Whereas these myths in the *Mahābhārata* counter infertility with the magic and power from the realm of the divine, modern medicine combats infertility with scientific technology. Kuntī and Mādrī's process of meticulously choosing a donor for one's potential baby is somewhat comparative to what occurs in modern sperm donation situations. When choosing a sperm donor, individuals and couples consider the attributes they desire in their potential child. They seek answers to all sorts of questions: What race is the sperm donor? Where is he from? What are his physical characteristics? What is his IQ? Grade Point Average? How much schooling has he completed? and What is his current profession? These same questions and others are asked of women willing to donate their eggs.[84] When going beyond conventional methods of childbearing, characters from ancient myths, as well as today, prefer not to simply go with the "luck of the draw." Rather, they attempt to manipulate as many factors as possible, so as to control the type of child that will eventually be born. Just as Kuntī and Pāṇḍu carefully select their divine sperm donors, modern individuals meticulously review the charts of potential sperm and egg donors.

POSTMORTEM SPERM DONATION

The creativity of antiquity and the technology of modernity share a similar concept, that of utilizing a dead man's sperm for impregnation. Recall Pāṇḍu's attempt to convince Kuntī to produce a child for him by participating in *niyoga.* As previously noted, Kuntī has eyes only for Pāṇḍu. She says: "For not even in my thoughts shall I go to any man but you. What man on earth is greater than you?"[85] Kuntī has no desire to be with any other man. It is in the context of this discussion that she reminds him of the following story.[86] King Vyuṣitāśva is a law-abiding man whose reputation is respected by men and gods alike. When he conducted sacrifices, the great seers of the land and all the gods, including Indra, attended. This king loves his wife, Bhadrā Kākṣīvatī, a woman of great esteem and unmatched beauty.

Tragically, one night while engaging in sexual intercourse with his wife, the king dies. Bhadrā is overcome with grief: not only has she lost her beloved husband, she is left without any sons. Clinging to his corpse, she continually laments her loss and wishes for her own death. Then a hidden voice speaks: "Rise up [. . .]. I shall father children on you, my sweet-smiling wife. On your own bed, on the eighth or fourteenth day of the moon, when you have bathed after your season, you shall lie with me."[87] The queen follows these instructions and through her husband's ascetic powers, which reach beyond the grave, she is impregnated by the king's corpse and eventually gives birth to seven sons.[88] Kuntī utilizes this story to remind Pāṇḍu that there are other options: They can have children without her having to have sexual relations with another man. For our purposes, this account is interesting because it provides yet another example of how this ancient text preserves imaginative means of having children that are surprisingly somewhat suggestive of contemporary practices—namely, the utilization of postmortem sperm.

The first modern postmortem sperm procurement was reported in 1980. The family of a thirty-year-old man requested his sperm be preserved following a deadly motorcycle accident. Dr. Rothman utilized a method by which he extracted and cryopreserved viable sperm from the deceased. Over a decade later, due to press coverage, the general public became more aware of such procedures when a newlywed wife requested the sperm of her deceased husband be preserved so that she would have the opportunity to bear his children in the future.[89] This newlywed was in a similar position to that of Queen Bhadrā. Their husbands had died leaving them both childless. Whereas in the myth Bhadrā was able to conceive magically through the ascetic powers of her husband, the North American woman in 1994 uses the advances in modern medical technology to have children.[90]

ADOPTION

Acquiring children through adoption finds parallels between Kuntī and Mādrī's story and modern situations. From the list discussing the means through which an heir may be obtained, some process of adoption may be assumed. In Kuntī and Mādrī's situation, there is a clear transfer of parental responsibilities. According to the story, one spring day Mādrī and Pāṇḍu walked alone in the forest. Pāṇḍu "could not control his lust, and lust overpowered him [. . .]. He forgot the curse and forced himself upon Mādrī." She struggled and with all her might tried to stop him, but was unsuccessful. In his moment of passion, the great king died in the arms of Mādrī.[91]

Upon Pāṇḍu's death, Kuntī and Mādrī both present arguments supporting their desires to follow Pāṇḍu in death. Kuntī says: "I am the elder wife by the Law, and the great fruit of the Law is due to me [. . .]. I shall follow my husband here who has succumbed to the dead. Stand up and let go of him! Look after the children." Mādrī counters by arguing that she is the one with whom Pāṇḍu was having sex, therefore she ought to be the one to follow him to "Yama's seat." Additionally she says:

> Nor will I go on living, treating your children the same as mine, noble lady, for evil would touch me that way! Therefore, you, Kuntī, must treat my twins as your own sons [. . .]. Watch over our children and think kindly of me [. . .].[92]

Mādrī "gifts" or "presents" her sons to Kuntī and implores her to take them as her own. From this time on, Kuntī adopts the twins and raises all five sons of Pāṇḍu as her own.

IN VITRO GESTATION AND ARTIFICIAL WOMBS

Gāndhārī's situation is every bit as intriguing as that of Kuntī and Mādrī. Gāndhārī's ingenuity in bringing about the birth of her children is interesting and brings to mind some controversial issues regarding reproductive technology. Our discussion needs to begin with an examination of the context in which she delivers her children. There is a common assumption that Gāndhārī is attempting to abort her fetus through her act of beating on her stomach.

In his chapter "On Abortion and the Moral Status of the Unborn," Julius Lipner utilizes Gāndhārī's situation as an example of abortion. Defining abortion in the "causative sense, that is, as the deliberate effecting of a miscarriage, a deliberate termination of pregnancy"—which usually results in the "morally reprehensible killing (*hatyā*)" of the fetus, Lipner demonstrates how abortion is clearly condemned in classical Indian texts.[93] From his study he concludes that:

> [. . .] from the earliest times, especially in the formative classical period described, both in canonical and collaborative orthodox Hindu literature, abortion (viz., deliberately caused miscarriage as opposed to involuntary miscarriage) at any stage of pregnancy, has been morally condemned as violating the personal integrity of the unborn, save when it was a question of preserving the mother's life. No other consideration, social or otherwise, seems to have been allowed to override this viewpoint.[94]

Lipner argues, "Gāndhārī aborts 'fainting with grief'" because "she is aware that she is transgressing the ethical code by her deed."[95] Lipner assumes that Gāndhārī's actions are motivated by the desire to terminate her pregnancy, an act that will bring about the death of her fetus. True enough, she wants to end her two-year-long pregnancy. However, are her actions motivated by the desire to bring about the "reprehensible killing" of her fetus? A close examination of her story will reveal that this may not be an accurate assessment of her motives. She is not necessarily trying to bring about the death of her baby, but rather is trying to discover what is going on in her body and perhaps even trying to bring about the *birth* of her fetus. If a simple abortion was her intention, then it is highly unlikely that she would have waited two years before attempting to terminate her pregnancy.

It is important to pay attention to the particular circumstances surrounding Gāndhārī's actions. Recall that by the time Kuntī calls upon Dharma, the first god she summons with her mantra to father a child for Pāṇḍu, Gāndhārī has already been pregnant for over a year. By the time of Yudhiṣṭhira's birth, Gāndhārī has endured pregnancy for two excruciatingly long years. The story reads: "When she heard that Kuntī had born a son, splendid like the morning sun; and when she felt the hardness of her own belly she began to worry."[96] Her worry, frustrations, and anger should not be underestimated. Because of her unusually prolonged pregnancy, Gāndhārī has not only endured the psychological and physical discomforts associated with pregnancy, she has also forfeited the claim of giving birth to the first-born son of the two brothers. This is not an issue to be taken lightly in this narrative; as previously indicated, questions regarding the legitimacy of rule are an underlying issue in the text as a whole. She takes action only after she hears that Kuntī has given birth to a son. According to the text, her actions do not appear to be motivated by a disregard for fetal life, but rather by the concern of a mother who is eager to discover the life of the unborn within her belly.

Additionally, the argument that Gāndhārī's actions do not display a disregard for fetal life are supported by her insistence that Vyāsa act to ensure that this pregnancy result in the birth of her children. Upon the delivery of the ball of flesh, Gāndhārī is understandably distraught. At first she is about to dispose of the "iron" ball of "clotted blood;" however, when given an opportunity to do otherwise, she takes it. She even disregards Vyāsa's warning of the destruction that will be brought about by the birth of her first son. She wants her prolonged pregnancy to result in the birth of children, not in their death. The motivations behind her actions are rooted in her desire to have and to see her long-awaited children.

Lipner makes it quite clear that abortions are prohibited except when the mother's life is in danger. He argues that Gāndhārī is well aware that she has transgressed the ethical code and that this is, in fact, why Vyāsa rebukes her upon his arrival. In this event, "the abortion does not have its natural consequence but is redeemed by Vyāsa's prescribing a surrogate gestation. All's well in the end."[97] According to Lipner, Vyāsa graciously redeems Gāndhārī's wrongful deed.

However, viewed from an alternate perspective, exactly how long would Gāndhārī be expected to endure this seemingly endless state of pregnancy before her actions would not be interpreted as "transgressing the ethical code"? Having working as a nurse in labor and delivery, I have witnessed women thirty-six, thirty-eight weeks pregnant who do not want to be pregnant anymore and want their baby out. At this point, most women are physically uncomfortable and they want to see their baby, they want the baby delivered so they can interact with it. According to the story, Gāndhārī was pregnant for two years. Though the *Mahābhārata* gives no indication that this pregnancy is in any way endangering Gāndhārī's life, at what point could she act and not be accused of "transgressing the ethical code"? The average human gestation is approximately forty weeks. Gāndhārī has already surpassed this norm by sixty-four weeks. Pregnancy places great demands, both physical and psychological, on the expectant mother. Surely Gāndhārī ought to be praised, not criticized, for patiently enduring this pregnancy for approximately 104 weeks!

The manner in which Gāndhārī obtains her 101 children is remarkable and brings to mind some very controversial issues regarding reproductive technology. Recall how Gāndhārī's product of conception is divided into 101 thumb-sized embryos.[98] These embryos all originate from the same substance—the same genetic material. Following Vyāsa's instructions, Gāndhārī does more than participate in something somewhat akin to "embryonic manipulation." Although the fertilization of Gāndhārī and Dhṛtarāṣṭra's gametes occurred in utero, the final gestation was in vitro,[99] so to speak. Gāndhārī and Vyāsa took each zygote (fertilized human egg) and "implanted" it into the ghee-filled clay pots. These pots become more than glass "test-tubes." They become "artificial wombs" (*ectogenesis*) that gestate the developing embryos until they are brought to term—an imaginative idea yet to be mirrored in modern medicine.

Within this narrative, Gāndhārī goes beyond the conventional methods of producing offspring and takes action that results in her having 101 children. The contemporary challenges of multiple-gestational pregnancies is considered to be a major area of concern for those involved with assisted reproductive technologies.[100] The use of Clomid (clomiphene citrate), IVF, GIFT, ZIFT, and other procedures often result in the development of multiple embryos and, subsequently, multiple births.[101] This situation leads to increased physical risks to the mother and to the developing fetuses. It also raises questions regarding the physical, psychological, and financial abilities of parents to care for the children who issue from multiple birth situations.[102]

We have examined only a few examples of how the birth narratives of the children of Kuntī and Gāndhārī contain imaginative elements that are somewhat similar to modern day medical practices. Beyond recording how characters in this epic struggled with infertility and employed various creative methods to overcome reproductive limitations, the *Mahābhārata* contains perspectives that have relevant contributions to make in the ongoing dialogues concerning specific issues in contemporary reproductive bioethics.

CHAPTER THREE

Narrative as a Source of Ethics

In the previous chapter we discussed the stories of how Kuntī, Mādrī, and Gāndhārī dealt with the challenges of conceiving. We saw how these ancient narratives preserve creative attitudes toward conception and child birth. This epic contains more than simply fascinating or entertaining stories; it preserves key elements of Hindu thought that informed the past and that may provide guidance for the present and the future.

We begin this chapter with an exploration of four topics extracted from the *Mahābhārata* that are relevant in contemporary discussions regarding assisted reproductive technology. After examining these topics with respect to the general issue of assisted reproductive technology, we compare and contrast Hindu perspectives with the attitudes present in the Hebrew Bible and with teachings of the Roman Catholic Church. Through this comparative exploration we see how perspectives grounded within Hindu traditions highlight important issues and questions that can have important implications.

As discussed in chapter 1, Hinduism is a religion overflowing with options, alternatives, and divergent beliefs. Its traditions neither owe their origin to a single religious leader or prophet nor do they have a single determinate creed or centralized hierarchical structure. This, combined with the fact that Hindu traditions tend not to establish clear categories of, and distinctions between, philosophy, religion, and the living of practical life itself, leads to the development of multifaceted traditions that embrace a variety of voices. It is said that many Hindus welcome pluralism and are bothered by attempts to eliminate alternative views. Arvind Sharma asserts that Hinduism is a "religion of options rather than prescriptions, of propositions rather than dogmas; a religion which prefers the article *a* (a truth) to *the* (the truth); a religion of guidelines rather than rules, and a religion which allows for more variations of the basic positions than its own Kama Sutra."[1]

Hindu traditions are pluralistic, syncretistic, and do not have a monolithic perspective on any topic. Though one will not find *the* Hindu perspective on assisted reproductive technology, this does not mean that Hindu ideas, attitudes, and insights relevant to the subject do not exist. Though the ancient Indian seers may have constructed systematic, all encompassing philosophical arguments, no one system was accepted as absolute or as exclusively expressing truth. The *Mahābhārata* preserves the moral philosophical thinking of the Indian traditions. Matilal argues that the "moral dilemmas presented in the *Mahābhārata* were in some sense universal, for most of them can be effectively used even today to illustrate arguments in moral philosophy."[2]

APPLICABLE TOPICS ADDRESSED IN THE *MAHĀBHĀRATA* NARRATIVES

1. Desirability of Progeny

The situations faced by the characters of Kuntī, Mādrī, and Gāndhārī reflect a common cultural emphasis on the importance of having children, specifically sons. According to the *Laws of Manu,* women are the "goddesses of good fortune" and "worthy of reverence and greatly blessed because of their progeny."[3] In *The Divine Hierarchy,* Lawrence Babb suggests the unfortunate conclusion that to "be a mother is to be a complete woman, and only with the birth of children is a woman's position in her husband's family fully secure."[4] Prompted by this cultural edict many women, including our three queens, have engaged in extraordinary means in order to procreate. Recall how, after renouncing his throne and practicing austerities for a number of years, Pāṇḍu became despondent. He says to his community of ascetics,

> For a childless man they say, my lords, there is no door to heaven. Therefore I who am childless am much troubled [. . .]. The sons of man are born on earth with four debts, which are to be paid to the ancestors, Gods, seers, and men [. . .]. With sacrifices he pleases the Gods, with study and austerities the seers, with sons and śrāddhas the ancestors, with benevolence men. I am acquitted by Law of my debts to seers, Gods and men; but not of my debt to the ancestors, and therefore I am troubled, ascetics. This is certain, that when my body perishes, so will the ancestors. It is to beget children that the best of men are born in this world. Should I have offspring in my field, just as I myself was begotten by the great-spirited seer in my father's field?[5]

Pāṇḍu has four moral/religious debts—one to the sages, one to the gods, one to men, and one to his forefathers. The last debt is fulfilled only through the birth of a son.[6] Sons save their forefathers from hell by performing the *śrāddha,* funeral ceremonies in which ancestors are ritually remembered and sustained through the presentation of offerings.[7]

Similar sentiments are reflected in the *Laws of Manu*: "As soon as his eldest son is born a man becomes a man with a son, and no longer owes a debt to his ancestors; that is why (the eldest) deserves to have the whole (estate)."[8] Elsewhere Manu is recorded as saying:

> A man wins worlds through a son, and he gains eternity through a grandson, but he reaches the summit of the chestnut horse through the grandson of his son. Because the male child saves (*trāyate*) his father from the hell called *put,* therefore he was called a son (*putra*) by the Self-existent one himself.[9]

Though a great king, accomplished in many ways, Pāṇḍu laments the fact that without children he will neither fulfill his obligations to his ancestors nor reach the summit of the sun (*mokṣa*).

In a discussion on the various qualities of marriages, Manu explains what sons from these marriages can accomplish. From one marriage a son can "free from guilt ten of the ancestors who came before him, ten later descendants, and himself as the twenty-first." From other marriages a son frees "seven ancestors and seven descendants," or "three of each."[10] Without sons, one's ancestors suffer. This is evident in the story of the ascetic Jaratkāru. Upon seeing the suffering of his forefathers, and hearing them rebuke him for his vows of asceticism and celibacy, Jaratkāru repents. He agrees to find a wife, get married, and have a son for the express purpose of relieving his ancestors of their suffering.[11]

Crawford comments on the economic, social, and religious significance of male children within traditional Hindu families. Through the *śrāddha* ceremony (a religious ritual performed for deceased ancestors), a son frees his family for the consequences of his parents' sins. Also through this rite, the son provides the way by which his deceased father joins the company of their forefathers. Crawford concludes, "It follows that a father not having a son to effectuate his passage into the assembly of the *pitṛ,* through *śrāddha* offerings, is indeed cursed."[12] The narratives within the *Mahābhārata* reflect this emphasis on the need to have children. Not only does a son assist the family in economic and social success in this life, he ensures success after death as well.

Though this priority of bearing children, in particular sons, is not unique to Indian religions, traditional Hinduism establishes childbearing as a duty for those in the householder stage.[13] The *Laws of Manu* provide explicit instructions regarding when to engage in sexual intercourse so as to optimize the chances of conception.[14] Furthermore, prior to taking up a life of renunciation (the fourth stage of life) and focusing on *mokṣa,* individuals must not only have provided for their family, they must also have children (sons) and grandchildren (grandsons).[15] The *Mahābhārata* clearly reflects this traditional Hindu ideology—that having children is an important priority, even definitive, for humans. According to Narayanan, this emphasis on having children opens the doors for contemporary couples to seek the use of assisted reproductive technology.[16]

2. Creativity and Conception

Beyond extolling the important role of sons, the examined narratives, and the *Mahābhārata* as a whole, appear to have few if any limitations on the utilization of creative means in one's attempts to produce sons. One can clearly argue that the *Mahābhārata* would not only permit the use of surrogacy, sperm donation, participation in gene selection, and embryonic manipulation, it would condone such practices. According to the text, none of the gods hesitates when he is called upon to respond to Kuntī's mantra. The text records no disapproval of Kuntī, Pāṇḍu, or Mādrī for utilizing the mantra.[17] The text records no hint of condemnation over how Queen Bhadrā obtains her children from her deceased husband; rather it praises her for her devotion and faithfulness. Gāndhārī is not criticized for her actions, even though she was warned that her eldest son would become a driving force behind the Great War that would bring devastation to the clan and nation as a whole. Desai states that myths "like this could be advanced to show the ethical acceptability of test-tube babies for Hindus." He goes on to include ovum donation and implantation of zygotes.[18] These *Mahābhārata* narratives imply that imaginative methods, in the case of modern technology, utilized to bring about the birth of children are, in and of themselves, acceptable. According to Desai, their use is quite arguably within ethically acceptable bounds for those who embrace Hinduism.

Though sexual intercourse did precede procreation for Kuntī, Mādrī, and Gāndhārī's, according to other stories within this epic, procreation is not necessarily dependent upon sexual intercourse. Queen Bhadrā obtained children from her dead husband. Also consider the circumstances surrounding the conception of Satyavatī, grandmother of Pāṇḍu and Dhṛtarāṣṭra. Thinking upon the loveliness of his wife, King Vasu inadvertently ejaculates. Eventually his sperm ends up in the river Yamunā, where a fish swallows it. One day, fishermen catch this fish and, upon cutting its belly, they find Satyavatī and her twin brother.[19] These stories and others demonstrate that this epic is open to and accepting of a variety of means to bring about the birth of children.

The *Mahābhārata* reflects an attitude that accepts creativity regarding the process of procreation; however, it does so within the bounds of propriety—it does not condone an "anything goes" attitude. Kuntī and Pāṇḍu's first choice demonstrates this point. Recall how Kuntī willingly calls upon three different gods to provide Pāṇḍu with three sons. Upon his request for a fourth son, she refuses. According to the passage, the law places limits on the number of children a man may legitimately obtain through *niyoga*.[20] Even in times of distress, when children may be more vulnerable and more likely to die, the law does not mention the option of producing a fourth son through this controversial practice. The purpose of *niyoga* was to provide progeny, not opportunities for illicit sex. Therefore, this practice placed limits on the number of partners and children a woman may have when utilizing *niyoga*.

Kuntī willingly applies the limitations placed on the practice of *niyoga* to her use of the mantra. There is no indication that the power of the mantra itself is limited. Theoretically, Kuntī could provide Pāṇḍu with an endless number of sons, while not being labeled a harlot, by simply calling upon the same gods again and again. This, however, is not her chosen course of action. Kuntī's objection to using her mantra a fourth time is related to her desire to stay within the limits of the law of *niyoga,* as well as not to be branded a harlot.[21] Kuntī's willingness to limit the use of her mantra provides a good example of restraint that should perhaps be a lesson for our present times. Kuntī's story highlights a particularly relevant and important issue to modern reproductive technology—that of designating appropriate limits of use. Like Kuntī's mantra, assisted reproductive technologies appear to have no limits within themselves. Therefore, similar to Kuntī, we ought to be responsible in our utilization of modern technology.

Upon Pāṇḍu's request, Kuntī allows Mādrī to utilize the mantra. Here again she limits its use by refusing her husband's second request on behalf of Mādrī. Admittedly, Kuntī's refusal of this second request is probably more related to the fact that she feels deceived and believes Mādrī is trying to get the better of her,[22] than it is related to her desire to stay within the law. Regardless, though the power in the mantra is apparently unbridled and limitless, Kuntī is careful not to misuse or abuse it. She carefully controls its use and distribution. Drawing on this story, one can conclude that though the *Mahābhārata* encourages creativity and would support the utilization of reproductive technologies, it also strongly advocates restraint. Though the text may not exclude creative means through which one may overcome infertility, it definitely limits the extent to which one ought to utilize such technology.

3. Women and the Control of Procreation

When discussing procreation and the challenges that are associated with it, it is interesting to note the active role women play in the process. The *Mahābhārata's* depiction of women, their roles in society, and their influence in reproductive issues reflects a complexity that persists into today. While there is no denying that this epic is infused with and upholds a dominating patriarchal social system, it nevertheless preserves stories that depict women in a variety of roles, positions of power, and with varying levels of influence.

Recalling the circumstances surrounding the conception of Pāṇḍu and Dhṛtarāṣṭra,[23] Dhand argues that there is a general lack of enthusiasm on the part of women to participate in the traditional practice of *niyoga.* She maintains that women have little voice in the matter, are passive instruments, and are at the mercy of their husbands, grandparents, or in-laws.[24] The reactions of Satyavatī's two widowed daughters-in-law, Ambikā and Ambālikā, to the thought of coupling with Vyāsa lends support to Dhand's claim that most women did not welcome *niyoga.* This story reveals how the experiences, thoughts, and feelings of many women are neither considered nor consulted, even in circumstances where their lives are most affected. This practice supports the oppressive idea that women/wives were property belonging to their husbands. If a family is in need of heirs, then the women are expected to perform their duty in order to satisfy the clan's needs.

While portions of the *Mahābhārata* depict women as powerless, passive characters, there are other situations where this is not the case. Though many women may have found *niyoga* distasteful, there are instances in this text where women, both widowed and even single, initiate the implementation of this ancient tradition. For example, when Pāṇḍu attempts to convince Kuntī to participate in *niyoga,* he refers to the story of Śāradaṇḍāyinī. Śāradaṇḍāyinī was a childless widow of a great hero. After preparing herself ritually, she "stood in the night at a crossroads and with a flower chose an accomplished Brahmin" to beget sons with her.[25] It was Satyavatī, not Bhīṣma, who developed the plan to save the family line through *niyoga* with Vyāsa. In this situation and others, women utilized *niyoga* for their own ends.

Kuntī's story provides yet another example of a woman taking control and determining her own reproductive destiny. Pāṇḍu urges her to participate in *niyoga.* It is very likely that she is aware of the story surrounding the birth of her husband and brothers-in-law, Dhṛtarāṣṭra and Vidura. Furthermore, she is probably well acquainted with the negative experiences of other women. Thus, it comes as no surprise that she flatly refuses Pāṇḍu's request. However, Kuntī's mantra enables her both to respond to Pāṇḍu's pleading and to spare herself the horrifying experiences of *niyoga,* which repulsed her mother-in-law. Kuntī is more than a passive participant in a difficult situation; she takes control. She refuses her husband's initial request and devises another plan. Sutherland argues that Kuntī's refusal to utilize *niyoga* a fourth time reflects "a faint but discernible legal and moral quandary which has begun to emerge in the law-makers' discussions of the conflict between the demand for a kinder and more ethical treatment of women as human beings and the need to command them for breeding purposes."[26]

Gāndhārī of course determined her own situation when she caused the products of conception to be delivered. Recall that it was her decision, even against the advice of Vyāsa, that leads to the incubation and birth of her one hundred sons and daughter. All of these women, within the confines of a patriarchal system, maximized their abilities to control their own procreative situations.

Another point of interest regarding the *Mahābhārata's* portrayal of women and their roles within the presumed patriarchal powers is the attitudes towards marriage relationships. Traditional texts, such as *Dharma-śāstra* and *Annśāsana,* preserve the recommendation that girls be married before they reach puberty, and in a husband-wife relationship, the wife is seen as no more than the submissive servant of the husband. This is not what we see within our epic narrative. For example, Satyavatī, Kuntī, and Draupadī (as well as others) are all presumably not child brides. Satyavatī and Kuntī both had children prior to their royal marriages. Though Draupadī's age is not mentioned, her twin brother had taken on adult responsibilities of state prior to her marriage to the Pāṇḍavas brothers. Additionally, Kuntī, Gāndhārī, and Draupadī's relationships with their husbands seem to preserve an attitude towards marriage where the wife is perceived as a copartner. She executes her *dharmic* duties and offers her support, advice, and assistance to her husband. The wisdom of these three women is sought by their husbands and even when grown and ruling various lands, their sons hold them in a position of honor and heed their council.[27]

The *Mahābhārata* also preserves a traditional practice wherein the woman, not the man, determines her future marital partner (*svayamvara*). As alluded to above, Kuntī participates in *svayamvara* when she selects Pāṇḍu to be her husband.[28] Draupadī devises a competition whereby her future groom must string a bow and shoot arrows through a contraption hitting a particular target. This contest brings Draupadī her husband of choice in the form of Arjuna.[29] While Yudhiṣṭhira is chosen by Devikā, Sahadeva is chosen by Vijayā.[30] Upon seeing Bhīma, Rākṣasī, a giant, human-eating demon, falls in love with him. Even after Bhīma kills her brother, Rākṣasī addresses Kuntī and argues that she and Yudhiṣṭhira should allow her to fulfill her desire to marry Bhīma.[31] The *Mahābhārata* recounts stories where women select their own husbands, thereby securing their own futures. It is Satyavatī's plan that addresses the crisis and ensures the continuation of the Bhārata clan when her sons die childless. Draupadī rescues her five Pāṇḍava husbands from a life of servitude. And Uttarā, Arjuna's daughter-in-law, ensures the continuation of the clan by carrying the only surviving male clan member. Though encased in a hierarchical patriarchy, this epic demonstrates how, ultimately, it is the Bhārata women, not only its men, who step up, save the clan, and ensure its continued existence.

4. Gods, Humans, and Procreation

The *Mahābhārata* preserves tensions between men and women as they struggle to control the process of procreation. The birth narratives of Kuntī, Mādrī, and Gāndhārī, along with many others, reflect an attitude toward procreation wherein gods and humans actively share in the procreative process. Though gods may participate in the process of procreation, they are neither in complete control nor are they always dictating the terms. Kuntī is dependent upon the power invested within her mantra. However, Kuntī and Pāṇḍu select which god they will call upon. The chosen god is then obligated to impregnate her. Though Gāndhārī is dependent upon the higher knowledge of Vyāsa, she is the one who determines that they should act.[32] These stories and others within this epic reflect a cooperative relationship between gods and humans in the process of procreation.

From the above discussions on the birth stories of Kuntī and Gāndhārī's children, the *Mahābhārata* clearly depicts the importance of having children for fulfilling one's obligations to other human beings, sages, ancestors, and gods. In this text, humans freely utilize ingenious means to fulfill the goal of having children. This epic portrays women as playing a variety of roles when it comes to procreation. They take the initiative and set plans into motion that result in their giving birth. Additionally, these narratives suggest that humans and gods are often coequals in the process of creating children.

Having examined some implications from this ancient Hindu text, it is appropriate, as a point of comparison, to turn our attention to specific texts that have significantly influenced modern "Western American" thinking on these issues, namely, the Hebrew Bible and the New Testament. Though the *Mahābhārata* does not share the canonical status of the Hebrew Bible and the New Testament, as indicated earlier, it is a formative text for India and for many within Hinduism. The point of comparison between these texts is that they are all formative for their respective religious traditions.

BRIEF COMPARATIVE ANALYSIS WITH THE HEBREW BIBLE AND NEW TESTAMENT:[33] GOD'S CONTROL OVER PROCREATION

The narratives in the Hebrew Bible approach the issues of human procreation in a very different manner from those found in the *Mahābhārata.* In the Hebrew Bible, God is unquestionably in ultimate control of the process of producing offspring. This text records countless stories of people praying to God for children and God opening or closing women's wombs. Take, for example, the story of Abraham and Abimelech, the king of Gerar. Responding to God's call, Abraham is traveling toward the region of the Negeb. Sarah, his wife, is very beautiful. As an alien traveling through foreign lands, Abraham fears that the godless inhabitants might kill him on account of Sarah. Thus, he instructs Sarah to identify herself as his sister, not as his wife. Abimelech sees Sarah while she and Abraham are residing in his city. Upon hearing that Sarah is Abraham's sister, Abimelech sends for her. That night God comes to Abimelech in a dream, threatens his life, and closes "fast all the wombs of the house of Abimelech" because the king had taken Sarah into his palace. Abimelech pleads his innocence before God; he had no idea that Sarah was Abraham's wife. The next day Abimelech returns Sarah, untouched, and confronts Abraham. Abraham confesses and then prays to God. God responds and heals the wombs of the women of Abimelech's household.[34]

Further on in the story, the power of God is seen again. "Now Abraham and Sarah were old, advanced in age; it had ceased to be with Sarah after the manner of women." Sarah laughs and scoffs at an angelic pronouncement that she and Abraham will have a son, saying: "After I have grown old, and my husband is old, shall I have the pleasure?" Even the patriarch expresses his doubts: "Can a child be born to a man who is a hundred years old? Can Sarah, who is ninety years old, bear a child?"[35] In due time Sarah gives birth to the promised son, Isaac. According to this story, and others, old age and menopause, though obstacles for humans, are not a hindrance to God.

Genesis 25 records the prayers of Isaac and Rebekah: "Isaac prayed to the LORD for his wife, because she was barren; and the LORD granted his prayer, and his wife Rebekah conceived." In another story, Rachel, Jacob's beloved wife, cries out: "Give me children, or I shall die!" Jacob angrily retorts: "Am I in the place of God, who has withheld from you the fruit of the womb?" Jacob is at a loss. Clearly, he feels there is nothing he can physically do to bring about the birth of a child. He is not God, granting or withholding the "fruit of the womb." Rachel gives Jacob her maid Bil'hah so she may bear children for Rachel. Still desiring her own children with Jacob, he and Rachel engage in the only other option they see open to them. They pray, and eventually God hears their cries and opens Rachel's womb.[36]

A similar spirit of divine control over procreation is reflected in the New Testament. The first chapter of Luke records the story of the elderly priest Zechariah and his wife Elizabeth. Both of them were righteous individuals but they were childless because Elizabeth was barren. While Zechariah is working in the temple, an angel approaches him declaring: "Your prayer has been heard. Your wife Elizabeth will bear you a son, and you will name him John." Zechariah, knowing that his wife is beyond childbearing years, questions the words of the angel. Shortly thereafter, Elizabeth conceives. Though Elizabeth and Zechariah had prayed for children, they had been unsuccessful and apparently had accepted the fact that they would remain childless. However, according to Elizabeth, God had "looked favorably on me and took away the disgrace I have endured among my people."[37] The stories of Zechariah and Elizabeth, and Abraham and Sarah, reflect a view of God as one who has ultimate control over human procreation; this God is able to open the wombs of woman who are physiologically beyond childbearing years.

In the sixth month of Elizabeth's pregnancy, God sends the angel Gabriel to visit Mary, a virgin betrothed to Joseph. Gabriel announces to Mary: "You will conceive in your womb and bear a son, and you will name him Jesus." When Mary objects and questions the angel's words, he responds: "The Holy Spirit will come upon you, and the power of the Most High will overshadow you; therefore the child to be born will be holy; he will be called Son of God."[38] In this case, Mary, still unmarried, has not even prayed for a child; nonetheless, God is indicating that she will have one. This text records the stories of both Mary and Elizabeth as extraordinary events. The conceptions and births of John and Jesus are unique and special. However, in the Hebrew Bible and New Testament, though humans are involved, God is ultimately in control of human procreation.

WOMEN'S ROLES IN THE PROCESS OF PROCREATION

Though God is ultimately in control of everything, and the Hebrew Bible and New Testament do not record instances where people manipulate products of conception to produce offspring, there are instances where women take particular actions to influence their situations. First, as already discussed, within the Hebrew Bible, one finds narratives depicting people beseeching God to enable them to have children. Hannah, the barren but most favored wife of Elkanah, bitterly cries and prays to God for a son at the Shiloh temple. In due time, the Lord remembers her, and she conceives and bears Samuel.[39]

Beyond praying, there are examples of women taking more of an initiative to move the procreation process along—especially when it comes to producing a proper heir. After God chose Abraham[40] and promised to make his descendants as countless as the stars in the sky, Sarah takes action that is akin to a form of maternal surrogacy. Knowing she is beyond childbearing years, she proactively presents her slave girl, Hagar, to Abraham in order that she may obtain a child through her servant.[41] Hagar gives birth to Ishmael and, until the birth of Sarah's own son Isaac, Ishmael is considered Abraham's heir apparent. Both of Jacob's wives, Rachel and Leah, also participate in a similar surrogacy situation. As mentioned above, after being unable to conceive, Rachel gives her maid Bilhah to Jacob, so "she [Bilhah] may bear upon my knees and that I too may have children through her." Leah, though she already has four sons, but not wanting to be outdone, follows suit by presenting Jacob with her maid Zilpah.[42]

Another example of a woman taking control of her situation regarding childbearing is found in the story of Tamar and Judah. Tamar marries the eldest son of Judah, Er. Because of his wickedness, Er dies prior to having any children. Judah instructs his second son, Onan: "Go in to your brother's wife and perform the duty of a brother-in-law to her; raise up offspring for your brother."[43] However, Onan, knowing that the children born of Tamar would not be his, "spilled his semen on the ground whenever he went in to his brother's wife, so that he would not give offspring to his brother." Onan also dies, so Judah promises Tamar his third and youngest son, Shelah. Judah sends Tamar back to her home while they wait for his son, Shelah, to come of age.

Tamar follows Judah's instructions and goes home. However, even when Shelah has grown up, Tamar is not given to him in marriage. So Tamar disguises herself as a prostitute. She sets up a tent near a road, which she knows her father-in-law, Judah, would be traveling. Upon seeing Tamar, but not recognizing her, Judah enters her tent thinking she is a prostitute. As payment for her services, he promises her a kid from his flock. Prior to having sexual intercourse with Judah, Tamar obtains several of his belongings as a pledge from him to ensure payment. She conceives. Three months later, when Judah is informed of Tamar's pregnancy, he is furious and says: "Bring her out, and let her be burned." As she is being brought out of her home, she retrieves Judah's belongings and informs him that their owner is the father of the child. Recognizing that the items belonged to him, Judah acknowledges that Tamar "is more in the right than I, since I did not give her my son Shelah."[44] According to this story, Tamar knew that Judah was not going to make good on his promise, so she took matters into her own hands to ensure that she would not remain childless.

The book of Ruth provides yet another example of both the implementation of levirate marriage and of a woman taking action to have children. The story begins with Naomi, her husband Elimelech, and her two sons moving from Bethlehem to Moab. Once established in Moab, Elimelech dies leaving Naomi alone with her two sons. Soon after, each of her sons marries a Moabite woman, Orpah and Ruth. They all live together for a period of about ten years, and then Naomi's sons die as well, each leaving their wives childless. While Orpah returns to her family, Ruth faithfully follows her mother-in-law back to Bethlehem. To provide for their food, Ruth works in the fields of Boaz, a wealthy kinsman of Naomi's husband. Once Naomi realizes that Ruth has met Boaz, she orchestrates events, providing Ruth the opportunity to request that Boaz redeem the rights of her dead husband. Boaz agrees to marry Ruth after determining that a closer next-of-kin is not willing to take on the responsibility. Upon the birth of Ruth's first child, the women in the village say to Naomi: "Blessed be the LORD, who has not left you this day without next-of-kin."[45] In this biblical story, both Naomi and Ruth play an active role in securing Naomi's familial line.[46]

Prayer, surrogacy, and levirate marriage are the only human initiated activities concerning procreation to be found in the Hebrew Bible and New Testament. Although there are examples of people manipulating familial and societal relationships in order to have heirs, there are no stories in the Hebrew Bible or in the New Testament where the product of conception is divided up into pieces and fetuses develop ex utero. Individuals pray to God for children, but humans do not have the power to actually manipulate God into giving them children. Unlike the narratives in the *Mahābhārata,* these biblical texts suggest an ultimate divine control over human procreation.

The Hebrew Bible provides the grounds for Jewish perspectives regarding assisted reproductive technology. These Scriptures, in conjunction with the New Testament, provide the foundation for views within Christian traditions. Though both of these texts depict a clear image of God as in control of procreation, there are a variety of interpretations as to how the God-human relationship and power over procreation function within modern expressions of Judaism and Christianity. No single perspective expresses the entire range of viewpoints that have developed within either religion.

A prominent, though not all encompassing, voice within Christianity is that of the Roman Catholic Church. As previously established in chapter 1, the Catholic Church has had, and continues to have, a significant influence on national and international discussions regarding infertility and procreation. For this reason, we focus exclusively on the teachings of Catholicism as a point of comparison with perspectives discussed within Hinduism.

ROMAN CATHOLICISM AND CONTROL REGARDING PROCREATION

While Hinduism does not have a fixed and formal doctrine concerning practically any matter, generally, there is neither an insistence that procreation and sexual intercourse necessarily go hand in hand, nor is there a categorical objection to the use of various forms of assisted reproductive technology. The structure of the Roman Catholic Church and the basic teachings of the *Magisterium* regarding God, humans, and procreation stand in stark contrast to their correlates within Hinduism.

The Church clearly affirms the biblical concept of divine control. The position of the Roman Catholic Church, as expressed through various theologians, asserts the dominion of a divine Ruler who cares about, and is in ultimate control of, this world and the events occurring in it; sex and procreation are no exception. Regarding the creation of human beings, Irenaeus states: "[. . .] each one of us receives his body through the skillful working of God."[47] Augustine affirms divine control over the creation of human beings in his *City of God*; Aquinas concurs in his *Summa Theologica* and in other writings. The Vatican clearly declares that in "the task of transmitting life, they [humans] are not free, therefore, to proceed at will, as if they could determine with complete autonomy the right paths to follow; but *they must conform their actions to the creative intention of God* [. . .]."[48] Again,

> to make use of the gift of conjugal love while respecting the laws of the generative process means to acknowledge oneself not to be the arbiter of the sources of human life, but rather the minister of the design established by the Creator. In fact, just as man does not have unlimited dominion over his body in general, so also, with particular reason, he has no such dominion over his generative faculties as such, because of their intrinsic ordination towards raising up life, of which God is the principle. "Human life is sacred," Pope John XXIII recalled; "from its inception it reveals the creating hand of God."[49]

When acts of marital sex are not followed by conception, this same text reads: "God has wisely arranged natural laws and rhythms of fertility, which already of themselves bring about a separation in the succession of births."[50] The Church utilizes biblical narratives to establish a solid concept of divine control. God is unquestionably in control of human procreation, "transmitting life," and individuals are not free to "proceed at will;" rather, they are obligated to conform their actions to God's intentions.

Concerning the proper role to be played by human participants, Pope Paul VI argues that God intends that sexual intercourse be inextricably linked to procreation and that these sexual relations are to occur only within the context of a marriage relationship. According to this Pope, marriage, "a teaching founded on the natural law, illuminated and enriched by divine Revelation [. . .], is not, then, the effect of chance or the product of the evolution of blind natural forces; it is a wise institution of the Creator to realize in mankind his design of love."[51] Regarding the inseparable aspects of sex and procreation he goes on to remark that:

> This teaching, set forth by the Magisterium on numerous occasions, is founded upon the inseparable connection, willed by God and which man may not

> break on his own initiative, between the two-fold significance of the conjugal act: the unitive significance and the procreative significance [. . .].[52]

Officially, the Vatican places procreation in a context wherein individuals are called upon to follow the path of God, to "conform their actions to the creative intention of God." Elsewhere, *Humanae Vitae* quotes the Second Vatican Council as saying: "Marriage and conjugal love are by their nature ordained to the begetting and rearing of children [. . .]."[53] According to the Magisterium, sex, marriage, and procreation are inextricably linked.[54]

The Magisterium teaches that, though God may regulate conception through "natural laws and rhythms of fertility," humans are not free to intervene. To do so would fail to consider the "vision of man and of his vocation, not only his natural and earthy vocation, but also his supernatural and eternal one."[55] According to the Church, "each and every marriage act must remain open to the transmission of life."[56] It is inappropriate, even a sin, to separate intercourse and conception. This argument provides the grounds upon which the Roman Catholic Church builds its doctrinal objections to such activities as sperm donation, IVF, and other forms of assisted reproductive technology. Sperm donation is prohibited because sperm is usually obtained through masturbation and thus apart from the sexual intercourse of the married couple. IVF also separates the act of sexual intercourse from fertilization; consequently, it too is prohibited.[57]

Immediate hominization, the belief that a soul immediately enters a zygote at the "moment of conception,"[58] is another reason these procedures and technologies are problematic. The Magisterium acknowledges the scientific understanding that conception is a process occurring over time, as opposed to a "moment." It also recognizes that the actual "moment" of ensoulment is unknown. According to the *Declaration on Abortion,* "From a moral point of view this is certain; even if a doubt existed concerning whether the fruit of conception is already a human person, it is objectively a grave sin to dare to risk murder." Nevertheless, the Vatican's rulings regarding hominization are grounded in the "theological concept protecting the embryo from the moment of conception, *whether the life is human or not, ensouled or not.*"[59] According to the Church, this position protects the embryo's right to life because it has the *potential* of human life throughout the process of conception. Through this argument the Vatican continues in its commitment to safeguard the dignity of human life.

While the Church acknowledges that the biblical texts themselves do not make a philosophical statement as to when human life begins, it highlights texts that speak of intrauterine human life. Luke 1:40-41 provides a prime example of such a passage. After the annunciation, Mary travels to visit her cousin Elizabeth, who is six months pregnant. Upon hearing Mary's greeting, Elizabeth's fetus, soon to become known as John the Baptist, leaps for joy within her womb. This text, along with others, is utilized by the Church to indicate that, prior to birth, a fetus is a human being. According to Noonan, this position reflects and enhances the values of a community sensitive to the living character of the embryo.[60]

In spite of the fact that there is no agreement as to when ensoulment occurs,[61] the Church argues for immediate hominization in the *Humanae Vitae, Gospel of Life,* and *The Declaration on Abortion.* According to the Magisterium:

> In reality, respect for human life is called for from the *time that the process of generation begins. From the time that the ovum is fertilized,* a life is begun which is neither that of the father nor of the mother; *it is rather the life of a new human being* with his or her own growth [. . .].[62]

As this excerpt indicates, according to the Church, the soul is infused into the embryo at the "moment" of conception. Thus, the resulting zygote is a human being. Through IVF, ZIFT, and other such technologies, a greater number of zygotes are produced and frozen than are actually implanted. Thus, the Church argues that, in essence, these procedures imprison a number of human souls. Additionally, in the process of cryopreservation and implantation, embryos are destroyed, resulting in the death of the destroyed ensouled zygotes. Finally, after individuals utilize these reproductive technologies, oftentimes there are "leftover" embryos. If one believes in immediate hominization, one is left with a dilemma as to how to dispose of these extra ensouled human embryos. Such official and unequivocal teachings as found in the Roman Catholic Church do not find their equivalent within Hinduism.

In this chapter, we utilized the *Mahābhārata* narratives of the births of Kuntī and Gāndhārī's children examine how an ethic from within Hinduism might respond to issues relating to assisted reproductive technology. Extrapolating from these paradigmatic stories, we see the importance that Hinduism places on having children and we find an acceptance of human creativity in attempts to bring about the birth of children. The god-human relationships portrayed in this text demonstrate a somewhat coequal existence. These issues were compared and contrasted with those found within the Hebrew Bible, New Testament, and Roman Catholic teachings. Utilizing the *Mahābhārata* narratives again, and keeping the above issues in mind, the following chapter explores six key elements of Hindu thought that underlie the construction of a Hindu ethic regarding assisted reproductive technology.

CHAPTER FOUR

Characteristics of Hindu Thought

From our discussion of attitudes regarding assisted reproductive technology preserved within the *Mahābhārata*, we can uncover some underlying characteristics of Hinduism. Prior to constructing a Hindu ethic regarding assisted reproductive technology, it is necessary to ensure a basic understanding of some of the underlying themes and key principles operating within Hindu religious traditions. As already emphasized, the *Mahābhārata* is a storehouse of the principles and characteristics that define Hinduism. Six important elements of Hindu thought relevant to the present discussion may be extracted from this text, namely: 1) an emphasis on the centrality of societal good; 2) a firm belief in the underlying unity of all life (*Advaita Vedānta*); 3) the expectations and requirements of *dharma*; 4) the multivalent nature of Hindu traditions; 5) a theory of *karma*; and 6) a commitment to *ahiṃsā* (no harm). These six characteristics of Hindu thought can profoundly influence the way individuals think about ethical issues and the way in which they make decisions.

CENTRALITY OF SOCIETY

A defining characteristic of Hindu traditions is evident in how Kuntī and Pāṇḍu utilize her mantra. Rather than acting immediately to satisfy their own desires, they carefully consider the needs and the greater good of the society in which they live. Through her mantra, Kuntī has the means to circumvent Pāṇḍu's curse and produce heirs.[1] Through it, she, and later Mādrī, have access to the entire pantheon of gods, each of whom could potentially be compelled to become her "sperm donor" should she choose to call upon him. However, Kuntī and Pāṇḍu are cognizant of the fact that this mantra provides them with a somewhat unique opportunity, which society may or may not accept. They could easily argue that utilizing the boon is similar to the traditional practice of *niyoga* and proceed to exploit the mantra's promised benefits without impunity. However, this is not their chosen course of action. Their hesitation indicates that they appreciate the difference between a "human sperm donor" and a "divine sperm donor." Only after devising a plan that ensures the social acceptability of their actions do they implement Kuntī's boon.

For their first child, Pāṇḍu selects the god Dharma because "he, among the Gods, partakes of merit. For Dharma would not join yoke with us if it were not lawful, and people will now think that this is the Law."[2] Dharma is chosen because he is a god of merit and, more importantly, if what they want to do is unlawful, Pāṇḍu is convinced that Dharma would refuse to participate. The god Dharma is the cosmic judge and discloser of truth. He "not only mythically personified the cosmic order or kept it going," he "also represented the principle of cognition of this order."[3] It is through Dharma's power that order is perceived and distinguished from chaos.

Consequently, if Dharma obliges Kuntī and Pāṇḍu's request, they can be assured that the rest of society will look upon their actions as lawful. Klaes confirms the idea that Kuntī and Pāṇḍu's choice of Dharma is related to their realization that they are participating in a risky adventure that can be accompanied by uncertain consequences. By choosing Dharma, "the most virtuous among the Gods," they can be assured that he will not allow them to do something that would contradict the order of the universe or go against society. Additionally, the son they would obtain from Dharma would certainly be a righteous and just ruler of the clan.[4] As recorded in the *Mahābhārata,* Yudhiṣṭhira is born under auspicious signs and is indeed a king who works to restore *dharma* in the world. Kuntī and Pāṇḍu's careful deliberation regarding the implementation of her boon highlights the priority they place on the importance of acting within the needs and concerns of society.

Hindu society is often described with the term, *varṇāśrama-dharma. Varṇa,* meaning "color," refers to the classes or castes and describes a stratified nature of society. There are the four traditional castes into which individuals are born, namely: 1) *brahmin,* the caste comprised of priests and scholars;[5] 2) *kṣatriya,* the caste of warriors and rulers; 3) *vaiśya,* merchants, artisans, and craftspeople; and 4) the *śūdra* caste, comprised of peasants.[6]

Additionally, traditional Hinduism speaks of four *āśramas,* or stages of life. One begins in the first stage as a *brahmacārin,* or student. The second stage involves establishing one's economic stability, getting married and having children; this is the *gṛhastha,* or householder stage. Third, after having grandchildren, particularly grandsons, one may enter the *vānaprastha,* or "forest-dweller," stage. This is a stage of life where one's thoughts turn inward and to spiritual matters. The final stage, reached by few, is that of the *sannyāsin,* or renouncer. This is an individual who completely renounces family, society, and work in search of *mokṣa,* spiritual liberation. The *varṇāśrama-dharma*[7] system is well established within Indian/Hindu society. It became one of the unifying elements, allowing for absorption of heterogeneous social and religious groups in the early development of what became known as Hinduism.[8]

Being married, in the childbearing stage of life, and fulfilling their duties as royalty, Kuntī and Pāṇḍu are participating in the second of four stages of life—the *gṛhastha* stage. Manu commends this householder stage of life as being the best.

> Just as all living creatures depend on air in order to live, so do members of the other stages of life subsist by depending on householders. Since people in the other three stages of life are supported every day by the knowledge and the food of the householder, the householder stage of life is the best.[9]

According to Manu, the *gṛhastha* stage is the most important because all the other elements of society are dependent upon it. As individuals engage in this stage of life, they are to do so with zeal and happiness because of the important supportive role this stage plays within society. One could argue that the principal goal of the *Dharmasūtra* and *Dharmaśāstra* texts[10] is the arrangement of life within a social system, so as to bring about a smooth functioning, well-ordered society.[11]

So central is the concept of society that David Kinsley associates being a Hindu, in part, with being a member of the Indian/Hindu society.[12] Radhakrishnan expresses this well when he writes:

> Human society is an organic whole, the parts of which are naturally dependent in such a way that each part in fulfilling its distinctive function conditions the fulfillment of function by the rest, and is in turn conditioned by the fulfillment of its function by the rest. In this sense the whole is present in each part, while each part is indispensable to the whole.[13]

This underlying assumption that all of society is interdependent leads to an ideal where individuals are encouraged to act in a manner that supports and works toward the greater good of society. According to the *Bhagavad Gītā,* preserving order within society is one of the primary motivating factors for Arjuna to take up his arms and fight.[14] This focus on the centrality of society is an important characteristic within a majority of Hindu traditions.[15]

UNDERLYING UNITY OF ALL LIFE

The centrality of society in turn reflects a foundational metaphysical belief evident within many Hindu traditions; namely, that there is an underlying unity of all life, the world, and all that exists. The *Vedas, Upaniṣads, Bhagavad Gītā, Advaita Vedānta* philosophy, and other literature and schools of thought within Hinduism teach this interconnectedness amongst all life and all things.

Ṛg Veda 10.90 describes how the world, humans, gods, animals, plants, and everything else comes forth from a cosmic primeval being, Puruṣa. The text reads:

> His mouth became the Brahmin; his arms were made into the Warrior, his thighs the People, and from his feet the Servants were born. The moon was born from his mind; from his eye the sun was born. Indra and Agni came

> from his mouth, and from his vital breath the Wind was born. From his navel the middle realm of space arose; from his head the sky evolved. From his two feet came the earth, and the quarters of the sky from his ear. Thus they set the worlds in order [. . .].[16]

From out of Puruṣa's mouth come the *brahmin* caste and the gods Indra and Agni. The earth and *śudras,* the servile class of society, originate from the feet of this cosmic being. Hopkins clearly articulates the significance of these connections. Just as the feet are the base for Puruṣa, so the *śudras* are the base of society, and the earth is the base of the cosmos.[17] This late Vedic hymn establishes an ultimate connection between the Vedic fire sacrifices, gods, humans, the world, and the cosmos.[18] Eck comments on how the Vedic "affirmation of oneness is not sociological or political but theological." According to her, "it is an affirmation about the very nature of ultimate reality. God or truth or Ultimate Reality is one, though people speak of that One in many ways and try to realize it in their lives through many paths."[19]

This Vedic worldview becomes the foundation from which the *Upaniṣads* teach that ultimately everything shares an underlying reality, a spiritual essence called *Brahman.* Ultimately *Brahman* encompasses everything. The *Muṇḍaka Upaniṣad* says of *Brahman*:

> In Him alone, as he shines, do all things reflect; this whole world radiates with his light. *Brahman* alone here extends to the east; *brahman,* to the west; it alone, to the south to the north, it alone extends above and below; it is *brahman* alone that extends over this whole universe, up to its widest extent.[20]

Elsewhere the *Kaṭha Upaniṣad* states: "Its roots above, its branches below, this is the eternal banyan tree. That alone is the Bright! That is *brahman*! That alone is called the Immortal! On it all the worlds rest; beyond it no one can ever pass."[21] The monistic upaniṣadic worldview is one of ultimate unity.[22]

Emphasizing this interconnectedness of all, Kṛṣṇa, representing the supreme personality of *Brahman* in this passage, proclaims the following:

> He who truly knows My manifested lordship and power is united with Me by unwavering devotion, of this there is no doubt. *I am the source of everything, from Me everything evolves.* Knowing this, the wise worship Me, endowed with faith.[23]

This belief that the Divine permeates everything radically connects all of life, human and otherwise. Thus, God and nature, the individual and others are all one, are all ultimately the unified.[24]

Regarding the connection between individuals and *Brahman,* the *Bhagavad-Gītā* builds on the upaniṣadic teaching and affirms that they are indeed the same. Human beings have within them an *ātman,* or soul,[25] that is *Brahman.* Therefore, Kṛṣṇa assures Arjuna that "The Self [*ātman*] neither slays nor is slain [. . .]. Just as a person discards worn-out clothes and puts on new ones, so too the embodied Self casts off old and worn-out bodies and enters into other new ones."[26] Kṛṣṇa continues: "The Self, which dwells in the body of everyone, O Bharata [Arjuna], is eternal and can never be slain."[27] In this text, Kṛṣṇa affirms that the *ātman,* being ultimately identical with *Brahman,* is immortal and indestructible.[28]

Śankara, the famous eighth century Hindu *Vedānta* philosopher, is attributed with proclaiming:

> I am verily that Supreme Brahman, which is eternal, stainless, and free; which is One, indivisible and nondual; and which is of the nature of Bliss, Truth, Knowledge, and Infinity [. . .]. Sitting in a solitary place, freeing the mind from desires, and controlling the senses, meditate with unswerving attention on Infinite Atman, which is One without a second [. . .]. He who has attained the Supreme Goal discards all such objects as name and form, and dwells as the embodiment of Infinite Consciousness and Bliss.[29]

Śankara argues for more than the nondual nature of the world and existence. According to him, the real, *Brahman,* is the indivisible Reality; an integration of the individual and the whole, of knowledge and of consciousness. *Brahman* "is life, human life, as lived."[30] This underlying belief in ultimate unity is one of many threads that make up the fabric of Hinduism. This thread is present in the ancient foundational texts of the *Vedas* and *Upaniṣads,* is seen throughout the *Mahābhārata,* is present in the works of philosophers such as Śankara, and is affirmed in the Hindu law codes.

The *Laws of Manu* seek to ground societal divisions and order in this idea of the Vedic cosmic person and the upaniṣadic teaching of ultimate unity:

> Then, so that the worlds and people would prosper and increase, from his mouth he created the priest, from his arms the ruler, from his thighs the commoner, and from his feet the servant. He divided his own body into two and became a man with one half, a woman with the other half [. . .]. You, who are the best of the twice-born, should know that the one whom he emitted was me, the creator of this whole (universe). Thus this whole (universe), stationary and moving, was created by those great-souled ones at my command through the use of inner heat—each according to its own innate activity [. . .].[31]

All of society is part of a cosmic body. In order for it to operate smoothly and to ensure cosmic order, each portion of society needs to fulfill its function; each individual needs to perform his or her duty. This principle of underlying unity is a primary belief within most, if not all, Hindu traditions.[32]

REQUIREMENTS OF *DHARMA*

Within Hindu traditions this thread of ultimate unity is tightly interwoven with the teachings on *dharma,* as is the concept of *varṇāśrama-dharma.* According to these traditions, just as all of society, the world, and the cosmos make up one "body," so also does each part have a particular role to play within the whole. This role, along with a number of other elements, is encompassed within the term *dharma. Dharma* is a central and ubiquitous concept in all of Indian civilization. Its very centrality, however, makes it a concept that is malleable; a concept given to "new twists and meanings at different times and by different groups, creating a dauntingly broad semantic range."[33] Whenever the topic of Hindu ethics is broached in academic circles, a discussion of *dharma* is inevitably included. Though *dharma* intersects with ethics, it is not equivalent to it. It has no direct English equivalent and its meaning is context specific.

The *Sanskrit-English Dictionary* of Sir Monier Monier-Williams provides the following definition of *dharma*: "that which is established or firm, steadfast decree, statute, ordinance, law; usage, practice, customary observance or prescribed conduct, duty; right, justice (often as a synonym of punishment); virtue, morality, religion, religious merit, good works."[34] *Dharma* is utilized in such a variety of ways as to elude concise definition. It has both a universal and individual level. It constitutes a principal Hindu equivalent of an "ethical category" on both a naturalistic and a normative level. According to Holdrege, *dharma* is a cosmic ordering principle that upholds the universe as a whole; simultaneously, on an individual/human level, it is infused with normative meaning.[35]

When discussing *dharma,* Hopkins refers to the large body of Brahmanical social and ritual responsibilities. According to him, *dharma* is "that which is established," or "what men ought to do."[36] Though in early times what people ought to do was related to sacrificial rituals, even as early as *Ṛg Veda* 10.90, the concept of *dharma* had a broader context of societal and cosmic order. Later texts on *dharma,* such as the *Dharmaśāstras,* focus on the particulars of social duty.[37] In this context, *dharma* refers to the privileges, duties, and obligations of individuals, and their standard of conduct in relation to their stage of life, their caste, and society.[38] Here *dharma* sustains individuals and connects them to one another.

In all of its multiple meanings, *dharma* is a term that ultimately relates in some manner to some sort of action or prescribed behavior. In the context of this study in comparative religious bioethics, the focus is on how *dharma* relates to the roles, decisions, and behaviors of individuals and groups. As discussed above, according to most Hindu traditions, individuals do not live independently of one another or of the society that surrounds them. As members of society, individuals have particular *dharmas,* particular roles and responsibilities.[39]

The narratives of Kuntī and Pāṇḍu reflect the focus on the needs of society, the belief that all are ultimately interconnected, and that all individuals have a role, a *dharma,* to fulfill. Even Pāṇḍu's desire for an assurance of heaven is not outweighed by the constraints of society and his sense of *dharma.* Recall how Pāṇḍu's quest for children began when he laments that "for a childless man [. . .] there is no door to heaven."[40] Though Pāṇḍu desires children and heaven, he and Kuntī proceed with their plan only after they are assured that their actions are lawful and considered legitimate by society. For Kuntī and Pāṇḍu, acting according to *dharma,* both in terms of God and in terms of their duties within society, is of utmost importance. Before they even begin to act, they want assurances that what they do is done in accordance with their *dharma*—in accordance with their privileges, duties, and obligations to society. In this narrative and others, the *Mahābhārata* as a whole clearly argues that fulfilling one's *dharma* is a priority; it is important for both the individual and society as a whole.

While *dharma* provides guidelines for how the individual and society are to function, these guidelines are not abstract universal principles. Rather, according to Manu, to be a moral individual is to particularize—to ask who did what, to whom, and when? Each caste has its particular duties and each stage of life has its particular *dharma.* What might be "right" for one individual at a particular stage of life might not be right in a different stage of life. Ramanujan emphasizes this context-sensitive nature of *dharma* when he compares it to a "Western" ideal of virtue. He highlights Hegel's observation, "While we say, 'Bravery is a virtue' the Hindus say, on the contrary, 'Bravery is a virtue of the Kshatryas.'"[41]

MULTIVALENT NATURE OF HINDU TRADITIONS

When the concern for society and acting according to one's *dharma,* as seen in Kuntī's story, is juxtaposed with the narrative of Gāndhārī and Dhṛtarāṣṭra, another key characteristic within Hindu traditions comes to light—that of its multivalent nature. While Kuntī and Pāṇḍu allow the needs of society to influence their decisions, Gāndhārī and Dhṛtarāṣṭra choose to act in their own interests. The latter couple is warned of the coming doom and destruction if their first born, Duryodhana, is allowed to develop and live. At Duryodhana's birth, Dhṛtarāṣṭra calls a council of his advisors and they tell him: "Clearly, this son of yours will spell the death of the dynasty! In abandoning him there is appeasement, great disaster in fostering him!"[42] They remind the king that he will still have ninety-nine sons and a daughter, and that he will secure the world and his dynasty if this baby is not allowed to develop. The counselors cite the law "For the family, abandon one son; for the village, abandon a family; for the country, abandon a village; for the soul, abandon the earth!"[43] In spite of their warnings and utilitarian justifications for abandoning the infant, the parents' desire for their first born son trumps the future of their dynasty and even society as a whole.

Since many of the narratives within the *Mahābhārata* underscore the importance of society and argue that individuals ought to act in a manner consistent with *dharma,* one might assume that the text would condemn Gāndhārī and Dhṛtarāṣṭra for doing just the opposite. However, this is not the case. The narratives record no criticism of this royal couple. Rather, they reflect genuine moral dilemmas faced by the characters and reflect the multivalent nature of the traditions. Bruce Long comments on this multivalent nature of Hinduism when he writes:

> One conclusion that we might draw from this diversification of philosophical perspectives and the inclination to intermingle ideas drawn from a variety of schools of thought evidenced throughout the *MBh.* is that the sages and scholars failed to discover any single principle of causation that could account for all exigencies of human life. Or, to state the matter affirmatively, like their Vedic forebears, the epic writers were prepared to embrace (or, at least, to tolerate) a diverse array of doctrines in the conviction that while reality is one, it can be designated by many names (*Ṛg Veda* 1.164.46).[44]

In its silence regarding Gāndhārī and Dhṛtarāṣṭra's actions, and the actions of others, the *Mahābhārata* acknowledges the complexity of life and demonstrates an understanding of the challenges posed by the ethical struggles in life. This commitment to multivalent thinking stands in stark contrast to Kantian philosophy, a system that presents clearly delineated categories through which human action is evaluated.

The stories of Kuntī, Mādrī, and Gāndhārī all acknowledge the complexities involved in actual life. According to Radhakrishnan:

> A Hindu thinker readily admits other points of view than his own and considers them to be just as worthy of attention. After all, if the whole race of man, in every land, of every colour, and every stage of culture, is the offspring of God, then we must admit that, in the vast compass of his providence, all are being trained by his wisdom and supported by his love to reach within the limits of their powers a knowledge of the Supreme.[45]

Rather than holding blindly to a straitjacket of philosophical ideals, the *Mahābhārata* acknowledges the various roles and responsibilities individuals hold at various times. There is flexibility in *dharma,* which reflects and embraces the flexible character of reality.[46] In his book *Dharma in Hindu Ethics,* Creel discusses the complexities of *dharma.* Though on the one hand the essence of *dharma* is "law, order, fixed pattern," when there is a conflict between *varṇāśrama-dharma* and *sadharana dharma,* the case of particular duties wins out over universal principles.[47] The holistic underpinnings of Hindu traditions and the complex nature of the situations described in the *Mahābhārata* and other texts highlight Hinduism's flexible and mercurial nature. These narratives take into account extraordinary and difficult circumstances and acknowledge that what might be good for one may not necessarily be good for others.[48]

Though the *Mahābhārata* may not establish a clear, consistent, all encompassing, philosophical treatise categorizing proper ethical behavior, it is nonetheless concerned with how individuals act and that they act appropriately. As discussed, *dharma* implies movement toward a higher order and sense of purpose. Each individual has duties to perform within society and each is called to perform that duty to one's utmost ability. According to the *Bhagavad Gītā,* it is better "to perform one's own duty (*dharma*) imperfectly than to perform the duty of another perfectly. Better to carry out one's own duty, even unto death, for to follow another's duty is perilous."[49] This focus on behavior and *dharma* is accompanied with a general guideline—one should act with the intention of guiding individuals in the right direction. However, specific prescriptions regarding what behaviors are proper or inappropriate and definitions of "right direction" are not listed. Rather, those judgments are to be determined by the circumstances surrounding the situation.

When taking individual situations into account, the result is often an inherently flexible system of beliefs. This might lead some to conclude that there are no boundaries or limitations to human behavior within Hindu traditions. Additionally, these traditions are sometimes viewed as being indifferent and supportive of a general attitude that "anything goes." This is not necessarily true. As Radhakrishnan expresses it, "Hinduism does not mistake tolerance for indifference. It affirms that while all revelations refer to reality, they are not equally true to it."[50] Though the *Mahābhārata* does not criticize Gāndhārī and Dhṛtarāṣṭra for choosing their son over the needs of society, and though it makes no apologies for their actions, it is neither indifferent nor, more importantly, does it "let them off the hook." Throughout its verses, the author of this epic clearly demonstrates that individuals always reap the consequences, and benefits, of their actions.[51] The entire text records not only the decisions and actions of individuals and groups, it painstakingly records the consequences of those decisions and actions. This highlights yet another primary element within Hinduism: namely that of *karma.*

THEORY OF *KARMA*

The multivalent nature of Hinduism also demonstrates a respect for the law of *karma,* which ensures that Gāndhārī and Dhṛtarāṣṭra cannot avoid the consequences of their decision not to kill Duryodhana. Contrary to popular understandings, *karma* is, in and of itself, neither fatalistic nor negative.[52] Linguistically, *karma* simply means "action."[53] As a theory or concept, it is complex and not surprisingly has a variety of interpretations even within the *Mahābhārata* itself.[54] The concept of *karma* can evoke a debate between destiny and human freedom.[55] In his essay "Human Action and Rebirth in the *Mahābhārata,*" Bruce Long demonstrates how passages in this epic reflect both the idea that human destinies are predetermined and the belief that humans, through their actions, determine their own destinies.[56] Regardless of whether one is living a life committed to acting in the world (*pravṛtti*) or to a life of asceticism (*nivṛtti*), *karma* is action. Action, whether past, present, or future, is inextricably tied to consequences, be they negative or positive, that will come to fruition either in this life or another. According to the *Mahābhārata,* everyone, regardless of gender, social status, or philosophical commitment, is subject to the constraints of *karma*; all will reap the fruits of the seeds planted by their actions.[57]

The *Bhagavad Gītā* declares that human beings cannot help but act. "*Indeed, no one can exist, even for a moment, without doing some action.* Everyone is forced to work, helplessly driven by the forces born of nature."[58] According to this passage, to be human and alive is to act. All action, all *karma,* is followed by results.[59] Consequently, Kṛṣṇa implores Arjuna:

> to do his allotted work, for action is indeed better than inaction and even the mere maintenance of your body is not possible without action. This world is bound by action (*karma*), except for work done as a sacrifice. Therefore, O son of Kuntī, do your work as a sacrifice and become free from the bonds of desire.[60]

Here the passage combines the principle of duty, one's allotted *dharma,* with that of *karma.* Again, though this text does not provide a specific handbook detailing exactly what one ought, and ought not, to do, it is pointing its readers in a particular direction.

Though various influences of *karma* may determine one's current state of being, *karma* "never determines one's mode of action. *Karma* is, therefore, more positive than normative and more descriptive than deterministic."[61] In discussing the principle of *karma,* Radhakrishnan indicates that "The cards in the game of life are given to us. We do not select them. They are traced to our past *karma,* but we can call as we please, lead what suit we will, and as we play, we gain or lose. And there is freedom."[62] According to this metaphor, there is freedom because all individuals are free to play their hands as they see fit. Thus, rather than being deterministic, this theory of *karma* calls individuals to take responsibility for their actions and to act.

This theory of *karma* condemns inactivity as the bane of all existence. According to Chapple, without activity, nothing will ever be accomplished. By not acting one is at the mercy of the situation, unable to fend off the unexpected, and unable to accomplish much of anything.[63] Though *karma* from past actions may influence an individual's current situation, it does not deem one powerless over the present or future. In his discussion regarding human effort in the *Mahābhārata,* Chapple recalls Yudhiṣṭhira's question to Bhīṣma, "Is the course of a person's life already cast, or can human effort shape one's life?" Bhīṣma responds by relating a story of a conversation between Brahmā, the Lord of creation, and the sage Vasiṣṭha. According to Brahmā:

> Nothing is born without seed;
> Without seed there can be no fruit [. . .].
> Just as a farmer plants
> A certain type of seed
> And gets a certain crop,
> So it is with good and bad deeds.
> Just as a field sown without seed is barren,
> So without human effort there is no fate.[64]

Here the *Mahābhārata* denies the idea of unexplainable fate and instead argues that human action, *karma,* is the cause of current situations and the determinate for the future.[65]

Acting in the present can transform the current and future course of *karma.* Kuntī, Mādrī, and Gāndhārī all took decisive actions that altered the course of their situations regarding having children. They obviously did not hold to the view that their course, their fate, was set and that any action on their part was futile. To the contrary, they initiated actions that set their lives on an entirely different course. This theory of *karma* connects human actions with their consequences, thus making humans directly responsible for both the positive and negative fruits of their actions. According to M. K. Gandhi, "All action will have its consequences; the consequences in one case, as we'll see, will be the bondage of *samsara,* in the other case it will be freedom from it."[66]

COMMITMENT TO *AHIṂSĀ*

The *Mahābhārata* and *Bhagavad Gītā* may not provide an explicit course to follow, such as is found in the ethical code of the Ten Commandments. However, they do supply general guidelines for shaping one's behavior. Kṛṣṇa instructs Arjuna to "always perform without attachment the work that should be done. By doing work without attachment, man attains the Supreme [. . .]. You should perform action also with the intention of guiding the people in the right direction."[67] Vinoba Bhave clearly argues against the notion that these texts do not provide specific instructions as to how one is to act. According to him, acting without attachment is a guiding principle that provides specific instructions as to how one *should* act. Violent actions, lying, and stealing are impossible to perform if one has renounced the fruit of action. Thus, according to Vinoba, "this is the condition of forbidden and interested actions. We must test all our actions on the touchstone of renunciation of fruit. Renunciation of fruit is the test for performing any action."[68] According to Vinoba, acting without attachment clearly means one's actions will neither be violent nor false. In the same tradition as Gandhi, Vinoba interprets the *Bhagavad Gītā* as presenting a very clear path for individuals to follow; a path of *ahiṃsā,* "no harm" or "nonviolence."[69]

More than nonviolence, Young asserts that *ahiṃsā* suggests the principles of nonmaleficence and beneficence.[70] Though the examined narratives do not directly address this concept of *ahiṃsā,* it is an important principle that directly relates to all five of the characteristics of Hindu thought discussed above. Kṛṣṇa says, the "gateway to hell which destroys the soul is threefold: lust, anger and greed. Therefore, one should renounce these three."[71] Actions grounded in *ahiṃsā* are free of lust, anger, and greed; they are actions of "protection, benevolence, friendship and compassion."[72]

If one believes that all of life is interconnected and interdependent, then a logical expression of this belief is *ahiṃsā.* According to Gandhi:

> Attacking an individual, even an enemy, is tantamount to resisting and attacking oneself. For we are all tarred with the same brush, and are children of one and the same Creator, and as such the divine powers within us are infinite. To slight a single human being is to slight those divine powers, and thus to harm not only that being but with him the whole world.[73]

Gandhi's belief in the underlying unity of all life fueled his commitment to *ahiṃsā*.[74] By acting in a spirit of *ahiṃsā*, one is acting in a manner that would most likely support the good of society and positively affect one's *dharma* and *karma*. According to Gandhi, *ahiṃsā* is more than the basis for action, it is the basis for truth.[75]

Traditions within Hinduism recognize that norms and values differ for those from diverse geographical areas and castes, from different genders and ages. There is also recognition that life itself is ever changing and dynamic and that no text, law, or philosophy can ever capture life in its entirety.[76] *Ahiṃsā* and the other five characteristics of Hindu thought are malleable in their application. These key concepts are in Hinduism's foundational and formative texts such as the *Vedas, Upaniṣads,* and the *Mahābhārata*. However, Young and Narayanan indicate that, though foundational, the Hindu texts are flexible and interpreted in various ways depending upon the time and situation, depending upon the context.[77]

Many operating within Hindu traditions tend to develop their ethics from the specific contexts and instances presented to them. This focus on the actualities of life accentuates the mercurial nature of Hinduism. According to Desai, the interpreters of these Hindu traditions demonstrate a passion for inclusiveness. They steer away from absolutes, are sensitive to context, and allow for qualification of each situation.[78] These traditions are pluralistic and welcome a plethora of options. Doniger O'Flaherty observes that "what makes Indian thought so fascinating is the constant rapprochement between opposed worldviews, hardly a true synthesis, but a cross-fertilization that seems to have no end, one mediation giving rise to another, each result becoming a new cause [. . .]."[79] This ability to hold a great amount of ambiguity—neither to feel compelled to arrive at a single conclusive answer nor to encapsulate the entirety of human experience into specific categories—provides fertile ground in which the complexities of life, rather than being problems, glitches, or inconsistencies that need to be overcome, are allowed to determine what is considered ethical and nonethical behavior.

The Hindu traditions reflected in the *Mahābhārata* are neither interested in establishing consistent philosophical theories or ethical principles nor are they committed to arriving at a single conclusion or answer. Perhaps this is in part because these traditions acknowledge that abstract philosophical theories cannot always assist those engaged in the process of living—those facing the emergencies of life. There seems to be an implied positive regard and confidence in an individual's ability to reason ethically. Murthy talks about how there is an emphasis on created faith and a confidence in human efforts.[80] Ideally this process of human reasoning is given some structure through the principles of *karma* and *ahiṃsā*.

By focusing on human action and the consequences of those actions, the *Mahābhārata* highlights the particularities and complexities of people's lives. This epic text makes no effort to clean up reality so as to satisfy the limitations of particular categories. By approaching each situation with a wide range of options, preconceived ideas of what ought or ought not be, are minimized. Each situation is assessed on its own merits and allowed to define the issues and direct one's course of action. Each situation places one in the center of a circle, with spokes like a wagon wheel going out in different directions, each presenting an array of choices. As Carstaires and Sharma indicate, these types of options and choices do not necessarily provoke anxiety for those living within the traditions reflected in the *Mahābhārata*.[81] Rather, these options provide opportunities for action, opportunities for individuals to fulfill their *dharma* and influence the course of *karma* for themselves and others.

Having discussed six key characteristics of Hindu thought and a few of their implications, we are now prepared to turn our attention to a particular case that highlights issues relating to assisted reproductive technology. In the following chapter, we apply these Hindu elements to an examination of the case of Jaycee Buzzanca. Through this process a Hindu ethic regarding assisted reproductive technology is constructed.

CHAPTER FIVE

Application of Hindu Thought

Although principles and characteristics extracted from the *Mahābhārata* are foundational for many Hindu traditions, we need to reemphasize that Hinduism, like other religious traditions, is not monolithic. It is a conglomeration of religious traditions that cherish their multivalent natures. Sharma remarks that Hindu traditions "consist of a frame of mind rather than fixed ideas;" their "answers are exploratory, rather than catechetical in nature."[1] Thus, when discussing ethics and how individuals ought to act, many speaking from within Hindu traditions tend to focus on the particular situation being examined rather than putting forth various generally applicable principles. Bearing this attitude in mind, we now examine a particular case—namely that of Jaycee Buzzanca—in light of Hindu ethics. Jaycee's situation not only challenges the legal limits of particular laws in the United States, it highlights many of the central ethical complexities that can accompany the use of assisted reproductive technologies.

Following a brief summary of Jaycee's situation, we examine her case in light of the six key elements of Hindu thought that we identified in the previous chapter, namely: (i) emphasis on societal good; (ii) the underlying unity of all life; (iii) the responsibilities of *dharma*; (iv) the multivalent nature of Hindu traditions; (v) a theory of *karma.*; and (vi) a commitment to *ahiṃsā.* Though these Hindu elements—specifically, the context-specific nature of *dharma*—preclude the formulation of an exclusive or definitive Hindu ethic, they do provide a beneficial set of lenses through which we can examine the ethical issues associated with particular medical technologies. Through this practical application of these characteristics of Hindu thought, Hindu responses to assisted reproductive technologies may be theoretically deduced. Again, as a point of comparison, these Hindu concepts will be juxtaposed with those of the Roman Catholic Church.

JAYCEE'S CASE[2]

The story of Jaycee Buzzanca begins in May 1989 with the marriage of John and Luanne Buzzanca. After years of unsuccessfully utilizing fertility treatments,

Luanne meets and convinces Pamela Snell to be a gestational surrogate mother for her and John's baby. Due to their own sterility, the Buzzancas obtain an embryo conceived through IVF with the sperm and ova from anonymous donors.[3] On 13 August 1994, this embryo is implanted into Ms. Snell's uterus. She, her husband Randy, and both the Buzzancas sign a surrogacy contract stipulating that neither the surrogate (Ms. Snell) nor her husband will interfere, retain, or assert any parental rights. Additionally, the contract provides that in the event that the "intended mother" (Luanne) dies prior to the child's birth, custody of the child will go to the "intended father" (John), and if the "intended father" dies, then the child will be placed with the "intended mother." If both Luanne and John were to die before the birth of the child, then the surrogate and her husband agreed to place the child into the custody of guardians, as stipulated in the Buzzancas' will.[4] This surrogacy contract clearly indicates that John and Luanne Buzzanca are the intended parents who will both care and provide for the resulting baby. The contract also unmistakably stipulates that Pamela and Randy Snell will neither make claims to parenthood nor bear any parenting responsibilities.

On 30 March 1995, John Buzzanca files for "dissolution of marriage," alleging that he and Luanne have been separated since September of 1994. In his claim, he indicates that there are "no minor children of the marriage." Less than a month later, Luanne files a response alleging that though there are no minor children at present, she and John are expecting a baby by way of a surrogate contract. Six days later, on 26 April 1995, Jaycee Louise Buzzanca is born. According to the conditions of the surrogate contract, and without any objections or hesitation, Ms. Snell willingly gives the baby, and custody of her, to Luanne, who subsequently takes her home. Several months later, Luanne files for sole custody of Jaycee, and requests *pendente lite* child support payments from John.

Not disputing the fact that he signed the surrogacy contract, John argues that the California Family Court lacks the jurisdiction to force him to pay child support because, according to its own definitions, it cannot establish that Jaycee is indeed a "child of the marriage." According to section 7610 of the Uniform Parentage Act,

> The parent and child relationship may be established as follows: (a) Between a child and the natural mother, it may be established by proof of her having given birth to the child, or under this part; (b) Between a child and the natural father, it may be established under this part; (c) Between a child and an adoptive parent, it may be established by proof of adoption.[5]

Johnson v. Calvert clarifies "under this part" to mean "genetic consanguinity." According to this Act, there are three ways in which individuals may establish legal familial relationships: 1) having a genetic connection with the child; 2) actually giving birth to the child; and 3) through the legal process of adoption.

Basing his ruling on the facts of the case and a close interpretation of the above Act, the trial court judge, Robert D. Monarch, came to the extraordinary conclusion that "Jaycee had no lawful parents." First, the judge accepted a stipulation that neither Pamela Snell, the surrogate, nor her husband were the "biological" parents.[6] Second, he concluded that the facts clearly indicate that Luanne could not be Jaycee's mother because she did not contribute the egg, or give birth to her, or legally adopt her. Additionally, John could not be Jaycee's father because he neither had a biological relationship with her, nor had he adopted her. Thus, Judge Monarch concurred with John's argument that the California Family Court lacked jurisdiction.

Jaycee's case is not a dispute over facts, but rather a dispute over the *legal significance* of the facts. John acknowledges that he willingly signed the surrogacy contract; however, he claims this contract is not sufficient evidence to indicate that he is Jaycee's father. The California Court of Appeals disagreed and reversed the lower court's decision. Applying the well established precedent of a Supreme Court case, *People v. Sorensen* (1968)[7] and the first surrogacy case, *Johnson v. Calvert* (1993),[8] the California Court of Appeals argued that the same reasoning guiding the courts in these cases applied to Jaycee's case. According to this Court of Appeals,

> Just as a husband is deemed to be the lawful father of a child unrelated to him when his wife gives birth after artificial insemination, so should a husband and wife be deemed the lawful parents of a child after a surrogate bears a biologically unrelated child on their behalf. In each instance, a child is procreated because a medical procedure was initiated and consented to by intended parents. The only difference is that in this case, unlike artificial insemination, there is no reason to distinguish between husband and wife. We therefore must reverse the trial court's judgment and direct that a new judgment be entered, declaring that both Luanne and John are the lawful parents of Jaycee.[9]

Through this ruling, the California Court of Appeals put an end to Jaycee's status as a "legal orphan."[10] In doing so, the court ruled that even in the absence of a genetic or biological relationship, parental relationships may be established when the intended parents initiate and consent to reproductive medical procedures.[11]

This court, like that of the Johnson court, arrived at its conclusion through examining the importance of an individual's intentions. The court did not focus on the question, "Is the surrogacy contract enforceable?" Rather it focused on the question of "What was John's intent when he signed the contract?" Jaycee would not exist had John and Luanne not intended for a child to be born. The California Court of Appeals, extrapolating from previous cases, utilized a degree of common sense to equitably resolve Jaycee's predicament. Though there is general agreement that the court arrived at the best decision for Jaycee's situation, there is concern and debate over its implications for, and application to, future cases.[12] Though the legal questions are beyond the scope of this paper, the ethical issues are not.

PRACTICAL APPLICATION: A HINDU ANALYSIS OF JAYCEE BUZZANCA'S CASE

In the context of assisted reproductive technology, Jaycee's case involves the utilization of donor gametes, IVF, and surrogacy. Of the many areas of concern regarding these technologies, let us focus our discussion on three. First, there is the question of whether these technologies ought to be used or not. Second, Jaycee's case underscores concerns relating to the tensions between individual rights and self-interest versus the rights and interests of others and of society as a whole. Third, opponents of assisted reproductive technologies often argue that these technologies threaten the existence of the marriage, the traditional family, and understandings of parenthood. Jaycee's case brings all these challenges to the forefront. It is true that fair-minded individuals can disagree over moral issues related to assisted reproductive technology. The disagreements involved in Jaycee's case provide opportunities for reexamination and expansion of previously held ideas. Through an application of the elements of Hindu thought drawn out of the *Mahābhārata* narratives, and the utilization of several other selected narratives from this epic, we address Hindu perspectives regarding these questions and concerns.

UTILIZATION OF ASSISTED REPRODUCTIVE TECHNOLOGY

One of the initial questions raised by assisted reproductive technologies—specifically, donor gametes, IVF, and surrogacy—is the ethical permissibility of their utilization.[13] While Roman Catholicism morally objects to all reproductive technologies on the grounds that they go against God's creative design by separating procreation from the act of sexual intercourse, some Protestant traditions may object to a few of the technologies, while finding others morally acceptable.[14] Similarly, responses within Hindu traditions also vary. As discussed in chapters 3 and 4, the attitudes expressed in the examined narratives of the *Mahābhārata* would presumably support John and Luanne's use of donor gametes, IVF, and surrogacy. However, we cannot say it enough: Hindu perspectives are neither simple nor monolithic.

Gupta and Lingam both object to various forms of assisted reproductive technologies on the grounds that they "abuse, disrespect, manipulate, and exploit women as objects." According to them, these technologies reinforce the idea that fertility is a primary indicator of a woman's status, and other "anti-women" ideals of society. Of critical importance to them is for the world to take note of and "support a woman's struggles to resist control by others and to achieve and maintain their integrity and autonomy over their bodies."[15] It appears that the primary area of concern for Gupta and Lingam is the position and role of women within society. Their objection is not necessarily to technology itself, but rather society's use of it in a manner that subjugates women and limits their abilities to identify themselves as they choose. This is a very important concern and the societal issues they raise need to be addressed. Again, their objection is not to the technology itself. Presumably, if a woman, maintaining her integrity and exercising her autonomy, chooses to utilize any number of assisted reproductive technologies, they would not object.

The majority of contemporary sources presenting Hindu views on assisted reproductive technology indicate that most speaking from within Hindu traditions argue for the permissibility of using assisted reproductive technologies. For example, the New York State Task Force on Life and the Law has a paragraph on Hindu perspectives. After acknowledging the lack of a central authority within Hinduism, the Task Force states the following:

> Most Hindu authorities, however, view the production of male offspring as a religious duty. Assisted reproduction is acceptable, therefore not only to address fertility problems but also the lack of male children. When all other infertility treatments have failed, assisted insemination with donor semen is permitted [. . .]. IVF using egg or embryo donors is also acceptable.[16]

Concurring with the Task Force's conclusions regarding Hindu perspectives, the *Encyclopedia of Bioethics* states, "the mythologies of ancestors appear to allow IVF, oocyte donation, embryo implantation, and surrogacy."[17]

A majority of contemporary Hindus argue for the ethical acceptability of gamete donation, IVF, and surrogacy. For example, Desai, relying on the *Mahābhārata* as a source, argues that gamete donation, IVF, implantation of fertilized ova, and surrogacy are all ethically acceptable for Hindus. Narayanan comes to the same conclusion in her essay, *Hindu Ethics and Dharma.*[18] Similar attitudes are present in the views of lay Hindus living in the United States. Of the six individuals interviewed for this study, all of them saw the utilization of assisted reproductive technology as morally acceptable. Mr. C and Mr. F, both with grown adult children, indicated that, though they have no ethical objections to the implementation of these technologies, they themselves would choose not to utilize them. Ms. B and Dr. D are married to each other. They underwent two cycles of IVF; the first failed, and the second, where they utilized intracytoplasmic sperm insertion (ICSI), resulted in the birth of twins.[19] From these examples from antiquity, the academy, and from lay Hindus, one finds a general acceptance of the use of various forms of assisted reproductive technologies. Within these Hindu perspectives, there is no presumption that procreation and sexual intercourse are inseparable activities. Neither is there any evident concern that utilizing creative means to procreate will defy the will of the gods or disturb the normative order of life.

Key arguments for or against the use of IVF, and other procedures that involve the extracorporeal creation and transfer of human zygotes or embryos, are based upon one's understanding of the moral status of an embryo. This moral status is an important focus of many, if not all, world religions, for it concerns the question of ensoulment and personhood. Questions of personhood are religious questions, not scientific. Science addresses questions regarding the genetic makeup of the embryo. Science determines if a particular embryo is human or if it is a platypus. Science does not ask, nor does it answer, a question such as: when is a human embryo ensouled?

These are issues for religion, and religious traditions share in their attempts to answer the question: At what point is the zygote, embryo, or fetus infused with a soul? At what point is it a person? Though all religious traditions attempt to answer this question, there is great disagreement within and between religious traditions regarding when ensoulment occurs and what that means in terms of our obligations.[20]

In spite of the limiting and polarized "prolife" "prochoice" debate in the United States, there are really at least three primary ethical positions regarding the ethical and moral status of a pre-embryo, or embryo. At one extreme, a pre-embryo, a zygote, is viewed as being a full human being, one that should be accorded all the rights of a person. At the other extreme is the idea that the pre-embryo, embryo, or even fetus is simply tissue, no different from any other human tissue, neither having any rights nor deserving of any protection.[21] A third, intermediate position, views the pre-embryo as developing life and deserving of respect. However, though considered and respected as life, the zygote and developing embryo is not equated with a fully developed adult human being. Because of the potential to become a full person, and because of its symbolic meaning for many, the pre-embryo, embryo, and fetus are afforded this middle ground of an ethical and moral status that is more than that accorded to tissue, but less than that of a person, a human being living ex utero. This third view acknowledges the developmental nature of the zygote and values and respects this developmental process.[22]

To begin this discussion regarding ensoulment with ideas familiar to many, let us pick up the discussion within the teachings of the Roman Catholic Church. Though the Church has always argued for the sanctity of human life, there has never been a unanimous view as to when ensoulment actually occurs. For example, while Augustine[23] and Ambrose[24] argue for immediate hominization, Tertullian presents conflicting views. In his support of *traducianism,* the theory that the soul is transmitted via the sperm, he argues that both the body and soul are conceived, formed, and born simultaneously so that "not a moment's interval occurs in their conception [. . .]. Now we allow that life begins with conception, because we contend that the soul also begins from conception."[25] Here he is clearly arguing for a theory of immediate hominization. However, elsewhere, in his *A Treatise on the Soul,* Tertullian states, "The embryo therefore becomes a human being in the womb *from the moment that its form is completed.*"[26] This does not coincide with his comments regarding *traducianism*; here his remarks support delayed hominization.

The great Thomas Aquinas espouses *hylomorphism,* a theory that expresses the Aristotelian idea that all natural or physical bodies are composed of matter and form as essential substantial principles.[27] Aquinas claims "the soul is in the embryo; the nutritive soul from the beginning, then the sensitive, and lastly the intellectual soul [. . .] the intellectual soul is created by God at the end of human generation."[28] According to Aquinas, as the embryo matures and grows, so does the soul. Only when the embryo has developed into a fetus and has human form does it have a human soul. Thus, in his theological application of *hylomorphism,* Aquinas concurs with Tertullian's support for the theory of delayed hominization.

Anselm also argues against immediate hominization because it is "inadmissible that the infant should receive a rational soul from the moment of conception. This would imply that every time an embryo perishes soon after conception, a human soul would be damned forever, since it cannot be reconciled with Christ."[29] Anselm points to one of the staggering implications of the theory of immediate ensoulment.

Despite this diversity of opinions expressed by its theologians throughout history, today, the Catholic Church teaches immediate hominization and makes the following argument regarding a zygote:

> [T]he fruit of human generation, from the first moment of its existence, that is to say from the moment the zygote has formed, demands the unconditional respect that is morally due to the human being in his bodily and spiritual totality. The human being is to be respected and treated as a person from the moment of conception; and therefore from the same moment his rights as a person must be recognized [. . .].[30]

In its argument regarding ensoulment, the Magisterium makes no moral distinction between zygotes, pre-embryos, embryos, and fetuses. The Church views the zygote as a full person from the "moment of conception," possessing a right to life and thus entitled to protection from harm. Since IVF and other technologies utilizing zygotes inevitably involve the destruction of at least some of them, the Church rejects the ethical permissibility of IVF and related technologies.[31]

The teachings of the Vatican concern themselves with the question: When does human life begin? Utilizing contemporary scientific knowledge regarding the nature of human in utero development, others argue that the question ought to be: At what point in the development of the embryo do we attribute to it the protection afforded a human being? Stating the question in this manner acknowledges the profound changes that begin as a sperm starts to penetrate the wall of the ovum, culminating, approximately forty weeks later, in a much larger and more complex full term fetus. The Ethics Committee of the American Fertility Society and others argue that the scientific facts of the developmental process ought to be considered as the status of the embryo is being determined. During the pre-embryonic stage, the early events in internal gestation involve physiological interactions between the multiplying blastocyst and the mother. At this point an embryonic rudiment is not even present. Each cell is totipotential, capable of becoming any type of subsequent cell. At this stage, if the cell mass undergoes twinning, a process whereby the cell is divided in half and allowed to grow, each half will develop into a full fetus. This is a situation in which identical twins are formed. However, at this point, if a divided cell goes through a process of reconjunction, where the halves are rejoined, the result is one embryo. The argument for immediate hominization simply does not coincide with these early biological stages of development.[32]

Once differentiation begins, a process where the embryonic cells "specialize," and are designated to become the bones, eyes, heart, or other parts of the fetus, then genetic individuality begins to be established. The first differentiation occurs slightly less than a week after fertilization. Implantation begins and the surface cells of the zygote form the placenta. Once the placenta is formed, the cells increase rapidly for approximately another week. By the end of the second week, a hominal organizer appears in the blastocyst. Differentiation of specific organ systems will not occur unless this organizer orders the pluripotential cells to differentiate into the specific organ systems that will form the human fetus. It is during this stage of the developmental process, after differentiation begins, that it makes sense to talk about ensoulment. Prior to this point, biologically, the multiplying zygote can undergo twinning or reconjunction any number of times. However, after differentiation, the cells of the zygote are programmed to develop into particular entities. Bearing these biological facts in mind, it appears reasonable to allow for moral distinctions to be made between a zygote, pre-embryo, embryo, and fetus.[33]

Let us add one additional note regarding the Church's teaching and science. If the Magisterium's argument of immediate ensoulment is juxtaposed with the widely recognized scientific fact that one-third to one-half of all fertilized ova never survive to implant in the uterus or differentiate to any advanced degree, then every day countless human beings are damned for eternity. In light of this theory of ensoulment and the medical facts, Karl Rahner responds by asking contemporary Catholic moral theologians, if today they still have "the courage to maintain this presupposition?" Rahner questions if these theologians are able to acknowledge that "50% of the 'human beings'—real human beings with an 'immortal' soul and an eternal destiny—do not, from the very start, get beyond this first stage of a human existence?"[34]

Classical Hindu texts reflect an understanding of the developmental nature of a zygote, embryo, and fetus. Preserving the *Atharvan* theory of fetal development, the *Garbha Upaniṣad* reads as follows:

> By the second night after the union of semen and blood the foetus is of the form of a round lump called Kalala, at the eighth night it is of the form of a vesicle called Budbuda, after a fortnight it assumes the form of a spheroid—*Piṇḍa,* in two months the head appears, in three months the feet, in four months the abdomen, heels, the pelvic portion appear, in the fifth month the spine appears, in the sixth month nose, eyes and ears develop; in the seventh month the feotus becomes endowed with life [. . .]; in the eighth month it becomes fully developed. In the ninth month when the foetus is well-developed with all of its organs, [. . .].[35]

Another account of embryonic development is found in the *Caraka-Saṃhitā*, a pre-Buddhist, Indian medical work dating from circa eighth century B.C.E. Once all the necessary elements are combined, the embryo takes on a form of jelly and "bears no particular form and the organs of the embryo are both manifested and latent," during the first month. During the second month "the embryo takes a compact form in the shape of a knot, elongated muscle or tumor (round and elevated). During the third month, all the senses and limbs along with their organs manifest themselves simultaneously," and so forth, the description continues.[36]

Along with presenting different accounts for the development of a zygote or fetus, these texts also contain differing arguments as to when ensoulment occurs. Lipner describes a major and a minor tradition in his brief discussion on Hindu perspectives concerning ensoulment.[37] The major tradition is found in *Caraka-Saṃhitā*. The developmental process begins once all the elements necessary to form an embryo are present, namely, the unimpaired sperm of a man, a healthy fertile woman's womb and ovum, sex during a fertile period, a free *jīva* (Soul), along with the mind to descend into the zygote.[38] According to this text,

> The fetus is produced out of the Soul [. . .]. This is now as *jīva* or animated Soul [. . .]. He [the *jīva*] is without the beginning and end, and He is unchangeable. By entering into the uterus, it gets combined with the sperm and the ovum thereby reproducing Himself in the form of a fetus [. . .]. The state of mere existence of sperm and ovum prior to be combination [*sic*] of the Soul cannot be called as fetus. They are entitled to be known as fetus only when the Soul gets combined with them.[39]

In this case ensoulment is simultaneous with the commencement of the process of conception. A zygote by definition is ensouled. According to Lipner, this major tradition views human beings as "composites of two essentially disparate but intimately conjoined principles—spirit (*ātman, puruṣa*) and matter (*prakṛti*). Personhood is established once there is a combination of the two."[40]

While the major tradition supports the idea of immediate hominization, Lipner describes the minor tradition as arguing that the soul unites with the embryo sometime *after* conception. In the *Garbha Upaniṣad*, cited above, it is in "the seventh month the feotus becomes *endowed with life*." Or, as Lipner translates it, the fetus "is *joined to the soul*."[41] According to this minor tradition, there may be grounds for distinguishing between an embryo prior to ensoulment and an ensouled embryo. However, Lipner comments on how the embryo does not undergo a "quantum leap" in its development. Rather, "in characteristic Hindu fashion, the language here is in terms of progressive MANIFESTATION of a personhood previously only latent, rather than origination of personhood *ab initio*."[42]

Regardless of when the soul (*ātman*) is believed to "enter" or combine with the zygote, Hindu texts reflect a respect for the developing fetal life and argue that it is deserving of protection from harm.[43] The fetus is conscious and even has a memory of his or her previous births. The fetus knows the difference between good and bad, and "repents, that on account of its previous Karma, it is suffering from the pains of life in a fetus, and resolves that if it can once come out, it will follow the path of knowledge." Unfortunately, as soon as the baby is "born, it comes into connection with the Vaiṣṇava Vāyu and forgets its previous births and resolutions."[44]

This story of the fetus forgetting past lives, and other narratives vividly depicting them as hearing, learning, and remembering, speaks volumes as to the status of the unborn fetus within Hindu traditions. At one point in the *Mahābhārata,* Kṛṣṇa tells his pregnant sister, Subhadrā, second wife to Arjuna, how a soldier can break into a particular military formation known as "the disc," called *chakra-vyuha.* According to the story, the fetus, Abhimanyu, is carefully listening to his uncle's instructions. Unfortunately, Kṛṣṇa's discussion is interrupted and he does not tell Subhadrā how one gets out of the military formation. At sixteen, Abhimanyu is on the battlefield and successfully penetrates the *chakravyha* of his enemies. However, he is ultimately killed because he lacks the knowledge of how to get out of it. This story clearly reflects an idea that a fetus, in utero, has the ability to hear and remember.[45]

Interestingly, these Hindu texts and traditions preserve both a commitment to the moral status of an embryo and a support for utilizing various means, *intra utero* as well as *ex utero,* for producing children. According to these traditions, it is not an either/or situation. One can have respect for embryo life and still utilize technologies such as IVF. According to these traditions, there is nothing inherently wrong with IVF, gamete donation, and surrogacy in and of itself.

The elements of Hindu thought discussed in the previous chapter would not have censured John and Luanne for taking advantage of the assisted reproductive technologies made available to them. Gamete donation, IVF, and surrogacy do not in and of themselves undermine a nondualist worldview. These technologies do not threaten a belief in an underlying unity of all life. Similar to the two couples of the epic narratives (Kuntī-Pāṇḍu and Gāndhārī-Dhṛtarāṣṭra), John and Luanne Buzzanca were a married couple in the householder stage of life. At this stage, one of their primary duties is to have children, thus securing the continuation of society. The Buzzancas were facing challenges in their attempts to produce children. Kuntī obtained donor gametes, as did the Buzzancas. The Buzzancas utilized IVF and a surrogate mother, while it could be said that Gāndhārī utilized "artificial wombs." The utilization of technology can be interpreted as enabling John and Luanne to fulfill their debts to their ancestors and society. In this manner, the good of society is supported. By having this child, according to traditional Hinduism, the Buzzancas would also be fulfilling a primary *dharma* of parenthood, thereby affecting their *karma* in a positive manner.[46] Thus, the utilization of assisted reproductive technologies can be ethically acceptable.

INDIVIDUAL VERSUS SOCIETAL RIGHTS AND INTERESTS

In the United States, central ethical issues regarding the uses of assisted reproductive technologies are often couched in terms concerning individual rights and interests versus those of society at large.[47] On the one hand there are those, championing autonomy and individual rights, who argue that procreation and infertility are private matters to be decided by each individual for himself or herself. According to these arguments, individuals have a right to enter into contractual agreements providing them access to the appropriate technologies and willing third parties. While the U.S. Constitution may imply that individuals have a right to procreate, the U.S. Supreme Court does not explicitly consider procreation a positive right—it is a negative right.[48]

On the other hand, there are those who view these matters from a broader societal perspective. Some of them caution against implementing these technologies because they go against the greater good of society.[49] In *Making Babies: Biomedical Technologies, Reproductive Ethics and Public Policy,* de Melo-Martin agues that viewing fertility, infertility, and procreation primarily as individual issues is inadequate. She is quick to point out that public policy relating to assisted reproductive technologies does not only affect the infertile, it affects society in a variety of ways. By focusing primarily on the individual, one is disregarding or underestimating social, ethical, and political factors, and this often leads to policy decisions that may not be in the public's best interest.[50] Admittedly, the issues of individuals and their relationships to others and society are very complex.

The paradigmatic narratives of the *Mahābhārata* and the elements of Hindu thought extracted from them both acknowledge and address these complexities, however with a slightly different focus. First, three of the six elements underlying unity of all life, centrality of society, and *dharma* directly address the above issue raised by de Melo-Martin. Infertility, fertility, and having babies are not considered private, individual issues. Rather, the Hindu narratives emphasize the opposite. The actions of individuals, particularly regarding procreative issues, affect their family, society, and ultimately all of life. Additionally, *dharma* relates an individual's actions to her particular situation and her relationship with society at the time. Take, for example, Kuntī's use of her mantra. Her initial use of the mantra, as an unmarried young woman, caused her to fear the response of society. However, with the same action, taken once she is married and has the responsibility of producing an heir, she is fulfilling her *dharma.*

Second, while the discussions in the United States are dominated by "rights" language, the language within the *Mahābhārata* and that utilized by many Hindus, even those living in North America, is one of "duty." Saral Jhingran points out that the *Dharmaśāstra* literature contains no discussions of individual human rights, except when speaking of Brahmins. When "rights" are discussed in these texts, they are the rights of a caste, not of individuals. Furthermore, these discussions regarding rights are undertaken in the context of defining the duties incumbent on one class with respect to another.[51] According to Creel, the Indian social system is comprised of a synthesis of groups rather than of individuals.[52] This reflects the notion that there is an underlying unity to all of life. We may be individual beings, but we do not stand in isolation, we are members of a family, of a society. Thus, it is in this context that Hindu traditions tend to focus on the needs of society as a whole, prompting questions of duty as opposed to rights. Rather than asking "What are my rights?" or "What are the rights of my society, vis á vis other societies or individuals?" those within Hindu traditions often ask such questions as: "What is my duty? What is my duty to myself, the family, and society?"

A dominant worldview depicted in the *Mahābhārata* narratives presupposes this centrality of society and an underlying unity of all life—divine, human, or otherwise.[53] This worldview is ideally "based on the sanctity of life of every creature, sympathy for sufferer, service without expectation, contentment and efficiency in all activities. These great principles become the soul and spirit of all people."[54] The concept that one's *ātman* is ultimately identifiable with *Brahman,* the divine ground of being, implies interdependence among all forms of life. In this worldview, humans are each part of a larger whole; thus, individual concerns extend beyond the individual to include her society and ultimately all beings.[55]

While this particular belief in the underlying unity of all life, and the subsequent priority of societal good, are commitments of religious faith within Hindu traditions, the idea that individuals are not radically insular is a concept shared by many and is not necessarily unique to Hindu belief systems. Louis Dumont, in *Homo Hierarchius: the Caste System and Its Implications,* indicates that the idea of fully developed individual selves has a relatively modern, even Christian ancestry. He writes, the "[a]ncient philosophers, up to the Stoics, did not separate the collective aspects of man from the others; one was a man because one was a member of a city, as much a social as a political organization." Plato, Dumont reminds us, said: "a true man is a man as collective being not man as a particular being."[56]

Though the dominant contemporary North American worldview places a priority on individual rights and autonomy, the idea of addressing and working toward societal good is not foreign to "Western" sensibilities. Emile Durkheim, the father of the field of sociology of religion, discusses the concept of interdependence in his book, *Elementary Forms of the Religious Life.* According to his model of modern society, individuals are dependent upon one another because of their particular areas of specialization. Thus, in order for society to function properly, members of society need to perform their various jobs. Admittedly, while on a metaphysical level Durkheim and the *Upaniṣads* may be working from very different views of reality, on a practical level their ideas of interdependence are quite compatible.

This notion that individuals are ultimately dependent upon one another, unfortunately, is somewhat obscured when undue emphasis is placed on individual rights. With freedom and autonomy comes responsibility. In her book, *Private Choices, Public Consequences: Reproductive Technology and the New Ethics of Conception, Pregnancy, and Family,* Lynda Fenwick comments on the commitment to autonomy within the United States. She calls upon all North Americans to take seriously the fact that autonomy goes hand in hand with responsibility. We each need to realize the impact that we have on one another, take responsibility, and make the hard decisions.[57]

Again, the idea that societal prerogatives ought to play a central role in the formation of ethical standards is obviously not unique to Hindu traditions. Cahill demonstrates how theological ethics, specifically in certain strains of Christian ethics, also tend to prioritize distributive justice and social solidarity over an individual's rights and liberty.[58] Thus, individuals do not have to subscribe to a Hindu ethic, particularly an *Advaita-Vedānta* belief that one's *ātman* is identical with *Brahman,* in order to acknowledge interconnectedness with others or to believe that the effects of their decisions and actions extend far beyond the immediate circle of the individual in the present moment.

In applying the presuppositions of an underlying unity and centrality of society to Jaycee's case, the discussion begins in a large arena that encompasses society, the United States' court system, and the individuals directly involved. Rather than beginning from a point of view that places society in a central position, both John Buzzanca and the California court system began their discussions from a position that holds autonomy and individual rights in a position of priority. Both John's attempt to legally relieve himself of any responsibility with respect to Jaycee, and the California Court of Appeals' decision that John was responsible for paying child-support are grounded in a modern, "Western," North American notion that places a premium value on autonomy and individual rights.[59]

The ethical and legal discussions surrounding the California Court's ruling on Jaycee's case reflect a concern for the complex implications of the ruling, both for society and for the rights and interests of the individual. While John was looking out for his own self-interest, the Court based its decision on what was best for Jaycee. Rather than asking what is best for only John or only Jaycee at any particular time, the Hindu ethical perspective being examined and analyzed here asks what is best for both of them within the context of society and the universe. This Hindu approach calls for us to take a step away from a preoccupation with our own self-interest and rights, and instead consider how our actions might affect others, both now and in the future. Acting in such a manner decreases the hold of selfish and egotistical states of mind and allows one to act from a position that is less distorted by an egocentric worldview.[60]

According to Sutton, the "ideology preached by the *Mahābhārata* is concerned specifically with sustaining virtue in *opposition to selfish* and hedonistic ways of life. This notion of virtue is a familiar one involving honesty, *being true to one's word,* generous, forgiving, kind-hearted, and tolerant."[61] From this perspective, John ought not to focus solely on his own self-interest or perceived legalistic rights. Rather, he ought to be a man of his word and honor the commitments he made to Jaycee when he signed the contracts that began the process that brought about her conception and birth. Callahan, though not speaking from within Hindu traditions, would agree to this call to responsibility. According to him, "Humans bear a moral responsibility for voluntary acts that have an impact on the lives of others; they are morally accountable for such acts."[62] Again, the concepts supported by *dharma, karma,* and *ahiṃsā* are not unique to Hinduism, nor are they entirely new to North Americans. With our focus on autonomy and individual rights, let us not lose sight of, let us even highlight, our responsibility.

While Hindu traditions place the needs of society in a position of priority, this is not to say that an individual's interests or rights are unimportant or ignored. Similar to the Buzzancas, the characters of Kuntī and Pāṇḍu wanted children, as did Gāndhārī and Dhṛtarāṣṭra. Gāndhārī even placed her interests in having children over and above Vyāsa's warnings of catastrophic destruction. Also like the Buzzancas, these kings and queens employed measures that ensured they would have children. However, unlike John Buzzanca, once they took action, the characters in the *Mahābhārata* did not attempt to abandon their responsibilities. They had willingly taken on the *dharma* of parenthood and they followed through by fulfilling their parental responsibilities.

John's position of wanting to abandon his responsibility to Jaycee is not without parallel in the *Mahābhārata.* The story surrounding the birth of Karṇa, Kuntī's first born through her encounter with Sūrya, the Sun god, provides a good example. According to the story, once Karṇa was born, Kuntī placed him "in a basket that was well-packed on all sides. And in that basket, comfortable, soft, sealed with beeswax, and finely covered, she tearfully set her child afloat in the River Aśva." Kuntī knew that propriety forbade her to have a child at this stage in her life, and she "lamented piteously and prayed" as she sent her son down the river: "May you be safe from the creatures of earth, atmosphere, and heaven, and from those that live in the water, little son. May your pathways be auspicious, and not adverse, and those who approach you, son be without malice [. . .]."[63] She foresees who will rescue him, adopt and care for him, and she prays for and blesses them. Though she is giving up her child, these are not the words and actions of a young woman recklessly abandoning her parental duties.

The actions of John and Kuntī *appear* similar. They were both abandoning their parental responsibilities. However, their situations are actually quite different. Unlike John, Kuntī was an unmarried teenager. John intended to be a parent; Kuntī did not. While John willingly set into motion a plan that resulted in Jaycee's birth, Kuntī was simply acting out of curiosity; her intent was not necessarily to have a baby. (Recall that she had just been given this boon and was curious to see if it would work). Upon his divorce, John, as a competent, presumably gainfully employed adult, apparently simply did not want parental responsibilities. Kuntī was young and feared the wrath and disapproval of her family and society. When she did abandon Karṇa, it was not without great preparation, prayer, and remorse. The multivalent nature of Hindu traditions allows these differences to influence how each case is evaluated. The actions of John and Kuntī may be similar; however, their intent and circumstances are not. Rather than focusing on a philosophical principle and attempting to make universal applications, Hindu traditions tend to examine various elements of the situation and evaluate each one accordingly.

The narratives of the *Mahābhārata* demonstrate that individuals are free to act in any manner they choose. However, all individuals, through the impersonal law of *karma*, must ultimately bear the responsibility for the consequences of their chosen actions. Although Kuntī is not explicitly criticized when she floats Karṇa down the river, the impersonal law of *karma* eventually comes full circle. Years later she suffers deeply when, after she fails to reconcile with Karṇa, he dies at the hand of Arjuna, Kuntī's fourth son and Karṇa's younger half-brother. Just as the Hindu notions of *dharma* and *karma* proactively and reactively hold individuals responsible for their actions, so ought our commitment to autonomy be accompanied by an equal commitment to holding individuals responsible for their actions.

ASSISTED REPRODUCTIVE TECHNOLOGY AND THE FAMILY

The use of these technologies and their effects on the family constitute another area of great disagreement. On the one hand, there are those who argue that these technologies offer options and support for couples who would otherwise be unable to have their own children. On the other hand, there are others who object to the utilization of assisted reproductive technologies on the grounds that they threaten the sanctity of marriage, the existence of the traditional family, and familial relationships.[64] Jaycee's situation is an excellent case to explore these various issues.

Regarding the threat to the sanctity of marriage, let us again begin with the teachings of the Roman Catholic Church. The Church claims that a child "has the right to be conceived, carried in the womb, brought into the world, and brought up within marriage."[65] Elsewhere the *Instruction* reads: "the act of conjugal love is considered in the teachings of the Church as the *only setting worthy* of human procreation."[66] According to this view,

> utilizing donor gametes is contrary to the unity of marriage, to the dignity of the spouses, to the vocation proper to parents, and to the child's right to be conceived and brought into the world in marriage and from marriage [. . .].

> Recourse to the gametes of a third person, in order to have sperm or ovum available, constitutes a violation of the reciprocal commitment of the spouses and a grave lack in regard to that essential property of marriage which is its unity.[67]

As previously indicated, the Roman Catholic Church prohibits actions or procedures that separate the act of sexual intercourse from procreation, and it prohibits procreation outside the marriage relationship. The Church argues that such activities damage the relationships within the family. The same arguments are applied to the utilization of IVF and surrogacy. One speaking from a perspective within the Catholic Church might point to Jaycee's case and use it as an example of how these technologies not only threaten but defy the existence and definitions of family.

While the Catholic Church insists that marriage, sex, and procreation must be connected, the position affirmed by the United Nations is much different. According to Article 16.1, the UN Declaration of Human Rights states: "men and women of full age, without any limitation due to race, nationality or religion, have the right to marry and found a family." In Hull's exploration of this UN statement, he indicates that the Committee regards heterosexual marriage as being the "most appropriate context for having children," all things being equal. However, the Committee acknowledges that factors in life are often *not* equal. Consequently, the UN Committee is unwilling to argue that not being married is grounds for constraining the liberty of individuals to reproduce. According to this UN Committee, "traditional" family structures are important; however, they need not be the sole environment into which children are born.[68]

In his essay "Bioethics and Fatherhood," Callahan argues that these technologies threaten familial relationships. He objects to various assisted reproductive technologies, particularly sperm donation, on the grounds that it is morally wrong because it "downgrades" fatherhood. Callahan asserts that it is morally irrelevant whether a donor does not want to be a father, or if the medical establishment simply wants his sperm and not a commitment of fatherhood. It is also morally irrelevant if society and the woman do not want the sperm donor to serve as a father. "If there are to be moral duties at all, the biological bond is as fundamental and unavoidable as can be." He continues: "Fatherhood, because it is a biological condition, cannot be abrogated by personal desires or legal decisions."[69] According to him, these technologies allow yet another father to go free and not fulfill his parental duties. Munson disagrees with Callahan, arguing that while biological connections are important, they are not sufficient conditions for being a moral or social father. According to him, the moral or social father is one who actually invests time and energy in the process of raising the child.[70]

The Catholic Church's concerns regarding assisted reproductive technologies extend beyond the preservation of the family. According to the Magisterium, assisted reproductive technologies such as donor gametes, IVF, and surrogacy not only cause a "rupture between genetic parenthood, gestational parenthood and responsibility for upbringing," they have negative "repercussions on civil society: what threatens the unity and stability of the family is a source of dissension, disorder and injustice in the whole of social life."[71]

Catholics are not alone amongst Christians in holding to the above commitments. Though James Dobson, founder of Focus on the Family, finds few areas of agreement with Roman Catholicism, they do share a commitment to the family and a belief in its connection to the strength of society. According to Dobson:

> The family is unraveling right in front of our eyes [. . .]. Let me say one more time that if the family and the Judeo-Christian ethic collapse, the entire culture will descend into the same black hole that consumed Greece, Rome and the other great empires of the world. It's just a matter of time.[72]

Both Dobson and the Catholic Church predict dire consequences for the United States if society allows for the continual unraveling of the "traditional" family.[73] They see assisted reproductive technology as a potential threat to the family, for these technologies allow for children to become a part of alternative relationships that, in turn, threaten the traditional family. Hindu traditions, and other traditions such as Confucianism, Neo-Confucianism, and Shintoism, agree that the family is the bedrock of society.[74] However, most within these traditions would not share this prohibition against the utilization of assisted reproductive technologies.

Admittedly, the utilization of assisted reproductive technologies creates new and complicated biological, social, and legal relationships. Jaycee's case provides a clear example of the complexities that may arise when technologies are utilized to bring about the birth of a child within a family. Through the use of IVF, donated gametes, and surrogate motherhood, potentially four couples, or a total of eight individuals, could have claimed parental rights for Jaycee: 1) the woman who donated her ovum and her husband; 2) the man who donated his sperm and his wife, 3) Pamela Snell, the gestational mother and her husband; and, finally, 4) Luann and John Buzzanca, the intended parents. This case clearly challenges the definitions of a traditional family and the legal definitions of motherhood and fatherhood. Though these technologies may increase the complexity of familial relationships, they, in and of themselves, are not necessarily a threat to the family.

Many within Hinduism, who are committed to the teaching of the underlying unity of all life and a focus on the good of society, tend to hold a broad definition of family. Consider the familial situations within the *Mahābhārata.* Prior to Pāṇḍu renouncing his throne and heading for the mountains with his wives, they all lived in the same palace with Dhṛtarāṣṭra and Gāndhārī, their grandmother Satyavatī, and probably a multitude of other family relations.

Following Pāṇḍu's death, Kuntī gathers "his" five sons and returns to live with Gāndhārī, Dhṛtarāṣṭra, their 101 children, other relatives, and a few of the great sages. This is an excellent example of an extended family, an idea that continues on in contemporary Hindu, and other, societies.

Of the six individuals I interviewed, all but one described their family as being part of an extended family. Mr. A, the one exception and a "convert" to Hinduism, defined his family as consisting of himself, his wife, and his children. However, he commented that his definition of family may differ "from the people in this congregation because I grew up in Western world. From a Hindu perspective, a family includes brothers, sisters, parents, [. . .] grandparents from both sides, cousins, and all of that." Ms. B describes her family as including herself, her husband and children, uncle and aunt living locally, her husband's three brothers in India, her half-sister's daughter, and very close friends. While Mr. C acknowledged that only his immediate family, himself, his wife, and children, were living in the United States, according to him "the whole village [where he was born and reared] is my family."[75]

After retiring from government work in India, Mr. F and his wife moved to the United States to rejoin four of his children, their spouses, and children. There are times when families immigrate to the United States and leave behind all familial ties. It is interesting to observe how, after establishing themselves within a particular area, they often construct an "extended family" that serves as an adopted family structure.[76] The belief in an underlying unity of life coincides with this concept of an extended family, be it via blood or constructed ties. On a metaphysical level, ultimately, everyone is family. Perhaps these extended family situations may be better equipped at absorbing the complications introduced through the use of assisted reproductive technologies.

The narratives of the *Mahābhārata* demonstrate how, even in the midst of complex familial relationships, the stability of society can stand.[77] Though technologies such as IVF and artificial insemination are relatively new inventions of modern science, discussions regarding who in society is responsible for the children are not. According to Manu:

> The son born in an appointed woman should take (his share) in the estate just like a natural son, for according to law, that seed and the offspring belong to the owner of the field. A man who maintains the property and the wife of his dead brother should beget a child for his brother and give his property to him alone.[78]

Though Manu is referring to the ancient practice of levirate marriage and not to modern forms of assisted reproductive technologies, the principles he discusses can still apply. The daughter, Jaycee, born in an appointed woman, Ms. Snell, should have her share of the estate just like a natural child of John and Luanne would. Unlike the perspectives of Roman Catholics and Callahan,[79] Manu's passage does not presume a necessary connection between biological relation and the responsibilities and duties of fatherhood.[80]

While the paradigmatic narratives of the *Mahābhārata* imply that a genetic connection between a child and his or her parents is significant, sometimes even preferred, it is not an exclusive requirement for establishing parental relationships. Consider the specific circumstances surrounding the "five sons of Pāṇḍu." Of the five sons, three are born of Kuntī and the younger twins are born to Mādrī. Upon Mādrī's death, Kuntī fulfills her promise to Mādrī and takes the younger twins as her own. The epic acknowledges Mādrī as the mother of the twins. However, following her death, they become the children of Kuntī. Chaitanya comments on how, even though Kuntī scrupulously tries to avoid the slightest discrimination in the way she treats her five sons, the youngest, Sahadeva, is her favorite.[81]

Also, consider how none of the five boys are genetically related to Pāṇḍu, and none of them even share the same father. Furthermore, the twins are not even biologically related to Kuntī. Nevertheless, they *all* recognize Kuntī as their mother and Pāṇḍu as their father. Both the text itself and the multiple generations reading it throughout the centuries recognize Yudhiṣṭhira, Bhīma, Arjuna, Nakula, and Sahadeva as brothers—as the five sons of Kuntī and Pāṇḍu.[82] From the story of the Pāṇḍava sons, one may infer that intent plays a role in establishing parenthood. Similar to John Buzzanca, Pāṇḍu participated in the original plan that brought about the births of the boys, and he was the intended father.

Interestingly, though lacking in actual genetic connection, the fact that the Pāṇḍava's family lineage and right to rule is secure is somewhat related to the *source* of the donated gametes. Recall when Pāṇḍu encourages Kuntī to participate in *niyoga,* his instructions are for her to find a Brahmin of *equal or greater* status than he. It is not insignificant that Kuntī and Mādrī are royal queens in their own right, and that *all* of their "donors" are divine. This secured a high social status for their sons. Such is not the fate of Vidura, Pāṇḍu, and Dhṛtarāṣṭra's younger brother. Vidura, the only son of Vyāsa that is free of a physical deformity,[83] is nevertheless ineligible to rule because his mother is the maidservant to Ambikā. Though the text does not demand a biological connection, it does imply that social status is an important factor. According to the text, these types of constraints are necessary to keep society functioning properly.

Narayanan points out that some contemporary Hindu couples place a great deal of importance on having a genetic connection to their children. Thus, for them, a husband or wife is generally the only accepted gamete donor.[84] This may imply hesitancy on the part of some Hindus to utilize anonymous gamete donations. Interestingly, none of the individuals I interviewed objected to sperm banks and the use of anonymous gametes. However, all of them indicated they would not choose to utilize them for themselves. When asked why, Ms. B indicated: "If the gene pool is going to come from somewhere else, I might as well get a child that is already here. I don't have the 'I have to have baby, or be pregnant' feeling."[85]

By virtue of the fact that Kuntī and Mādrī were Pāṇḍu's wives, and that he, while alive, fulfilled his parental duties, his *dharma,* to the Pāṇḍava brothers, he is considered their father. According to the *Mahābhārata,* while biology and social status are not insignificant, of greater importance are those who intend to take on the parental *dharmic* responsibilities. Karṇa's story provides another example of how parentage is determined more by intent and by who actually fulfills the *dharmic* role of parenthood.

According to the story, after Rādhā and her charioteer husband, Adhiratha, adopted Karṇa, they nurtured him and raised him as their own. When Karṇa is presented with the facts, that Kuntī, a queen of much higher status than his adopted parents, is his mother, he is not moved. Although Kuntī gave birth to him and is genetically related to Karṇa, he feels no obligation to her. Following Kṛṣṇa's failed attempts, Kuntī tries to convince Karṇa to join her other sons and fight side by side with his Pāṇḍava brothers.[86] Since he is Kuntī's eldest son, by joining the Pāṇḍavas, their whole kingdom would be his. However, according to Chaitanya, Karṇa is not a son to Kuntī in the same way that Yudhiṣṭhira or Arjuna are and he, Karṇa, is well aware of this fact. He is courteous and respectfully rejects her offer and her pleas. He acknowledges that children have a duty to their parents. However, since she never fulfilled her parental duties as a mother toward him, he feels no obligation to reciprocate in kind.[87] The relationships reflected in this story imply that gestational, genetic mothers or biological fathers do not take precedence over those who actually take the children into their care and parent them. In Jaycee's situation, it was John and Luanne who had made the commitment to parent her.

Having examined Jaycee Buzzanca's case through a prism of Hindu thought, we found some informative emphases and perspectives regarding the utilization of gamete donation, IVF, and surrogacy. Traditional as well as contemporary societies condone and encourage individuals to have children. Interestingly, even in our current situation, where many claim that overpopulation is one of the world's greatest threats to existence, having children is important and valued by society. According to one interviewee, having children is of "great importance because your children have to be better than you. The role of children is to improve society, and that's the way it should be."[88] In light of this societal emphasis, as well as the personal desires of individuals to raise children, the traditions reflected in the *Mahābhārata* are sympathetic to John and Luanne's initial desires to have children. Additionally, this emphasis on the good of society calls John and Luanne to focus on their duties to Jaycee and society.

The belief in the underlying unity of all life has many implications for this discussion. Since everything is part of this underlying unity, an interconnection among all humans, among all life, is presupposed. Perhaps this belief underlies the concept of the extended family prevalent within many Hindu communities. Familial relationships are ultimately not dependent upon genetics. This implies that there are no moral objections to John and Luanne's use of donor gametes. It also implies that the fact that Jaycee is not genetically related to either of them does not lessen their familial connection to her. This underlying belief, coupled with the principles of *dharma, karma,* and *ahiṃsā,* bind John and Luanne closer to Jaycee than any court ruling ever could.

Additionally, these principles call John to fulfill his responsibilities and at least financially support Jaycee. His arguments that Luanne is not Jaycee's legal mother, and that therefore he is not her father, hold little to no weight in this situation. He participated in setting events into motion that resulted in the birth of Jaycee. Presumably, he is an adult, in the householder stage of life, fully aware of his circumstances, and in control of his actions. Consequently, he has obligations to Jaycee. *Karma* and *karmic* consequences ultimately hold every individual responsible for his or her actions.

In Jaycee's case, under these particular circumstances, the hitherto mentioned characteristics of Hindu thought support the implementation of assisted reproductive technology, and establish that John and Luanne are parents to Jaycee, in spite of their lack of genetic connection. Additionally, they establish that both John and Luanne are responsible for Jaycee's well-being. However, the multivalent nature of Hindu traditions and the context-specific nature of *dharma* together require an examination and careful consideration of the particular conditions of each case that is brought up for questioning. These traditions will not simply impose the interpretations and conclusions of this case onto others. A majority of those operating within Hindu worldviews have little desire to attempt to impose set categories onto reality. Rather, they have an incredible ability to allow each situation to set and define its own parameters.

While in Luanne and John's case, utilizing assisted reproductive technology was considered appropriate, this does not translate into an uncritical acceptance of assisted reproductive technologies. In this particular case, where no one else contested it, Luanne was granted the responsibilities of motherhood. This in no way implies that gestational motherhood is secondary. While in Jaycee's case, genetics was not considered a defining factor, this does not negate the importance of genetics in other situations. While John was being held responsible in this situation, there might be circumstances under which someone in a similar case might not be. The multivalent nature of Hindu traditions admits that a "right" course of action is often dependent upon the particulars of the situation. Admittedly, cases and bioethical issues may appear more complex and difficult when a multivalent attitude prevails. However, this attitude preserves a commitment to viewing and honoring the views of life from various perspectives. In this contemporary, pluralistic world, this emphasis may be one of Hinduism's greatest contributions to the contemporary field of bioethics.

Conclusion

Through an examination of narratives within the *Mahābhārata,* we found that its characters reflect a creativity and moral openness that is common to many within Hindu traditions. As we explored this influential Indian epic, we discovered principles, ideas, and characteristics of thought that together distinguish a Hindu approach to doing applied ethics, specifically to examining ethical issues regarding assisted reproductive technology. We have seen how particular aspects of Hindu traditions are reflected in selected birth narratives of the main characters of the *Mahābhārata,* and we have applied these ideas to the case of baby Jaycee. Throughout this process, we have demonstrated that religious ideas often play a central role in the ethical decision making process for bioethical issues and we have demonstrated how perspectives grounded within Hindu traditions can contribute to bioethical discussion, particularly discussions regarding assisted reproductive technology.

THE HERMENEUTICS OF CROSS-CULTURAL AND INTERDISCIPLINARY STUDIES

We gain a richer understanding of moral questions and a better grasp on answers when we examine bioethical issues from the vantage point of several different perspectives. By grounding our exploration of Hindu perspectives within a few paradigmatic *Mahābhārata* narratives, we have attempted to stay true to the spirit of many Hindu traditions: traditions that often do not have strict boundaries between philosophy, religion, ethics, and the practical aspects of daily life. This Hindu mythology, interpreted in conjunction with foundational Hindu texts, and established teachings within the traditions, provides a rich source from which to engage and capture the essence of Hindu traditions, teachings, and people.

In a discussion regarding comparative studies, Antonio de Nicolas comments on how we call the studying of "others" comparative. "Thus," he says, "we have not succeeded in encountering the other, but rather we have pushed through this method the possibilities of other men and ours to the verge of almost human triviality."[1] de Nicolas suggests that rather than seeking authentic understanding, comparative studies often seem to trivialize other cultures. By conducting this study regarding reproductive ethics, we have provided a method for arriving at an authentic cross-cultural engagement. Narratives such as those within the *Mahābhārata* are powerful and provide an opportunity for people from diverse cultures, religions, historical periods, and geographical lands to actually engage each other. The stories allow people to truly encounter each other as embodied, whole individuals, not simply as abstract thoughts.[2]

It is true, as Ricoeur observes, that we are limited; we are limited by our own orientation and our interaction with the text itself. Our very questions and the issues we raise reflect our contemporary times and technological advances. However, we also find, as Ricoeur claims, that myths, though seemingly disconnected from modernity, provide a grounding for understanding and "ritual action." Stories capture the essence of what it means to be human; as we engage the narratives of the past, we engage the experience and wisdom of those who came before us. Through studying these myths, we gain insights that contribute to our understanding of ourselves, of those around us, and of life.[3]

Of the myriad topics, themes, and issues discussed within the *Mahābhārata,* we focused on issues relating to creative ways of having children. We limited our examination and interpretation primarily to the birth narratives of the five Pāṇḍava brothers and their one hundred Kaurava cousins. These specific narratives were significant for how they portrayed how children could come into being, and this in turn had profound implications for attitudes and perspectives on bioethical issues relating to assisted reproductive technology.

BIOETHICS, CASUISTRY, AND CULTURAL COMPETENCY

As previously discussed, bioethical issues are raised in three primary arenas: the academy, the clinical setting, and in public policy. We focused on the discussions in the academy and the clinical setting. Often, truth is related to the experiences of the living and suffering. The harm done by neglecting the experiences of the individual and the good done by compassionate care of the individual, demonstrated through writing, personal accounts, or particular theoretical models, can, through interpretive, interactive dialogue, lead to a new ethic of responding to suffering. Furthermore, ethics involves the study of experiences as they relate to living a moral life.[4] Thus, the cross-fertilization between the academic ivory towers and the experiences occurring at hospital bedsides is immensely important for bioethics.

From this exchange, philosophers, theologians, and theorists may benefit from the perspectives of those who confront the complexities of actual life and death situations. Jonsen and Toulmin, in *The Abuse of Casuistry: A History of Moral Reasoning,* argue that, as the academy focuses more on metaethics, it often fails to address the complexities present in clinical situations. According to them, the philosophical rule, or principle-based approach to ethics, can often oversimplify the issues.[5] While metaethical analysis may affirm the importance of particular principles and even illuminate ethical discussions, it is of limited value in the clinical setting if it is unable to address the particular needs, questions, and concerns of the suffering patients and their families.

Additionally, clinicians would benefit from taking up the challenge to carefully consider and critique the grounds and implications of their decisions and actions. The academy highlights the importance of this kind of reflection and provides the tools with which to process difficult issues. Healthcare providers are working with people whose hopes and fears regarding their reason for hospitalization are tied up with their beliefs regarding life, suffering, and death.

Finally, patients would also benefit from an exchange between the academy and the clinical setting. Patients can benefit from the wisdom preserved and passed on in the various schools of thought, ethical theories, and religious traditions. From these, patients and their families may also obtain tools for interpreting and expressing their own experiences. Additionally, they may find some comfort in the knowledge that they do not struggle in isolation; others have come before them, asking similar questions, and seeking answers.

As previously mentioned, cultural competency emphasizes the importance of healthcare professionals having the ability to hear, understand, and address the various questions and concerns of their patients. This is a challenging task in the contemporary pluralistic, multicultural, and multireligious environment of the United States. Clinicians cannot be aware of every tradition. However, by being open and exposed to other worldviews, clinicians can increase their ability to administer competent care to all their patients. To this end, this study contributes Hindu perspectives to our contemporary bioethical discussions on assisted reproductive technology.

Working from within the *Mahābhārata,* six key Hindu characteristics were extracted which embrace a diversity of thought and experience; they welcome pluralistic, multicultural, and multireligious dialogues and engagements. Together, they provide a variety of avenues through which bioethical issues and clinical situations may be examined. The presupposition of an underlying unity of all life, coupled with the multivalent nature of Hinduism, lead these traditions to genuinely invite and engage a variety of perspectives. Eck remarks: "Unity in diversity is a keynote of Hindu civilization: so many paths, so many gods, so many sects, and yet the deeply held affirmation of one common humanity animated by the one reality called Brahman." As she says, these Hindu traditions have something unique to offer America, which is "a worldview based on religious pluralism. It is a worldview in which the various religious ways, paths, and understandings of God, are not conflicting but consonant."[6]

When there is an underlying belief that everything is ultimately one, ultimately *Brahman,* the attitude of tolerance goes beyond just being polite. Mr. A describes it well when he says:

> The Hindu perspective at least allows the possibility or gives credence to other religious traditions. When my father-in-law [who is a Christian] walks in here [the Hindu temple], he's polite. But basically, I think he thinks we're idolaters; we're worshipping graven images. So I don't think he *really* believes we're worshipping the same God as he is, and that we're somehow or other connected with, I don't know if he'd say the devil, or anything that bad, but it's off. It's not right.

Mr. A continues:

> Whereas, if a Hindu were to go into a Christian church, or even a mosque for that matter, I don't think in the deepest part of their soul they're seeing that this is off, they're seeing it's a different way, but it's the same God.[7]

While ideologically exclusive, fundamentalist groups exist within Hinduism, this attitude of genuine acceptance and inclusion of differing perspectives is pervasive throughout many paths within Hindu traditions.

Mr. F responds with the following to the question, "How would you define a good Hindu?"

> Practicing Hindu is a tolerant man. He believes that God appears in so many forms. What is required is faith in God. It may be in a form or formless. We may have an idol or not. Some Hindus believe only in one God. Others believe in so many gods [. . .]. He [a Hindu] believes that God may be worshiped in so many different ways. You can worship God simply by working and doing your professional work. You see, God is difficult to specify. Just like the blind man who feels the elephant. One man says it is like a trunk, another man says it is like a broom. The man who feels the ear says it is like a fan. So each one feels God is omniscient, feels one aspect of it, and says that is God. Actually you need to integrate all that.[8]

This ability to hold and be comfortable with differing accounts and interpretations of God, of *Brahman,* translates into differing accounts and interpretations of particular situations. In our contemporary pluralistic world, this attitude and ability provides an exemplary model for engaging in bioethical discussions.

This metaphor of the blind men and the elephant has several implications for Hinduism's notion of human ability. One could argue that this story is in fact saying that each of us suffers from some sort of blindness. Consequently, we are prevented from seeing the whole picture of reality; we as human beings are limited. To this, Śankara and others would respond that it is true. The assumption that there are even qualities and forms is a result of *avidyā,* ignorance. *Avidyā* is itself a result of *māyā,* or illusion, of not seeing things the way they really are.[9] However, in recognizing human blindness there is strength and wisdom.

This story is often told to elucidate the belief in the underlying unity of life and the multivalent nature of Hinduism. The point of the story is not only the recognition of human blindness. Rather, the lesson emphasizes the importance of genuinely hearing other descriptions of the elephant, of reality. Implicitly, there is an assumption that we are all engaging reality; we all have a handle on a part of the truth. There is also a presupposition of trust and faith in the human ability to perceive reality, reason, and act.

In the contemporary context of bioethics, both interpretations of this metaphor have implications that may be found to be constructive for working through difficult bioethical issues and situations. First, there is an admission that no one, not the patient, the philosopher, the physician, or the theologian is omniscient. Second, complete knowledge and certainty is not expected. The admission and acceptance of limited knowledge can be beneficial in that it can potentially decrease an individual's anxiety over always "having to be right." More importantly, it may provide opportunities to learn something new or see something from yet another perspective. Third, there is a call to listen and hear the perspectives of others. If the blind men were to integrate all their findings, as Mr. F suggests, they would all have a more complete understanding of an elephant. Finally, there is an allowance for the actual circumstances of particular clinical situations, or cases, to frame the issues and influence one's decisions and actions.

A case-based approach to decision-making, and to bioethics in particular, has a long, though somewhat dubious, history. Jonsen and Toulmin present a history of casuistry, a "method for the practical resolution of moral issues,"[10] that directly addresses issues present in actual situations. Within their discussion, Jonsen and Toulmin point out how moral philosophers in Great Britain and the United States moved away from case-based reasoning toward a focus on metaethics, on developing universal, abstract, systematic ethical theories and foundational principles. They demonstrate how these attempts to design general, abstract, philosophical theories are themselves bound to historical and social backgrounds. These theories, they argue:

> need to be understood not as making *comprehensive and mutually exclusive* claims but, rather as offering us *limited and complementary* perspective on the whole broad complex of human conduct and moral experience [. . .], none of these theories tells us the whole truth [. . .] about ethical thought and moral conduct. Instead, each of them gives us part of the larger picture we require, if we are to recognize the proper place of moral reflection and discussion [. . .].[11]

Though the various philosophical theories claim to ground ethics in "axiomatic superprinciples," they are ultimately framed by the historical and social settings of the time in which they were developed. Rather than providing us with the elephant in its entirety, these theories provide us with insights into different parts of the elephant.

After discussing the zenith and then decline of casuistry, Jonsen and Toulmin conclude by calling for a revival of a "new casuistry." Our study supports this call and the two claims they make regarding this approach to ethics. First, in ethics, particularly bioethics, casuistry is unavoidable. Second, Jonsen and Toulmin assert, "*moral knowledge is essentially particular,* so that sound resolutions of moral problems must always be rooted in a concrete understanding of specific cases and circumstances."[12] The six characteristics of Hindu thought are elements that engage the practical aspects of life; they demonstrate the necessity of a casuistic approach to considering the ethical circumstances of particular situations while retaining commitments to particular principles. These six Hindu characteristics also encapsulate the tendency within Hindu traditions to intermingle elements such as philosophy, religion, knowledge, and experience. For many within these traditions, experience and knowledge, religion, philosophy, and ethics are inseparable. Consequently, the particulars of specific situations are important when evaluating ethical and moral issues.

There is a clear difference between casuistry and "situation ethics." While the former has a long, conflicted history within Catholic moral reasoning, the latter experienced a brief period of popularity during the 1960s. While casuists operate with a number of moral paradigms, principles, and maxims, situationists do not necessarily acknowledge one general principle. Situationists may accept a role for maxims; however, they are only considered guidelines, not determining factors. Casuists pay attention to circumstances as one feature among many regarding the moral life; situationists usually reduce the moral life to the circumstances. Another difference is that casuists will analyze a new case by comparing and contrasting it with previous or paradigmatic cases. Situationists will focus more exclusively on the concrete case before them.[13]

Jonsen and Toulmin maintain that this casuistic approach to ethics falls within the Aristotelian tradition. By heeding "Aristotle's advice to take a more substantive and practical approach to ethics, we can broaden our view and recognize in what multiple ways moral arguments are rooted in experience." Moral arguments, according to them, "form 'networks' whose multiple roots and inner connections give them—in the jargon of the electronic engineers—the 'redundancy' they need if they are to be provided with effective strength in practice."[14] Rather than being left with different, disconnected philosophical descriptions of an elephant, the six elements of Hindu thought, and this casuistic approach, encourage a blending of a variety of views, leading to a fuller understanding of the elephant, of the circumstances, and the issues at hand.

Jonsen's description of a good casuist seems quite applicable to one operating out of the characteristics of Hindu thought. According to him, an individual engaged in bioethical struggles "should be cognizant of particulars," and "should have a solid, even scientific understanding of topics." In addition:

> He or she should recognize the obscurity of the situation and thus depend on other involved parties to illuminate as best they can. He or she must be able to hear and hold in mind a variety of arguments about the maxims appropriate

> to complex situations. He or she should be able to tolerate uncertainty about the right course and, within that uncertainty, find a reasonable course of action; that is, the course recommended by the most persuasive argument in the circumstances, with due recognition of other arguments that are plausible. A good casuist must, then, have all the intellectual virtues recommended by Aristotle: science, prudence, intuition, wisdom [. . .].[15]

The strength of casuistry and of the multivalent nature of Hindu traditions is their commitment to engaging in the actual struggles occurring in the clinical setting. Each practical experience is taken seriously. More importantly, they are the focal point from which the bioethical discussions emerge. Though academic bioethical discussions may occur in a vacuum, in isolation from actual experiences, the clinical struggles do not.

DeGrazia and Beauchamp present a critique of casuistry that some may wish to apply to the Hindu ethics being examined in this study. They caution that casuists are less independent of principle-based reasoning than they care to admit. They also argue that casuists have difficulties when it comes to justifying judgments in particular cases. According to DeGrazia and Beauchamp, this case-based approach risks not being able to make progress, especially in controversial issues, and can potentially overlook general fundamental issues.[16] However, Hindu ethics, as we have discussed it, is dependent on the key characteristics and principles of Hindu thought. While there is a focus on the particular circumstances in Hindu decision-making processes, there is an unwavering commitment to causing the least amount of harm possible. There is also an eye to the overall good of society. While *dharma* lays out particular guidelines for how people should live, these guidelines are not set in stone. As individuals mature and societies evolve, roles and expectations of *dharma* change and shift depending on one's circumstances. While some may question the lack of universal principles and lack of attention to "means-end" and "actor-action" dichotomies within this Hindu ethic, one need only examine the theory of *karma*. In the theory of *karma*, these dichotomies dissipate because the "ends inhere in means and actors are products of actions."[17] No one is free from the ultimate consequences of his or her actions.

IMPLICATIONS AND ADDITIONAL APPLICATIONS OF HINDU BIOETHICS

The six elements of Hindu thought have implications for bioethics in the academy, the clinical setting, and in the public policy arena. Hindu presuppositions in the academy may contribute to the exploration of bioethical issues in at least two ways. First, they broaden the discussions by the inclusion of perspectives from non-Western, pluralistic, South Asian traditions. In this age of globalization and multiculturalism, this inclusion is an important element for the academy. These Hindu perspectives provide ethicists, philosophers, and theologians additional material from which to draw when considering various issues. Second, these characteristics of Hindu thought, grounded in practical experiences as they are, may be utilized to remind the academy that the issues being discussed, though perhaps abstract and theoretical in the classroom, are often actual situations that individuals are struggling through within the clinical setting and within their lives.

Within the clinical and public policy arena, the six characteristics of Hindu thought can be very useful. As previously mentioned, the dominant religious voices currently influencing clinical and public policy are those from within various Roman Catholic and other conservative Christian groups. Those from within these traditions tend to hold tightly to principles they consider absolute. Additionally, these individuals seem to believe that the principle to which they cling prescribes a particular course of action. Take, for example, teachings such as the sanctity of all human life. Roman Catholic commitments to this principle have profound implications for how they engage the clinical setting and public policy debates and decisions.

Grounding their stance in the principle of respect for life, the National Conference of Catholic Bishops issued the "Ethical and Religious Directives for Catholic Health Care Services." It is these directives that prohibit Catholic hospitals from offering many reproductive health services such as contraception, tubal-ligations, vasectomies, abortion, and IVF or other infertility services. These restrictions are of great concern for the public at large because as hospitals, HMOs, and medical facilities struggle financially, many are bought by, or merge with, Catholic health systems. According to statistics offered by the Catholic Health Association (CHA) of the United States, one out of every ten acute care hospitals in this nation is now operated by Catholic operated healthcare systems. From 1990 through 1998, there were 127 Catholic/non-Catholic hospital mergers and affiliations throughout the nation. Forty-three of these occurred in 1998 alone. While some creative efforts are made to preserve at least minimal reproductive services, in approximately half of these mergers all or most of the disputed reproductive healthcare services were discontinued at previously non-Catholic facilities. Consequently, women in the communities where these mergers occur, regardless of their religious convictions, are no longer able to access many reproductive health services. As of May 2005, there are 599 CHA member hospitals nationwide. The decisions of the National Conference of Catholic Bishops directly influence the healthcare made available to women across this country.[18]

In the United States, where autonomy, freedom of choice, and self-determination are primary values, issues involving fetuses often become very polarized. On the one hand, there are those, represented by the conservative religious voices, who place the principle of the sanctity of human life over and above autonomy and argue for a "prolife agenda." On the other hand, there are other voices, both religious and secular, that uphold autonomy and individual freedom and defend a "prochoice agenda." These labels of "prochoice/prolife" represent a simplistic understanding of the issues involved and greatly limit the discussions. There is a struggle between balancing the principle of autonomy with other principles, and with what is good for society as a whole.

Public policy issues such as third trimester abortions, fetal stem cell research, cloning, and even foreign aid are likewise affected by an unwavering commitment to the principle of the sanctity of human life. Arguing for the sanctity of human life, representatives of the Catholic Church and others demand the prohibition of third trimester abortions and jail time for physicians participating in such procedures. They also call for a ban on fetal stem cell research and cloning, arguing that these technologies fail to recognize the sanctity of the life of the fetus. Their objections to foreign aid are often grounded in their objections to the funding of family planning services offered by many Non-Governmental Organizations (NGO). According to these arguments, society is better served by eliminating particular reproductive options from which individuals may choose.

The Hindu ethic presented within this book also presumes the sanctity of human life, of all life. The commitment to *ahiṃsā* is held in conjunction with the other five characteristics of Hindu thought. However, within Hindu traditions, a commitment to the sanctity of life does not automatically prescribe only one acceptable course of action. Rather than upholding a particular principle as universal and monolithic in meaning and applicability, the six characteristics of Hindu thought work together to form an ethic that proves to be very helpful for negotiating a path through the complicated issues mentioned above. Rather than defending agendas of "prolife" verses "prochoice," these characteristics highlight the nuances of the situation and the arguments. They invite thoughtful consideration of the complexities of issues at hand.

For example, in regard to fetal stem cell research and cloning, the Hindu belief in the underlying unity of all life acknowledges the sanctity of fetal life, of all life. A human fetus is not simply inconsequential tissue easily discarded, nor is it a fully matured adult human being. Taking life, even fetal life, has its *karmic* consequences; therefore, Hindu principles would most likely support objections to the creation of fetuses for the sole purpose of experimentation. However, the acknowledgement of the sanctity of life applies both to the fetus and to the practical situations within society and the overall good for society. While it may not be good for society to indiscriminately kill embryos and fetuses, finding cures for Alzheimer's and Parkinson's disease, organ failure, and other diseases is a potential good for society. Therefore, one could justify utilizing fetal tissue from miscarriages, abortions, or remaining frozen embryos from reproductive technologies. Again, all actions are accompanied with *karmic* consequences; thus, medical scientists need to carefully consider their *dharma,* the harm and the good that will result from their work.[19] The characteristics of Hindu thought do not prescribe only one course of action to accompany a commitment to the principle of the sanctity of life. Additionally, one's commitment to a principle such as the sanctity of life does not preclude one from considering the situation at hand, what would cause the least harm, one's dharma, and so on.

The complex issues involved with foreign aid provide another example of how the six characteristics of Hindu thought work in concert to preserve the sanctity of life while also considering the concrete situations occurring in the world. There are connections between particular religious convictions and objections to various forms of foreign aid. Roman Catholic objections arise from the fact that this aid often includes family planning services. According to the Church, services such as distributing condoms and other forms of contraception threaten the development of, or life of the fetus and thereby threaten the sanctity of life.[20] On the topic of foreign aid, the Hindu ethic developed within this work would take into consideration a broad range of issues, not the least of which would be the sanctity of life, and a commitment to *ahiṃsā.* However, while upholding the principle that life is sacred, this ethic also holds up the sacredness of the lives of women who are suffering from the effects of multiple pregnancies. The lives of individuals who are suffering from HIV/AIDS and other sexually transmitted diseases, as well as all those suffering from the effects of overpopulation and poverty, are also included in one's commitment to *ahiṃsā.* Each of these topics, fetal stem cell research, cloning, and foreign aid, merit a full examination in light of various potential Hindu perspectives.

In ethical perspectives within Hinduism, commitments to the principles of the sanctity of human life, autonomy, and self-determination are combined when suggesting clinical practice and public policy. Though we are individuals, we live in societies, are interdependent, and are affected by each other's actions. Rather than focusing on prohibiting various actions, the Hindu ethic examined in this work emphasizes the presupposition that all are ultimately interconnected, that each of us has a particular *dharma,* a commitment to *ahiṃsā,* and that *karma* ultimately holds each of us responsible for all of our actions. When applied to academic bioethical discussions, experiences in the clinical setting, and public policy, the Hindu focus presented here offers potentially insightful conclusions. Although these perspectives will most likely not produce a definitive, difficulty-free conclusion, they can contribute to the process of decision making and thereby move the field of bioethics forward in our contemporary pluralistic world.

Endnotes

INTRODUCTION

1. It has been well over ten years since the city burned for four days following the not guilty verdicts of four Los Angeles Police Department officers in the Rodney King beating trials. Though many issues contributed to the unrest, some attribute the conflicts to a lack of understanding between groups and individuals. Reflecting on the past and looking to the future, Reverend Cecil Murray councils, "move to make room and we'll fly; fail to make room and we'll crash." Scott Simon, National Public Radio's *Weekend Edition,* KPCC, 4 May 2002.

2. While "medical ethics" refers to the study of ethics within the discipline of medicine and medical care, "bioethics" is a more inclusive term. The latter term focuses on the worlds of medicine, life sciences, psychology, biotechnology, and genetics, and on the serious challenges and questions that arise from within these worlds. For a fuller discussion on the development of the field of bioethics see Thomas A. Shannon, *Introduction to Bioethics,* 3rd ed. revised and updated (New York: Paulist Press, 1997); Helga Kuhse and Peter Singer, "What is Bioethics? A Historical Introduction," in *A Companion to Bioethics,* ed. Helga Kuhse and Peter Singer (Malden: Blackwell Publishers, 2001); Allen Verhey, ed., *Religion and Medical Ethics: Looking Back, Looking Forward* (Grand Rapids: Eerdmans Publishing Company, 1996).

3. Shannon, *Introduction to Bioethics,* 5.

4. J. Lipner's term, "A Hindu View of Life," in *The Meaning of Life in the World Religions,* ed. Joseph Runzo and Nancy M. Martin (Oxford: Oneworld Publications, 2000), 118.

5. Because of the high premium placed on the separation of church and state, the United States government does not collect religious information from its citizens. However, in recent years The Graduate Center of the City University of New York has conducted two nation-wide surveys. The first, National Survey of Religious Identification (NSRI), was taken in 1990, and the second, American Religious Identification Survey (ARIS), was taken between February and April, 2001. While the NSRI questioned 113,723 individuals regarding their religious preferences, it did not ask the respondents questions regarding their religious beliefs, involvement, and religious composition of

their families. Taking the results of the 1990 survey into account, the ARIS interviewed fewer people, 50,281; however, additional, more detailed questions were asked. For the sake of analytical depth, the ARIS also interviewed a subsample of approximately 17,000 households, asking them additional questions regarding religious beliefs, affiliation, etc. The Graduate Center of the University of New York, *American Religious Identification Survey* http://www.gc.cuny.edu/studies/innovations.htm (23 April 2002). The results and analysis of the NSRI study are available in Barry A. Kosmin and Seymour P. Lachman, *One Nation Under God: Religion in Contemporary American Society* (New York: Crown Trade Paperbacks, 1993).

6. Diana L. Eck, *A New Religious America: How a "Christian Country" Has Become the World's Most Religiously Diverse Nation* (New York: HarperSanFrancisco, 2001), 36. Early in her book, Eck points out how the religious diversity of America began with the variety of peoples indigenous to this land. The Wampanoags of the Northeast, Seminole of the South, Blackfeet of the plains, and Apache of the Southeast all had their own cultural and religious traditions. See also Roger Finke and Rodney Stark, *The Churching of America 1776–1990: Winners and Losers in Our Religious Economy* (New Brunswick: Rutgers University Press, 1992). One of the first questions in the ARIS was an open-ended question, "What is your religion, if any?" This question generated over one hundred different answers, which the surveyors classified into sixty-five different categories. Beyond membership in organized religious traditions, the ARIS asked a question regarding whether the interviewees considered their outlook on life to be essentially religious or secular. To the question: "When it comes to your outlook, do you regard yourself as 1) Secular, 2) Somewhat Secular, 3) Somewhat Religious, or 4) Religious" respondents were able to indicate if they were unsure or a little of both. While seventy-five percent described their outlook as religious or somewhat religious, only sixteen percent indicated their outlook was secular or somewhat secular. http://www.gc.cuny.edu/studies/key findings.htm (23 April 2002).

7. Eck, 22.

8. *Ibid.*

9. Rozzano Locsin, "Building Bridges: Affirming Culture in Health and Nursing," *Holistic Nursing Practice* 15:1 (October 2000), 1. Downloaded from http://gateway2.ovid.com (31 May 2001).

10. Mary K. Canales and Barbara Bowers, "Expanding Conceptualizations of Culturally Competent Care," *Journal of Advanced Nursing* 36:1 (October 2001), 102–111. Downloaded from http://gateway1.ovid.com (18 March 2002). While in this book, we focus on diversity within the United States, there are others who take up the challenges of diversity and healthcare on a global level. For example, see Howard Coward and Pinit Ratanakul, *A Cross-Cultural Dialogue on Health Care Ethics* (Ontario CN: Wilfrid Laurier University Press, 1999).

11. For a discussion on the meaning of the *Magisterium,* see John Mahoney, SJ., *The Making of Moral Theology: A Study of the Roman Catholic Tradition* (New York: Oxford University Press, 1987), 116–121.

12. For a recent work on applied Hindu ethics see S. Cromwell Crawford, *Hindu Bioethics for the Twenty-first Century* (New York: State University of New York Press, 2003).

CHAPTER ONE

1. Kuhse and Singer, 4.

2. Prakash N. Desai, *Health and Medicine in the Hindu Tradition: Continuity and Cohesion* (New York: Crossroad, 1989), 12; see also Kenneth G. Zysk's book, *Medicine in the Veda: Religious Healing in the Veda* (Delhi: Montilal Banarsidass Publishers, 1998).

3. Tao Lee, "Medical Ethics in Ancient China," in *Cross Cultural Perspectives in Medical Ethics: Readings*, ed. Robert M. Veatch (Boston: Jones and Bartlett Publishers, 1989), 132. For more on medicine in China see Charlotte Furth, *A Flourishing Yin: Gender in China's Medical History, 960–1665* (Berkeley: University of California Press, 1999).

4. Marin E. Marty, "Religion, Theology, Church and Bioethics," *Journal of Medicine and Philosophy* 17:3 (June 1992): 280–81; Ronald L. Numbers and Darrel W. Amundsen, *Caring and Curing: Health and Medicine in the Western Religious Traditions* (New York: Macmillan Publishing Company, 1986).

5. Kuhse and Singer, "What is Bioethics?," 4–5. Isabel de la Fuente Fonnest and others argue that there's a strong relationship between individual attitudes toward assisted reproductive technologies, professions, and religious convictions. "Attitudes Among Health Care Professionals on the Ethics of Assisted Reproductive Technologies and Legal Abortion," *ACTA Obstetricia et Gynecologica Scandinavica* 79 (January 2000). Downloaded from http://gateway.ovid.com (21 February 2001).

6. Tao Lee, 133.

7. *Caraka-Saṃhitā* as cited by K. R. Srikanta Murthy, "Professional Ethics in Ancient Indian Medicine," in *Cross Cultural Perspectives in Medical Ethics: Readings,* ed. Robert M. Veatch (Boston: Jones and Bartlett Publishers, 1989), 131.

8. Albert R. Jonsen, "American Moralism and the Origin of Bioethics in the United States," *Journal of Medicine and Philosophy* 17:3 (June 1992): 113.

9. Jonsen, "American Moralism and the Origin of Bioethics in the United States," 114. See also, Max Weber's *The Protestant Ethic and the Spirit of Capitalism.*

10. *Ibid.,* 124–125.

11. Inmaculada de Melo-Martin, *Making Babies: Biomedical Technologies, Reproductive Ethics and Public Policy* (Boston: Kluwer Academic Publishers, 1998), 52–54.

12. Lynda Beck Fenwick, *Private Choices, Public Consequences: Reproductive Technology and the New Ethics of Conception, Pregnancy, and Family* (New York: Dutton, 1998), 300.

13. Kuhse and Singer, "What is Bioethics?" 3; Verhey, "Introduction," 2; Smith, "Religion and the Roots of the Bioethics Revival," 9; Baruch Brody, "Religion and Bioethics," in *A Companion to Bioethics*; Kuhse and Singer, "What is Bioethics?," 4–6; Lisa Sowel Cahill, "Religion and Theology," in *Methods in Medical Ethics,* ed. Jeremy Sugarman and Daniel P. Sulmasy (Washington: Georgetown University Press, 2001); Daniel Callahan, "Religion and the Secularization of Bioethics," *Hastings Center Report* 20:4 (July/August 1990), 2.

14. Unethical experiments conducted on human subjects, such as those conducted at the Tuskegee Institute, impelled the U.S. Congress to establish the National Commission for the Protection of Human Subjects of Biomedical and Behavioral Research. Along with publishing the *Belmont Report,* which articulated the ethical principles that the Commission felt should govern research on human subjects, the Commission also instituted the establishment of Institutional Review Boards (Kuhse and Singer, 10). While Cahill and Lammers emphasize that various Christian and Jewish theologians and philosophers were members of these committees, Callahan argues that the reports generated by these committees, specifically the 1978 *Belmont Report* issued by the National Commission, did not have a trace of religious influence in their wording.

15. Baruch Brody, "Religion and Bioethics," 4–6; Cahill, "Religion and Theology;" Verhey, "Introduction;" Smith, "Religion and the Roots of the Bioethics Revival."

16. Smith, "Religion and the Roots of the Bioethics Revival," 15.

17. Cahill, "Religion and Theology," 50.

18. Courtney S. Campbell, "Religion and Moral Meaning in Bioethics," *Hastings Center Report* 20:4 (July/August 1990): 5.

19. Marty, 273–274; David DeGrazia and Tom Beauchamp, "Philosophy," in *Methods in Medical Ethics,* ed. Jeremy Sugarman and Daniel P. Sulmasy (Washington: Georgetown University Press, 2001), 32–33; Callahan, "Religion and Secularization of Bioethics," 4. Jampes P. Wind, "What Can Religion Offer Bioethics," *Hastings Center Report* 20:4 (July/August 1990): 18.

20. Stephen E. Lammers, "The Marginalization of Religious Voices in Bioethics," in *Religion and Medical Ethics: Looking Back, Looking Forward,* ed. Allen Verhey (Grand Rapids: Eerdmans Publishing Company, 1996), 19–43. See also Marty, "Religion, Theology, Church, and Bioethics." These authors agree that marginalization does not mean total absence of religious voices.

21. Callahan, "Religion and the Secularization of Bioethics," 2.

22. Richard Holloway, *Godless Morality: Keeping Religion Out of Ethics* (Edinburgh: Canongate, 2000), 14, 19–20.

23. Stephen L. Carter, *The Culture of Disbelief: How American Law and Politics Trivialize Religious Devotion* (New York: Anchor Books, 1993), specifically chapters 2–5.

24. Cahill, "Religion and Theology," 50–51; Campbell, "Religion and Moral Meaning in Bioethics," 5–6; Lammers, 37–39.

25. Callahan, "Religion and Secularization of Bioethics," 3; Lammers, 37–39; Campbell, "Religion and Moral Meaning in Bioethics," 5.

26. Cahill, "Religion and Theology," 63–64.

27. Lammers, 27–28.

28. Though every patient, family member, and healthcare provider may not turn to organized religion in these times, most of them, in some way, interpret and engage their experience on both a conventional and ultimate level. In this work, "religion" is not necessarily a separate entity. Along with referring to the actuality of living life, it refers to the space in which individuals struggle with the realities of life, seek for meaning, and

relate to ultimate and unconditioned reality. Though organized, official religious traditions are included in this space, it is not exclusive to them. This broad understanding of religion is reflective of a Hindu influence.

29. Campbell, "Religion and Moral Meaning in Bioethics," 5; Callahan, "Religion and the Secularization of Bioethics," 2.

30. Callahan, "Religion and the Secularization of Bioethics," 2.

31. Wind, "What Can Religion Offer Bioethics," 18; Catherine Myser, "How Bioethics is Being Taught," in *A Companion to Bioethics,* ed. Helga Kuhse and Peter Singer (Malden: Blackwell Publishers, 2001), 486.

32. Warren Thomas Reich, "A New Era for Bioethics: The Search for Meaning in Moral Experience," in *Religion and Medical Ethics,* ed. Allen Verhey (Grand Rapids: Eerdmans Publishing Company, 1996), 112.

33. Callahan, "Religion and Secularization of Bioethics," 2; Wind, "What Can Religion Offer Bioethics," 18; Marty, "Religion, Theology, Church, and Bioethics," 283.

34. Thomas Fox captures the tensions in his description of the conference proceedings in the eighth chapter of his book, *Sexuality and Catholicism* (New York: George Braziller, 1995).

35. Ethics Committee of the American Fertility Society, "Ethical Considerations of The New Reproductive Technologies," *Fertility and Sterility* 53 (April–June, 1990), S1.

36. Though the Roman Catholic Church presents official, authoritative teachings, there is discussion, debate, even dissent within and between her leaders. For example, three years prior to the publication of the *Instruction,* the Pontifical Academy of Sciences, a group consisting of moral theologians who advise the Pope, held a conference regarding IVF. After three days of presentations on the various aspects of IVF, all the moral theologians, save one, indicated that they would not consider IVF a sin and they had no moral objection to it. The lone dissenter, Monsignor Carlos Cafarra, objected on the grounds that IVF allowed for procreation outside the bonds of marriage and that sexual intercourse within marriage is the only legitimate way to procreate. Jones and Cockin, "On Assisted Reproduction, Religion and Civil Law." Obviously the voices of the other moral theologians at this conference did not prevail. As is discussed in chapter 5, the *Instruction* clearly objects to IVF and other forms of assisted reproductive technology. Though extremely interesting, discovering the reasons for, and reasoning behind, the positions of the Roman Catholic Church are beyond the scope of this study.

37. Congregation for the Doctrine of the Faith, "Instruction on Respect for Human Life in Its Origin and on the Dignity of Procreation," in *Ethical Issues in the New Reproductive Technologies,* ed. Richard T. Hull (Belmont: Wadsworth Publishing Company, 1990), 35–36 (emphasis added). This document can also be found at hppt://www.Vatican.va. Henceforth this work, *Instruction on Respect for Human Life in Its Origin and on the Dignity of Procreation,* is referred to as *Instruction* and is cited as it appears in Hull.

38. The document resulting from these second meetings is included as Appendix E in a third report published in 1990. Due to significant developments in the field of

assisted reproductive technology, the Ethics Committee convened for a third time in 1989. The Ethics Committee of the American Fertility Society, "Ethical Considerations of the New Reproductive Technologies," 95S–104S.

39. *Los Angeles Times,* 24 July 2001.

40. *Los Angeles Times,* 21 July 2001.

41. *Los Angeles Times,* 19 July 2001.

42. Evan Thomas and Eleanor Clift, "Battle for Bush's Soul," *Newsweek,* 9 July 2001, 28–30.

43. *Los Angeles Times,* 24 July 2001.

44. Margaret Farley, "The Role of Experience in Moral Discernment," in *Christian Ethics: Problems and Prospects,* ed. Lisa Sowle Cahill and James F. Childress (Cleveland: Pilgrim Press, 1996), 135–36.

45. In many respects, this is the methodology employed in this study. Chapters 3 through 6 of this work are centered around two situations. The first "cases" come from paradigmatic narratives of ancient India. Then, once the foundation is laid through an examination of these stories, a modern case study is examined in light of what was extracted from antiquity.

46. According to The Graduate Center of the City University of New York's ARIS Study, the Christian population of the United States has declined from 86% in 1990 to 77% in 2001. The following provides three examples of the change in populations from 1990 to 2001: number of those identifying with Islam rose from 527,000 to 1,104,000, Buddhist rose from 401,000 to 1,082,00, and the number of Hindus rose from 227,000 to 766,000. http://www.gc.cuny.edu/studies/keyfindings.htm.

47. Cheryl A. Howard, Sally Andrade, and Theresa Byrd, "The Ethical Dimensions of Cultural Competence in Border Health Care Settings," *Family and Community Health* 23:4 (January 2001): 36–49. Downloaded from http://gateway2.ovid.com (31 May 2001); Emilio J. Carrillo, Alexander R. Green, and Joseph R. Betancourt, "Cross-Cultural Primary Care: A Patient-Based Approach," *Annals of Internal Medicine* 130:10 (18 May 1999): 829–34; Giselle Corbie-Smith, "The Role of Cultural Competence in Addressing Health Disparities," *SGIM Forum* 24:10 (October 2001): 1; Canales and Bowers, 102.

48. Howard, Andrade, and Byrd, 2.

49. Barbara Leonard and Gregory A. Plotnikoff, "Awareness: The Heart of Cultural Competence," *American Association of Critical-Care Nurses* 11:1 (February 2000): 51–59. Downloaded from http://pageway2.obid.com (31 May 2001). A similar definition for cultural competency, developed by a subgroup within the California Department of Health Services, is as follows: "learning, accepting and respecting the values, norms and traditions of cultural groups [and] appreciating the differences and similarities within, among, and between groups." California Department of Health Services, "Cultural and Linguistic Requirements Subgroup: Recommended Standards for the Medi-Cal Managed Care Program" (California Department of Heath Services, 1993), as cited in Salimbene.

50. Salimbene, 23–25. In their article, Leonard and Plotnikoff discuss Starn's Five Components of Cultural Competency: 1) An awareness and acceptance of the fact

that there are cultural differences; 2) Self-awareness; 3) Understanding the dynamics of cultural differences; 4) Knowledge of the client's family culture; and 5) Adaptation of services to support the client's culture. Leonard and Plotnikoff, 2.

51. Joseph Fins, "Encountering Diversity: Medical Ethics and Pluralism," *Journal of Religion and Health* 33:1 (Spring 1994): 23–27; Canales and Bowers, 102–11.

52. Anne Fadiman, *The Spirit Catches You and You Fall Down: A Hmong Child, Her American Doctors, and the Collision of Two Cultures* (New York: Farrar, Straus, and Giroux, 1997).

53. In her article "Cultural Competence: A Priority for Performance Improvement Action," Salimbene describes other examples of where sensitivity to particular cultural and religious beliefs can make a difference in the quality of medical care. She uses eye contact and patting children on the head as two such examples. Though in mainstream North American culture, a lack of eye contact could be interpreted as "holding something back" or not telling the truth, in many traditional Asian cultures, it is a sign of disrespect to look directly at a person in positions of authority. Often, a nurse or doctor will pat a child on the head as a sign of affection and reassurance. This gesture, in some Korean families, could be very disquieting because touching someone's head can be interpreted as an attempt to steal the child's soul.

54. Canales and Bowers, 102–11. Emphasis added.

55. Marie Ngetiko Fongwa, "Advancing Healthcare Practices: Linking Quality with Culture," *Journal of Nursing Administration* 30:6 (June 2000): 291. Downloaded from http://gateway2.ovid.com (31 May 2001); Locsin, 2; Leonard and Plotnikoff, 2.

56. Canales and Bowers; Carrillo, Green, Betancourt.

57. Eck writes, "'We the people of the United States' now form the most profusely religious nation on earth" (5).

58. Canales and Bowers; Salimbene. Working in Neurosurgery Intensive Care and in Labor and Delivery, I understand first hand how cultural competence is not dependent upon actual knowledge of an individual's culture. This is not to say that actual cultural knowledge is not helpful; it is. However, being culturally competent is not dependant upon knowledge, but rather on empathy, respect, and a desire to hear and understand the patient.

59. Arvind Sharma, "On Hindu, Hindustān, Hinduism and Hindutva," *NVMEN* 49:1 (2002): 1, 8. The Persians utilized the term "Al-Hind" to designate places where non-Muslim lived, thus also providing it with an obvious religious connotation. It was not until around the sixteenth century that particular people, who wanted to distinguish themselves from their Muslim neighbors, appropriated the term "Hindu" as a self-description. Hindu now became a specific "religious" description, referring to a way of life ultimately grounded in or derived from the Vedas.

60. Julius J. Lipner, "A Hindu View of Life," 112. Desai, *Health and Medicine in the Hindu Tradition,* 7.

61. Radhakrishnan, *The Hindu View of Life* (New Delhi: Indus, 1993), 91.

62. As cited in Lipner, *A Hindu View of Life,* 117.

63. As cited in Doniger O'Flaherty, *Women, Androgynes, and Other Mythical Beasts* (Chicago: University of Chicago Press, 1980), 6.

64. Sharma, "On Hindu, Hindustān, Hinduism and Hindutva," 8.

65. John Stratton Hawley, "Who Speaks for Hinduism and Who Against?" *JAAR* 68:4 (December 2000): 712.

66. Radhakrishnan, 13. The British used the term "Hindu" to "characterize *all things in India* (specifically elements and features found in the cultures and religions of India) which were *not* Muslim, *not* Christian, *not* Jewish, or, hence, *not* Western." Utilizing the term "Hindu" to refer to "all things in India" is indicative of the all-encompassing nature of Hindu traditions (Frykenberg 1989:31, as cited in Sharma, 17).

67. Desai, *Health and Medicine in the Hindu Tradition,* 6–12.

68. Barbara A. Holdrege, "Hindu Ethics," in *A Bibliographic Guide to the Comparative Study of Ethics,* ed. John Carman and Mark Juergensmeyer (New York: Cambridge University Press, 1991), 12.

69. Vasudha Narayanan, "Hindu Ethics and Dharma," in *Ethics in the World Religions,* ed. Joseph Runzo and Nancy M. Martin (Oxford: Oneworld, 2001), 177.

70. Lipner describes how there is a constant conversation between official and unofficial Hindu traditions. On the one hand, characteristics of the orthodox traditions find expression in the popular forms of Hinduism, while, on the other hand, the popular traditions take on formalized characteristics (117).

CHAPTER TWO

1. J. A. B. van Buitenen, *The Bhagavad Gītā in the Mahābhārata* (Chicago: University of Chicago Press, 1981), 6–7.

2. *Mokṣa* is often translated as salvation; however, release or liberation from the cycle of rebirth better captures the Indian context.

3. van Buitenen, *The Bhagavad Gītā in the Mahābhārata,* 8–9.

4. In his discussion on the *Mahābhārata,* Krishna Chaitanya acknowledges that the text is "not scripture by strict orthodox canons;" however, he adds, "it has been treated as such by long tradition." Chaitanya, Krishna, *The Mahābhārata: A Literary Study* (New Delhi: Clarion Books, 1985). Julian F. Woods, *Destiny and Human Initiative in the Mahābhārata* (New York: State University of New York Press, 2001), viii.

5. *MBh.* I.57.74 & XII.327.18; Shalini Shah, *The Making of Womanhood: Gender Relations in the Mahābhārata* (New Delhi: Manohar Publishers, 1995), 2; Bruce M. Sullivan, "The Religious Authority of the *Mahābhārata*: Vyāsa and Brahma in the Hindu Scriptural Tradition," *Journal of the American Academy of Religion* 62:2 (Summer 1994): 378.

6. J. A. B. van Buitenen, *The Mahābhārata: I. The Book of the Beginning* (Chicago: University of Chicago Press, 1975), xxv. James Fitzgerald, "India's 5th Veda: The *Mahābhārata*'s Presentation of Itself," in *Essays on the Mahābhārata,* ed. Arvind Sharma (Netherlands: E. J. Brill, 1991), 154; Elizabeth Seeger, *The Five Brothers: The Story of the Mahābhārata* (New York: The John Day Company, 1948).

According to scholars, there never has been nor will there probably ever be, a census of *Mahābhārata* manuscripts. There are two major traditions of the text, northern and southern. The most extensive search to produce a critical edition in Sanskrit was conducted by the Bhandarkar Oriental Research Institute. The project began in 1917 and was completed in 1966 under the editorialship of V. S. Sukthankar. John Dunham, "Manuscripts Used in the Critical Edition of the *Mahābhārata*: A Survey and Discussion," in *Essays on the Mahābhārata,* 1–2; Alf Hiltebeitel, *The Cult of Draupadī,* vol. 1 (Chicago: University of Chicago Press, 1988), xx; Indira V. Peterson, "Arjuna's Combat with the Kirata: Rasa and Bhakti in Bharavi's Kiratarjuniya," in *Essays on the Mahābhārata,* 213.

In his introductory chapter, Norbert Klaes presents a brief yet comprehensive summary of critical studies regarding the *Mahābhārata* (*Conscience and Consciousness: Ethical Problems of Mahābhārata* (Bangalore: Dharmaram Publications, 1975)). The historical development of this text is interesting and informative. However, for the purposes of this work, it is inconsequential as to when the particular narratives being examined were incorporated into the text. Whether they were part of the original core of the story or redacted at a later date (sometime between 200–400 C.E.), they nonetheless provide fertile ground for an exploration of issues relating to infertility and human reproduction.

This study utilizes J. A. B. van Buitenen's English translation of the *Mahābhārata.* This is an annotated and critical English translation based on the Sanskrit edition edited by Sukthankar. Occasionally stories and details important to this work are taken from another translation, that of Kisari Mohan Ganguli, *The Mahābhārata,* vol. I–XII (New Delhi: Munshiram Manoharlal Publishers Pvt. Ltd., 1993). Unless otherwise stated, all direct quotations of the text are taken from J. A. B. van Buitenen's translation. *MBh.* is the abbreviation used to indicate the *Mahābhārata.*

7. *MBh.* I.56.35.

8. *MBh.* I.56.14–16.

9. Radhakrishnan, 87.

10. S. Cromwell Crawford, *Dilemmas of Life and Death: Hindu Ethics in a North American Context* (New York: State University of New York Press, 1995), 6.

11. Bimal Krishna Matilal, *Moral Dilemmas in the Mahābhārata* (New Delhi: Shri Jainendra Press, 1989), vii. Harold Coward regards the *Mahābhārata* as representative of authoritative classical texts on *dharma.* According to Vishnu Sukthankar, the preeminent importance of this text is universally acknowledged. Regarding the epic, he writes: "it is the most valuable product of the entire literature of ancient India, . . . it is one of the most inspiring monuments of the world, and an inexhaustible mine for the investigation of the religion, mythology, legend, philosophy, law, custom, and political and social institutions of ancient India." Vishnu S. Sukthankar, *The Adiparvan: Being the First Book of the Mahābhārata the Great Epic of India* (Poona: Bhandarkar Oriental Research Institute, 1933), iii.

12. Vinoba, *Talks on the Gita* (Varanasi: Sarva Seva Sangh Prakashan, 1995), 1–2.

13. Gary A. Tubb, "Santarasa in the *Mahābhārata,*" in *Essays on the Mahābhārata,* ed. Arvind Sharma (Netherlands: E. J. Brill, 1991), 171. Vyāsa is also traditionally credited with arranging the *Vedas* into the four books, composing other texts and, according to the narrative, he himself fathers the primary patriarchs of the narrative, Dhṛtarāṣṭra and Pāṇḍu. He also fathers a third half-brother, Vidura—a minor figure in the story (*MBh.* I.1.50–65).

14. Sullivan, 377.

15. Shah, 2.

16. Fitzgerald, 151–152.

17. In May 2001, Concordia University hosted The Second International Conference on the *Mahābhārata.* This conference attracted scholars from Australia, Canada, England, India, Israel, Mexico, the United States of America, and other countries. The papers presented covered a variety of topics ranging from textual and character analysis to applications regarding weapons of mass destruction and assisted reproductive technologies. Presenters were South Asian specialists, linguists, ethicists, and scientists.

The *Mahābhārata* is the primary source for contemporary scholars exploring various aspects of Hindu thought. In *Destiny and Human Initiative in the Mahābhārata,* Julian Woods utilizes this text as the focus of his discussion on Hindu concepts of human destiny and free will. Norbert Klaes, in his book *Conscience and Consciousness: Ethical Problems of Mahābhārata,* examines the character of Yudhiṣṭhira, the oldest son of Pāṇḍu. Through his presentation, he demonstrates how the text presents and works through various ethical dilemmas. While Nicholas Sutton utilizes this ancient epic in his discussion of religious doctrines of Hindu traditions, Bimal Krishna Matilal uses it as the foundation for his presentation of the moral dilemmas in life. The utilization of this text throughout Indian history, particularly its most renounced section, the *Bhagavad-Gītā,* is evidence of the timeless, applicable nature of the *Mahābhārata.*

18. van Buitenen, *The Bhagavad Gītā in the Mahābhārata,* 17–18.

19. Ainslie T. Embree, 227; Hopkins, 89.

20. van Buitenen, *The Bhagavad Gītā in the Mahābhārata,* 9–10.

21. In his essay "The Life-Ethics of the Bhagavad Gītā as Interpreted by Rāmānuja," Klostermaier argues that Rāmānuja "sees in bhakti the highest calling of a human persona and reads the *Gītā* as a text that inculcates love to God as the first and foremost duty." In *Life Ethics in World Religions,* ed. Dawne C. McCance (Atlanta: Scholars Press, 1998), 57.

22. Gandhi's call was one advocating nonviolence, while Tilak's call involved the taking up of arms to fight the British.

23. Hiltebeitel discusses the various forms in which the *Mahābhārata* is depicted. His text includes photographs of various statutes, plays, paintings, temples, and ceremonies that either depict particular scenes from this epic or are inspired by it, 262. Jean-Claude Carriére, vii, xv.

24. Americans have Superman, Wonderwoman, Batman and Robin, as well as biblical figures such as Abraham, Sarah, Samson, and Esther. Indians and Hindus have Bhīṣma, Draupadī, Arjuna and his younger twin brothers, as well as exemplary figures like Yudhiṣṭhira, Gāndhārī, and Kuntī. In keeping up with available technology, a comic book version of the *Mahābhārata* may be found in cyberspace simply by conducting a search using "*Mahābhārata*" as a key word.

25. The *Mahābhārata* is the source of a number of one act plays that reshape and emphasize the characters from the epic. "Karnabhara" is an example of a such a play based on the character of Karṇa. Translated by Barbara Stoler Miller, "Karnabhara:

The Trial of Karna," in *Essays on the Mahābhārata,* ed. by Arvind Sharma (Netherlands: E. J. Brill, 1991).

26. A *wayang* is a flat or rounded puppet utilized in the presentation of a play. For a discussion on the making and symbolism of the *wayang* puppets, see R. L. Mellema, *Wayang Puppets: Carving, Colouring and Symbolism* (Amsterdam: Koninklijk Instituut voor de Tropen, 1954).

27. *Los Angeles Times* staff writer Kevin Thomas makes the following comment on Peter Brook's production of the *Mahābhārata*: "Brook and his collaborators have brought to life one of the world civilization's literary cornerstones, an awe-inspiring expression of mankind's attempt to make sense of the often baffling and terrifying human experience and to illuminate the faith, values and conduct essential for human survival and fulfillment." *Los Angeles Times,* 29 June 1990.

28. Steven Pressfield, *The Legend of Bagger Vance: A Novel of Golf and the Game of Life* (New York: Avon Books, 1995).

29. Steven J. Rosen, *Gita on the Green: The Mystical Tradition Behind Bagger Vance* (New York: Continuum, 2000). In the Foreword to Rosen's book, Pressfield acknowledges that the structure of his book, *Legend of Bagger Vance,* is modeled on the *Bhagavad-Gītā,* 11.

30. Eck, 94–96. Some of Ralph Waldo Emerson's works reflect the influence the *Bhagavad Gītā* had on him. It was after reading and digesting this text that he wrote "Ethical Scriptures." Likewise, Henry David Thoreau was influenced by this text.

31. Fitzgerald, 151.

32. M.K. Gandhi, *The Gospel of Selfless Action or The Gītā According to Gandhi* (Ahmedabad: Navajivan Publishing House, 1946), 127–28.

33. van Buitenen, *MBh,* xvi.

34. *MBh.* I.92.45–55.

35. *MBh.* I.94.45–95.

36. *MBh.* I.96.1–60.

37. *MBh.* I.57.65–75.

38. *Niyoga* is an ancient Indian custom. P. V. Kane defines *niyoga* as an "appointment of a wife or widow to procreate a son from intercourse with an appointed male" (Kane 1974, II,1:399). This practice of *niyoga,* and its disputed history, is discussed in more depth below.

39. *MBh.* I.99.1–100.20.

40. *MBh.* I.103.1–20.

41. *MBh.* I.105.1–9.

42. *MBh.* I.105.10–30; Sutherland, 95–98. For those interested in the larger context of these narratives, consult van Buitenen's translation, or for a shorter version see Elizabeth Seeger's *The Five Brothers: The Story of the Mahābhārata* (New York: The John Day Company, 1948).

43. *MBh.* I.105.1–8.

44. *MBh.* I.109.5–30.

45. The importance of children, particularly sons, is discussed in chapter 4.

46. *MBh.* I.111.10–20.

47. *MBh.* I.110.25–113.35. Though Kuntī reveals the fact that she has this mantra, she does not disclose to Pāṇḍu that she utilized it shortly after receiving it. Being overwhelmed with curiosity, she decides to call upon the Sun God to see if the mantra actually works. The Sun God appears and impregnates her with a son. However, since Kuntī is as yet an unmarried maiden, the birth of her first son, Karṇa, is deeply problematic. So, in order to "hide her misconduct and out of fear of her relations," she fashions a small raft and floats Karṇa down the river. He is discovered and saved by a peasant couple who raised him as their own (*MBh.* I.04.9–15). Kuntī hides this secret in her heart.

48. Reasons for their selections will be discussed below.

49. *MBh.* I.114.1–5.

50. *MBh.* I.114.5–35.

51. *MBh.* I.114.65.

52. *MBh.* I.114.65. This *MBh* passage is reflecting the limitations of the law when after a third partner, the woman is considered "loose" and after a fourth she is called a "harlot." This limit to the number of partners a woman may have in her attempts to produce children for her infertile (or dead) husband holds true even in times of distress. This practice is discussed in the *Dharmasūtras,* specifically *Gautama* 18.4-8. Along with limiting the number of partners, this practice also insists that there be no "love" between the woman and man fulfilling his obligations (M. B. Emeneau and B. A. van Nooten, "The Young Wife and her Husband's Brother: *Ṛg Veda* 10.40.2 and 10.85.44," *Journal of the American Oriental Society* 111.3 [1991]: 484–86).

As just mentioned above, Kuntī's first use of her mantra resulted in the birth of Karṇa. Now, in this situation with Pāṇḍu, Kuntī willingly calls upon three different gods to provide him with three sons. She refuses to call upon a fourth, declaring that the law does not permit such actions, even in times of distress. Apparently she is discounting her first use of the mantra, which resulted in the birth of Karṇa. If Kuntī's first use of the mantra is counted, then Indra is the fourth god she calls upon, and she is, in fact, a "harlot." However, Kuntī has kept Karṇa's existence a secret (a secret that will bring her great heartache in the end, as she watches her sons from Pāṇḍu fight and, unbeknown to them, kill their half-brother). Therefore, as far as Pāṇḍu is aware, her objections are legitimate. Beyond Kuntī's desire to hide her earlier "indiscretion," she has grounds upon which she may discount her first encounter with the Sun God. The text indicates that, following the birth of Karṇa, the Sun God "restored her virginity to her," thus making it as if she had never utilized the boon in the first place (*MBh.* I.104.10–14).

53. *MBh.* I.115.1.

54. *MBh.* I.115.15–24.

55. *MBh.* I.107.5–9.

56. Krishna Chaitanya, 160.

57. *MBh.* I.107.10–15.

58. *MBh.* I.107.15–16.

59. The record of Vyāsa's warning to Gāndhārī is in Ganguli's translation of the *Mahābhārata.* Kisari Mohan Ganguli, *The Mahābhārata,* vol. 1 (New Delhi: Munshiram Manoharlal Publishers Pvt. Ltd., 1993), 241–42. This warning is not found in van Buitenen's translation.

60. *MBh.* I.107.16–25.

61. Ganguli 1993, 243–44. Again, van Buitenen's translation records neither the desire for nor the birth of Gāndhārī's daughter.

62. *MBh.* I.107.34f.

63. *MBh.* I.111.25–30. The text reads, "six sons who are of the blood and heirs [. . .] six who are neither heirs nor of the blood." Though the former list contains six options for obtaining a son, the latter list actually has seven options. Similar, though not identical, lists appear in The *Laws of Manu,* 9.158–160. Again, there is mention of twelve options for obtaining a son, "six are both relatives and heirs, and six are relatives but not heirs." The six sons that are both relatives and heirs are listed as being the "Natural, born in the (husband's) field, adopted, made, secretly begotten, and rejected." The following six (again, there are actually seven options), are relatives but not heirs, "Born of an unmarried girl, born of a pregnant bride, bought, born of a remarried woman, self-given, and born of a servant woman." Wendy Doniger O'Flaherty and Brian Smith, eds. and trans., *The Laws of Manu,* (New York: Penguin Books, 1991), 9.158–160. The *Laws of Manu* is a Hindu law text, "an encompassing representation of life in the world—how it is, and how it should be lived" (xvii). All citations of the *Laws of Manu* are taken from the Doniger O'Flaherty and Smith translation.

64. *Manu* 9.33–55. The editors of the *Laws of Manu* indicate that Manu is ambivalent regarding this practice. According to them, though Manu acknowledges that *niyoga* is a legal emergency measure to provide heirs for a dead husband, he dislikes the practice and tends to liken it to unofficial adultery. In 9.181, Manu points out that the natural father has a serious claim to the child born through *niyoga* (Doniger O'Flaherty and Smith, footnote to 9.58, p. 203). There are many rules and regulations regarding this practice. See Gail H. Sutherland's article, "*Bīja* (Seed) and *Kṣetra* (Field): Male Surrogacy or Niyoga in the *Mahābhārata,*" *Contributions to Indian Sociology* (n.s.) 24:1 (1990): 77–103.

65. *Manu,* 9.59–63.

66. *Manu,* 9.143, 147.

67. *Manu,* 9.147.

68. Emeneau and B. A. van Nooten, 484–86.

69. Sutherland, 100.

70. *Manu,* 9.32.

71. *MBh.* I.113.40.

72. Klaes, 19.

73. *MBh.* I.113.40.

74. Yudhiṣṭhira's reputation for honesty is held in such high regard that Kṛṣṇa utilizes it to defeat Droṇa. Under Droṇa's leadership the Kauravas are gaining

ground and the five sons of Pāṇḍu are weary. Kṛṣṇa informs Yudhiṣṭhira and his brothers that Droṇa's commitment to fight will evaporate if they tell him his son, Aśvatthāman, is dead. Thus, they implement the following plan: Bhīma kills an elephant by the name of Aśvatthāman in the presence of Yudhiṣṭhira. He then sends a message to Droṇa informing him that his son is dead. Disbelieving the messenger, Droṇa boils with rage against the Pāṇḍavas. Kṛṣṇa, egging Yudhiṣṭhira on, tells him that Droṇa will exterminate everyone if he, someone whose truthfulness Droṇa trusts, does not confirm the story. With much hesitation and doubt, Yudhiṣṭhira goes before Droṇa. When Droṇa asks if Aśvatthāman is indeed dead, Yudhiṣṭhira admits he saw Bhīma kill Aśvatthāman. As Droṇa lays down his weapon and Bhīma kills him, Yudhiṣṭhira mumbles under his breath, "whether he is an elephant or a man I did not say." Immediately after deceiving Droṇa, Yudhiṣṭhira's chariot, which used to hover a few inches above the ground, sank to the surface of the earth (*MBh.* VII.164.68ff).

75. *MBh.* I.129.5–10. Klaes comments on how the tendency of this passage to moralize the crowning of Yudhiṣṭhira as king is particularly striking.

76. *MBh.* I.114.8–9. Parenthesis added.

77. *MBh.* I.114.5–11. The text records an amazing occurrence that happened shortly after Bhīma's birth. Kuntī is frightened by a tiger and stands up suddenly, forgetting that Bhīma is sleeping in her lap. Even as a baby, his strength is so incredible, his little body as hard as diamonds, that when he falls from his mother's lap he shatters the mountain upon which he lands, but he himself is unharmed. Seeing the pulverized mountain, Pāṇḍu marvels in amazement (*MBh.* I.114.11–15). Elsewhere, stories record Bhīma's unmatched physical strength and character: As a child, he overpowers his cousins, brothers, and others (*MBh.* I.119.15–40). His unmatched strength is demonstrated as he literally carries his family to safety: "Then Bhīmasena, whose speed and power were terrific, took his brothers and his mother and carried them all. He put his mother on his shoulder, the twins on his hips [. . .]. He shattered the trees with his impact and rended the earth with his feet [. . .]" (*MBh.* 1.136.15f).

78. *MBh.* I.114.15.

79. *MBh.* I.114.20–25.

80. At Arjuna's birth, a disembodied voice declares his greatness by saying: "The mighty leader of his people shall vanquish the barons, and with his brothers the hero shall offer up the three sacrifices" (*MBh.* I.114.34–35). It is said of Arjuna, "in battle he became no less hard to face than the sun" (*MBh.* I.1.84). *MBh.* I.123.1–40 records the story of how Arjuna became the greatest archer of his time.

81. By the end of the Great War, Bhīṣma, Droṇa, the five Pāṇḍava brothers, Duryodhana, his clan, Karṇa, and all the others who fought, die and traverse heaven and hell (which are interesting stories to explore in and of themselves). The lone survivor of either clan is a descendent of Arjuna and Kṛṣṇa. Through his second wife, Subbadrā, who is Kṛṣṇa's sister, Arjuna has a son, Abhimanyu. Abhimanyu marries Uttarā and, while she is pregnant with his son, Pariksit, Abhimanyu dies on the battlefield. Thus, the Pāṇḍava family line continues through Arjuna's grandson.

82. *MBh* I.115.15.

83. *MBh.* I.115.15–20. Nakula and Sahadeva are endowed with "beauty, courage, and virtue beyond all other men, they shall shine with surpassing luster, with comeliness and opulence."

84. In her book *Private Choices, Public Consequences,* Lynda Beck Fenwick mentions the Repository for Germinal Choice in Escondido, California. This is a sperm bank, founded in 1963, which specifically provides sperm for donor insemination from men of recognized intellectual achievement (268).

Daily Trojan, the University of Southern California student newspaper, consistently runs ads soliciting women to "donate" their eggs. One heading reads as follows: "Pay your tuition with eggs." It continues, "If you're a woman between 18 and 32, you can earn money easily, anonymously. Donate your eggs to an infertile couple." The ad then goes on to indicate that a woman willing to participate will receive "$5,000 and up, depending on your education and other qualifications." *Daily Trojan,* 12 April 2002.

85. *MBh.* I.112.5.

86. Interestingly, in this narrative, both Kuntī and Pāṇḍu ground their arguments in traditional stories.

87. *MBh.* I.112.30.

88. *MBh.* I.112.34.

89. Susan M. Kerr, Arthur Caplan, Glenn Polin, et al., "Postmortem Sperm Procurement," *The Journal of Urology* 157:6 (June 1997): 2154–58.

90. Fenwick discusses issues that arise from utilizing sperm postmortem. She presents the case of Ed and Nancy Hart. After four years of marriage and unsuccessful attempts to have children, Ed was diagnosed with esophageal cancer. Prior to receiving treatment for his cancer, Ed deposited sperm samples in a fertility clinic, to be utilized at a later time by his wife Nancy. Following Ed's death in June 1990, Nancy became pregnant with his sperm and Judith was born a year after her father's death. The state of Louisiana refused to recognize the baby as Ed's child because Ed was not alive when the child was conceived. This began years of legal battles between Nancy and state and federal governments. When Judith was five years old her entitlement to social security benefits was finally recognized. Fenwick asks the probing question, "Should society be willing to underwrite survivors' benefits for children who did not actually survive their father's death but rather came into existence after death?" (195–198).

A more recent example of the difficulties that can arise from utilizing postmortem sperm was presented on NBC. On August 5, 2001, NBC's 11:00pm Nightly News ran a story of five-year-old twin girls born two years after their father's death. Their mother was suing the Social Security Office for benefits that were denied. This governmental office ruled that the girls were illegitimate, and thus not eligible for benefits, because their father's death ended his marriage to their mother.

91. *MBh.* I.116.1–9.

92. *MBh.* I.116.20–30.

93. Julius J. Lipner, "The Classical Hindu View on Abortion and the Moral Status of the Unborn," in *Hindu Ethics: Purity, Abortion, and Euthanasia* (New York: State University of New York Press, 1989), 42–43. Crawford's reading of the *Mahābhārata*

and *Rāmāyaṇa* leads him to conclude that, in this literature, life begins at conception and preserving this life is of utmost importance (Crawford, 1995, 25).

94. Lipner, 60. Crawford and Young express similar understandings (Crawford, 1995, 25; Young, 19–20).

95. Lipner, 47–48.

96. *MBh.* I.107.10.

97. Lipner, 48.

98. *MBh.* I.107.15–25.

99. Lipner also makes reference to this being a possible early substitute for in vitro gestation (47).

100. New York State Task Force on Life and the Law, *Assisted Reproductive Technologies: Analysis and Recommendations for Public Policy* (New York: New York State Task Force on Life and the Law, 1998), 149.

101. According to statistics cited in the New York State Task Force's report, "Infertility treatment is the major factor that has been implicated in the nationwide surge in the number of multiple births. Between 1974 and 1994, the rate of triplet and higher order multiple births increased fourfold." Nationally and internationally, multiple births attributed to assisted reproductive technologies are as high as sixty-seven percent (*Ibid.*, 149–50).

102. The McCaughey and Chukwu families received international media attention (and subsequent commercial sponsorships) following the successful delivery of septuplets and octuplets, respectively. Following the birth of the McCaughey's thirty-one-week septuplets, ranging in birth weight from two pounds five ounces to three pounds four ounces, the Governor of Iowa came through with his promise to build Bobbie and Kenny McCaughey a new, bigger home. Other gifts included university scholarships for all seven of the children, ten years of portrait photographs, a lifetime supply of Pampers, and seven years of cable TV. Not every individual can count on family and communal support in raising up to eight children all at once. Additionally, few receive television coverage and the resulting financial sponsorship support (Arlene Judith Klotzok, "Medical Miracle or Medical Mischief?: The Saga of the McCaughey Septuplets," *Hastings Center Report* 28:3 (1998): 5. http://www.cnn.com/US/ 9711/11/quad.crazy/; http://www.medicalpost.com/mdlink/english/members/medpost/data/3519/13A.HTM (2 May 2001).

Critics make an astute observation when they comment on how the public welcomes the situations of these multiple births, despite the medical complications and the emotional and financial burdens that accompany them. Multiple gestational pregnancies expose both mother and babies to a great deal of risk. Ovarian overstimulation, a complication associated with various fertility medications, can cause swelling and bleeding of the ovaries and severe fluid retention, and in rare situations this can lead to heart failure. These women are at higher risk for fatal blood clots during pregnancy and delivery. The babies of multiple gestational pregnancies often suffer from chronic lung disease, strokes, mental retardation, and blindness. (Klotzok, 6) In her article "Access to Justice: 'Planned Parenthood': Adoption, Assisted Reproduction, and the New Ideal Family," Susan Appleton juxtaposes the public's outpouring of awe, excitement, and support in situations of multiple births, with circumstances where families have more children than they can handle without outside assistance. The same public that applauds the family with multiple gestational births condemns the latter family as being "irresponsible." According to Appleton, the only thing that distinguishes the babies born as a result of assisted reproductive technology is that their parents went to considerable trouble to have them. Susan Appleton, "Access to Justice: 'Planned Parenthood': Adoption, Assisted Reproduction, and the New Ideal Family," *Washington University Journal of Law and Policy* 1:85 (1999).

CHAPTER THREE

1. Arvind Sharma, "When it Comes to Karma" in *Ethical Issues in Human Cloning: Cross-Disciplinary Perspectives,* ed. Michael C. Brannigan (New York: Seven Bridges Press, 2001), 98.

2. Matilal, 5.

3. *Manu* IX.26.

4. Lawrence Babb, *The Divine Hierarchy: Popular Hinduism in Central India* (New York: Columbia University Press, 1975), 76.

5. *MBh.* I.111.10–17. Pāṇḍu's reference to having offspring in his "field" is reminiscent of the metaphor in *Manu.* He is also referring to Vyāsa's participation in *niyoga,* when he sowed seeds in Pāṇḍu's dead father's "field," that is, in the wombs of Vicitravīrya's widows, Ambikā and Ambālikā.

6. *Manu* does make provisions for those who have daughters but no sons. "A man with no son may make his female child an appointed daughter [. . .]. Whatever children are born in her will offer the refreshment for the dead for me." According to the text, "A son is just like one's self, and a daughter is equal to a son" *Manu* IX.127–130. Elsewhere in the same chapter, "There is no distinction between a son's son and a daughter's son in worldly matters, for a daughter's son also saves him in the world beyond, just like a son's son" *Manu* IX.139.

7. Sutherland, 80.

8. *Manu* IX.106–107.

9. *Manu* IX.137–138. The "chestnut horse" is the highest world of the sun (see IV.231). The importance of having children is also discussed in *Baudhāyana Dharmasūtra* 16.1–14.

10. *Manu* III.37–38.

11. *MBh.* I.13.20–21.

12. Crawford, 1995, 26–27.

13. Traditional "Hinduism" speaks of four stages of life (*āśramas*) that an individual (particularly men) progresses through. These stages are discussed below in chapter 4.

14. *Manu* III.45–50.

15. Traditional "Hinduism" speaks of four goals of life. These goals of life are discussed below in chapter 4.

16. Narayanan, "Hindu Ethics and Dharma," 192.

17. Recall that Kuntī is not even criticized when, out of curiosity, as a young, unmarried teenager, she calls upon the sun god to ascertain if the mantra actually works. *MBh.* I.04.9–15.

18. Prakash N. Desai, *Health and Medicine in the Hindu Tradition: Continuity and Cohesion,* 68.

19. *MBh.* I.57.35–55.

20. *MBh.* I.114.65.

21. *MBh.* I.104.10–14.

22. The text clearly indicates that Kuntī is annoyed, even feeling threatened by Mādrī's cunning choice of calling on the Aśvins. Kuntī's response to Pāṇḍu's second request on behalf of Mādrī is as follows: "I said to her, 'For this once,' and she got two! I was deceived! I fear that she will best me. That is the way of women! I had not known, the more fool I, that by invoking two Gods the fruit would be doubled" (*MBh.* I.115.23–24). This passage captures Kuntī's distrust of Mādrī and it reveals a sense of competition between the two wives. Kuntī is the first and elder wife, and beautiful in her own right, but Mādrī is younger and exceedingly beautiful. As the story continues in the *Mahābhārata,* it is, in fact, Mādrī's irresistible beauty that brings about the death of Pāṇḍu.

Additionally, this dialogue between Kuntī and Pāṇḍu implies that Kuntī would desire to have more children. She is angry and calls herself a "fool" for not realizing that by calling on twin gods her "fruit would be doubled."

23. Satyavatī, acting to ensure the continuation of the family line through the wives of her son, Vicitravīrya, summons Vyāsa from a life of renunciation to engage in *niyoga* with her two childless, widowed daughters-in-law, Ambikā and Ambālikā. *MBh.* I.99.1ff.

24. Arti Dhand, "The Subversive Nature of Virtue in the *Mahābhārata*: A Tale about Women, Smelly Ascetics, and God," *Journal of the American Academy of Religion* 72:1 (March 2004): 40–42.

25. *MBh.* I.111.32–36. Dhand discusses situations where even unmarried women can act out of a desire to have children, see *MBh.* I.78.32.

26. Sutherland, 100.

27. Sutton, 431–33. In this discussion on marriage and the position of these three queens, Sutton makes an interesting point: Though all the sons, Pāṇḍavas and Kauravas, are powerful political leaders, they all remain deferential to their mothers; they revere them and listen to their advice. However, there is a difference between how the Pāṇḍavas and Kauravas respond to their mothers. While the Pāṇḍavas, the "righteous" ones, act on the orders of their mother as if she were dictating divine commands, the Kauravas more or less ignore the council of Gāndhārī and are ultimately destroyed.

28. *MBh.* I.105.1–4.

29. *MBh.* I.174.5ff. During these bridegroom festivities, Arjuna's skills as an archer put Duryodhana to shame and crystallize the latter's hatred of the former. This event serves as a focal point of the growing animosity between the sons of Pāṇḍu and the sons of Dhṛtarāṣṭra.

30. *MBh.* I.9282–89.

31. *MBh.* I.139.10ff. It is interesting to note that while Rākṣasī saluted both Yudhiṣṭhira and Kuntī, her words were actually addressed to Kuntī.

32. Recall how, being able to foresee the future destruction brought about by Gāndhārī's first born, Vyāsa attempts to dissuade her from proceeding with their plan.

33. All citations from the Hebrew Bible and New Testament are taken from the *New Revised Standard Version* (New York: Oxford University Press, 1991).

34. Genesis 20.

35. Genesis 17:17.

36. Genesis 30:1–2, 22–23.

37. Luke 1:8–24.

38. Luke 1:30–35.

39. I Samuel 1:17–20.

40. At this point in the story, Abraham's name is still Abram, and Sarah's is Sarai. However, to avoid confusion, I utilize the new names given to them as recorded in Genesis 17:5, 19.

41. Genesis 16:1–4.

42. Genesis 30: 3–13.

43. The biblical idea of *levirate* marriage (from the Latin *leviratus,* brother-in-law) is somewhat related to the practice of *niyoga.* The difference is that the biblical practice involves an actual marriage whereas the Hindu practice of *niyoga* does not. In both cases, however, the goal of the tradition is to provide heirs.

44. Genesis 38.

45. Ruth 4:14.

46. According to the Gospel of Matthew, this familial line is of great importance. Boaz and Ruth's son, Obed, is the father of Jesse. Jesse is the father of King David. As the family lineage is traced through the generations, it eventually leads to Joseph, husband of Mary, mother of Jesus.

47. Irenaeus, *Against Heresies,* 2.33.5.

48. Pope Paul VI, *Humanae Vitae* (San Francisco: Ignatius Press, 1978), II.10. Emphasis added.

49. *Humanae Vitae,* II.13.

50. *Ibid.,* II.11.

51. *Ibid.,* I.4, II.8.

52. *Ibid.,* II.12.

53. *Ibid.,* II.9.

54. Though the *Humanae Vitae* reaffirmed positions of previous pontiffs regarding the procreative function of sex within marriage, according to Fox, the encyclical is somewhat reformative in its affirmation, and blessing, of the unitive function of sex (Fox, 74–76).

55. *Humanae Vitae,* II.7

56. *Ibid.,* II.11

57. *Instruction,* 25–28. Some married couples creatively attempt to stay within the boundaries of the Church's teachings by having sexual intercourse with a pierced condom. This maintains the connection between the act of intercourse and the possibility of procreation, while simultaneously allowing for the collection of semen.

58. *Declaration on Abortion* (3.13) Washington: Office of Publishing and Promotion Services United States Catholic Conference, 1974 (Fox 1995, 99). Emphasis added.

59. Fox 1995, 99. Emphasis added.

60. John T. Noonan, "The Catholic Church and Abortion," *The Dublin Review* 514 (Winter 1967/68): 305. In *Evangelium Vitae,* Pope John Paul II elaborates on the "incomparable worth of the human person," wherein humans are called to a "fullness of life [. . .]. The loftiness of this supernatural vocation reveals the greatness and the inestimable value of human life even in its temporal phase."

61. If one examines the writings of the Church fathers through the ages, one finds a variety of different perspectives as to when ensoulment occurs. This is discussed further in chapter 5.

62. *Declaration on Abortion,* 3.12. Emphasis added.

CHAPTER FOUR

1. As previously discussed, the need for heirs goes beyond simple desires of having a son—even beyond fulfilling the necessities of having a male child to replace the king after his death. Recall that Pāṇḍu's discussion with Kuntī takes place after he laments the fact that "for childless men there is no door to heaven." According to the text, the motivating factor behind his desire for children is heaven.

2. *MBh.* I.113.40.

3. Klaes, 19.

4. *Ibid.,* 20.

5. The name of this caste reflects the close proximity in which this group was identified with *Brahman,* the all-encompassing essence of the universe. To avoid confusion, *brahmin* refers to the caste or *priests,* while *Brahman* refers to the essence of the universe.

6. Thomas J. Hopkins, *The Religious Life of Man: The Hindu Religious Tradition* (Belmont: Wadsworth Publishing Company, 1971), 84.

7. The concept of *dharma* is discussed below.

8. Hopkins, 74–84.

9. *Manu,* 3.77–78.

10. These are texts that establish Brahmanical rules for society.

11. Hopkins, 74–75.

12. Kinsley, 152–75.

13. Radhakrishnan, 76.

14. *Bhagavad Gītā,* I.39–40.

15. The focus on ensuring the good of society does not exclude the needs and desires of individuals. See the discussions below regarding the choices of Gāndhārī and Dhṛtarāṣṭra and the multivalent nature of Hinduism.

16. *Ṛg Veda* 10.90.12–14. The *Ṛg Veda* is the earliest "Hindu" text containing hymns of praise to various Vedic gods. All translations of the *Ṛg Veda* are taken from Wendy Doniger O'Flaherty, *The Rig Veda: An Anthology* (New York: Penguin Books, 1981).

17. Hopkins's more complete discussion of *Ṛg Veda* 10.90 is found on pp. 22–25.

18. According to Hopkins, this late Vedic worldview understood that the "phenomenal world, the world of thought and action, was neither permanent nor self-existent; it was a manifestation of names and forms brought forth by the creative powers of *brahman* and *tapas*" (Hopkins, 36). However, early Vedic hymns expressed a different worldview, one in which there was a clear distinction between humans and gods. Early Vedic hymns depict a world where the gods are in control and humans aimed to improve their lives on this earth through praising and appeasing these gods. An example of this attitude is found in *Ṛg Veda* 1.32. For a discussion of these various strands of Vedic thought, see the first two chapters of Hopkins.

19. Eck, 80.

20. *Muṇḍaka Upaniṣad* 2.2.10–11. The *Upaniṣads* are primarily philosophical dialogues between gurus and their students. All translations of the *Upaniṣads* are taken from Patrick Olivelle, *Upaniṣads* (New York: Oxford University Press, 1996).

21. *Kaṭha Upaniṣad* 6.1. *Bṛhadāraṇyaka Upaniṣad* 1.4.10 reads: "In the beginning this world was only *brahman*, and it knew only itself (*ātman*), thinking: 'I am *brahman*.' As a result, it became the Whole [. . .]." *Chāndogya Upaniṣad* 8.3.3–4 provides yet another example of where the text is clearly linking the *ātman* (one's true self/"soul") with *brahman* and then arguing that *brahman* is the real totality of all.

22. Hopkins utilizes the following metaphor in his description of this Upaniṣadic worldview, "Since all things are ultimately the Existent, individual differences are no more significant than are the individual rivers that in the end all flow together to make the single ocean" (Hopkins, 44). As Klaes clearly states, ultimately there is "no essential difference; but only a difference of degree, between the lokas [worlds] of the Gods and the life on earth" (Klaes, 55). Radhakrishnan recalls how when Yājñavalkya, an Upaniṣadic sage, "was called upon to state the number of gods, he started with the popular number of 3306, and ended by reducing them all to one Brahman. 'This indestructible enduring reality is to be looked upon as one only'" (Radhakrishnan, 22).

23. *Bhagavad-Gītā*, X.7–8. Emphasis added.

24. O. P. Dwivedi, "Dharmic Ecology," in *Hinduism and Ecology: The Intersection of Earth, Sky, and Water*, ed. Christopher Key Chapple and Mary Evelyn Tucker (Cambridge: Harvard University Press, 2000), 4–6.

25. The common word for "self" in the Sanskrit language is the reflexive pronoun, *ātman*. Within the upaniṣadic literature, *ātman* had a more specific meaning: the essential part of a human being, a person's most fundamental reality. Generally, *ātman* refers to the "inner self," and is distinguished from the physical body (Hopkins, 37).

26. *Bhagavad Gītā* II.19.

27. *Ibid.,* II.30.

28. Crawford describes *Brahman* as "the ultimate source of the external world" and *ātman* as "the inner self of man." "Brahman of the macrocosm is none other than the atman of the microcosm." S. Cromwell Crawford, *The Evolution of Hindu Ethical Ideas* (Hawaii: University Press of Hawaii, 1984), 37.

29. *Atmabodha* 36–38, 40. Translation obtained from *Atambodha (Self-knowledge),* trans. by Swami Nikhilananda (New York: Ramakrishna-Vivekananda Center, 1970). Authorship of this text is somewhat unclear, although Indians traditionally attribute it to Śankara.

30. Antonio T. de Nicolas, "The Unity and Indivisibility of the Self (Brahman)," *Main Currents in Modern Thought* 29:4 (1973): 134.

31. *Manu,* I.31–32, 41.

32. *Ibid.* Though this idea of an underlying unity is shared by most Hindu traditions, how this belief is interpreted and explained can be radically different.

33. Patrick Olivelle, *Dharmasūtras: The Law Codes of Apastamba, Gautama, Baudhayana, and Vasistha,* (Varanasi: Motilal Banarsidaas, 2000), 14.

34. Sir Monier Monier-Williams, *Sanskrit-English Dictionary* (New York: Oxford University Press, 1995), 510. Though in their translation of the *Laws of Manu,* Doniger and Smith usually translate *dharma* as "duty," they also render it to mean "religion," "justice," "law," and "right." (Doniger and Smith, 3).

35. Holdrege, 12–14.

36. Hopkins, 73.

37. *Ibid.,* 73–75.

38. Pandurang Vaman Kame, *History of Dharmasastra* (Poona: Bhandarkar Oriental Research Institute, 1974) vol. 2, part I, 1–3; Hopkins, 72–75.

39. *Manu* I.88–91 prescribes various tasks for the four castes. For example, *brahmins,* priests, are ordained for teaching and learning, sacrificing for themselves and for others, and giving and receiving. The *kṣatriya* is responsible for protecting his subjects, having sacrifices performed, studying, giving, and being ruler. Protecting livestock, farming, having sacrifices performed, studying, trading, and lending money is the focus for the *vaiśya.*

40. *MBh.* I.111.11. Recall the discussion in chapter 3 regarding the importance of progeny.

41. A. K. Ramanujan, 46.

42. *MBh.* I.107.30ff.

43. *MBh.* I.107.30–35.

44. Bruce J. Long, "The Concepts of Human Action and Rebirth in the *Mahābhārata,*" in *Karma and Rebirth in Classical Indian Traditions,* ed. Wendy Doniger O'Flaherty (Berkeley: University of California Press, 1980), 42.

45. Radhakrishnan, 16.

46. Crawford emphasizes how often the "dharmic thing to do is to be guided by the demands of the situation." Crawford, *Hindu Bioethics for the Twenty-First Century,* 27.

47. A. B. Creel, *Dharma in Hindu Ethics* (Calcutta: M. K. Mukerjee Temple Press, 1977), 6.

48. M. C. Joshi, *Hindu Religion and Ethics* (New Delhi: Aryan Books International, 1994), 257; Jhingran, ix.

49. *Bhagavad Gītā,* III.35.

50. Radhakrishnan, 36. See also chapter one of Crawford's *Hindu Bioethics.*

51. As Duryodhana matures, he envies the five sons of Pāṇḍu and is never dissuaded from his desire to take over as the ruling king. Though the actual responsibility for the Great War falls on many shoulders, Madeleine Biardeau places responsibility as far back as on King Śāṃtanu himself (see discussion in Woods 2001, 10–14). Duryodhana's persistent hatred of his cousins and his desires for the throne eventually lead to the actual engagement of war. At the conclusion of this war, practically everyone from both sides of the clans—family, friends, leaders, and teachers—dies.

52. Christopher Chapple, *Karma and Creativity* (New York: State University of New York Press, 1986), 2–3; Desai, 32; Radhakrishnan, 52.

53. The word *karma* derives from the Sanskrit verbal root *kṛ* (do, make, perform, accomplish). It is the nominative singular neuter form of the word *karman* meaning "act, action, performance, deed" (Chapple, 2).

54. See the collection of essays published in Wendy Doniger O'Flaherty's *Karma and Rebirth in Classical Indian Traditions* (Berkeley: University of California Press, 1980).

55. In "Life Ethics of the *Bhagavad Gītā* as Interpreted by Rāmānuja," Klaus Klostermaier argues that a concept of predeterminism is intrinsically linked with a theory of *karma* and rebirth (55).

56. Long, 38–60.

57. In the introduction to his translation of the *Bhagavad Gītā,* Murthy describes the doctrine of *karma* as being "fundamentally the application of the scientific law of causation to the spiritual plan. Every act performed by an individual has its inexorable consequences" (Murthy, 11). Klaes understands the law of *karma* to be underlying all expectations and doubts in life. According to him, this law applies to both the usefulness of the effects/fruits of action in balancing the order of human society and its fruitfulness for the actual individual who is producing its cause (Klaes, 54). Hopkins relates the doctrine of *karma* to the belief in rebirth and argues that both are important because "all actions had continuing effects and all were important in determining the future conditions of the embodied self [. . .]. The totality of men's actions determined the conditions of their rebirth and their progress toward release" (73–74).

58. *Bhagavad Gītā,* III.5. Emphasis added.

59. Holdrege likens the *"law of Karma"* to a cosmic law of retribution that dispenses justice to all living beings in accordance with their deeds. *Karma* is "an inexorable law of cause and effect that extends the principle of natural causality to the realm of human morality" (Holdrege, 14).

60. *Bhagavad Gītā,* III.8–9.

61. Murthy, 11.

62. Radhakrishnan, 54.

63. Chapple, *Karma and Creativity,* 62.

64. *Ibid.,* 59–60. *MBh.* XIII.6.5–7, Chapple's translation.

65. Again, as Long reminds us, the text also preserves the idea that the gods are puppeteers and human beings their wooden puppets (46–47).

66. Gandhi, 173.

67. *Bhagavad Gītā,* III.19–20.

68. Vinoba, 218.

69. Vinoba says the following: "Some people complain, 'The *Gita* merely teaches us to perform actions renouncing the fruit, but it does not tell us what actions to perform.' But it only appears so; it is not really so. Because, once it is said, 'Perform action after renouncing the fruit,' it becomes clear what actions we should perform and what not. Violent actions, actions filled with falsehood, actions like theft—it is quite impossible to perform them after renouncing the fruit. The moment such actions are tested on the touchstone of renunciation of fruit, they simply disappear. When the light of the sun spreads, all objects begin to look bright, but does the darkness too appear bright? No, it disappears altogether. This is the condition of forbidden and interested actions. We must test all our actions on the touchstone of renunciation of fruit. Renunciation of fruit is the test for performing any action" (Vinoba, 218).

70. Young, "Hindu Bioethics," 12.

71. *Bhagavad Gītā,* XVI.21.

72. Young, "Hindu Bioethics," 12.

73. Gandhi, 206.

74. Young makes an interesting observation. According to her, while many Hindus ground their commitment to the value of life in the belief that there is an underlying unity to all life, many Christians ground their argument regarding the sanctity of life ultimately in God. Since God created each individual, each life is valued. While the Hindu concept emphasizes the collectivity of humanity and all of life, this Christian perspective focuses on the individual, wholly other from the rest of creation (Young, 16).

75. For more on *ahiṃsā* and its importance in Indian religious traditions see Christopher Key Chapple, *Nonviolence to Animals, Earth, and Self in Asian Traditions* (New York: State University of New York Press, 1993).

76. Narayanan provides a modern example of how the classical dharmic texts are superseded by local practice. In a legal case, *Krishna Singh v. Mathura Ahir* (AIR 1980 SC 707; 1980 All LJ 299), the Supreme Court of India debated the question: May a *śūdra* become a *sannyāsin*? According to the classical texts, only men from the top three castes are allowed to go through all four stages of life. *Śūdras* and women are excluded from participating in the final stage, that of renunciation. Thus, according to the texts, a *śūdra* may NOT become a *sannyāsin.* However, traditions associated with Rāmānuja and many Śaiva orders have a number of *śūdra* ascetics, *sannyāsins.* The Supreme Court

of India ruled, "though the orthodox view does not allow shudras to become sannyasis, the existing practice in India is contrary to such a view and [. . .] at the present time a Hindu of any caste can adopt the life of a sannyasi." Additionally the Court abrogated, by virtue of mandates embodied in Part III of the Constitution of India, the ban on *śūdras* becoming *sannyāsins.* According to Narayanan, this ruling indicates that, though *dharma* and classical legal texts are important, local customs and living traditions are even more important (186–88).

77. Young, "Hindu Bioethics," 5. See also Crawford's *Hindu Bioethics.*

78. Desai, 19.

79. Doniger O'Flaherty, *Karma and Rebirth in Classical Indian Traditions,* xxv.

80. K. R. Srikanta Murthy, *Professional Ethics in Ancient Indian Medicine,* 127.

81. Doniger O'Flaherty, *Women, Androgynes, and Other Mythical Beasts,* 66; Sharma, "When it Comes to Karma," 98.

CHAPTER FIVE

1. Sharma, "When It Comes to Karma," 98.

2. The case as it is presented here draws on the following sources: *Jaycee B. v. Superior Court* 42 Cal. App. 4th 781; 1996 Cal App. LEXIS 101; *In re Marriage of John A. and Luanne Buzzanca* 61 Cal. App. 4th 1410; 1998 Cal. App. LEXIS 180; Laura A. Brill, "When Will the Law Catch Up with Technology? Jaycee B. v. Superior Court of Orange County: An Urgent Cry for Legislation on Gestational Surrogacy," *The Catholic Lawyer* 39:241 (Summer/Fall 1999); Jerald V. Hale, "From Baby M to Jaycee B.: Fathers, Mothers, and Children in the Brave New World," *Journal of Contemporary Law and Family Studies* 24:335 (1998); Ilana Hurwitz, "Collaborative Reproduction: Finding the Child in the Maze of Legal Motherhood," *Connecticut Law Review* 33:127 (Fall, 2000).

3. Currently there are two types of maternal surrogacy. First, traditional surrogacy is when a woman agrees to be artificially inseminated with the sperm of a married man and, if all goes as planned, upon the birth of the child, she relinquishes it to the father and his wife. In this circumstance, the surrogate and father are both genetically related to the resulting child. The famous case of Baby M is an example of traditional surrogacy. In this case, however, the surrogate mother, Mary Beth Whitehead, reneged on the agreement and sued for parental rights of the baby she carried. Second, gestational surrogacy refers to a situation where the surrogate has no genetic link to the embryo she has agreed to carry and allow to develop to term. In this case, through the process of IVF, a couple's egg and sperm, or donor gametes, are united and the resulting zygote is implanted into the surrogate's womb (Hale 1998, 336–39). The Buzzancas and Ms. Snell are participating in the latter form of surrogacy. While *Johnson v. Calvert* was the first surrogacy case to come before the courts, Jaycee's situation is the first case where all of the parties involved (the surrogate, her husband, and contracting/intended parents—the Buzzancas), did NOT have any genetic relationship to Jaycee. Additionally, this case is unique in that, unlike Johnson and Moschett, Ms. Snell is neither reneging on her agreement nor seeking to establish parental rights regarding Jaycee.

4. *Jaycee B. v. Superior Court,* 722.

5. 7610 of the Uniform Parentage Act, quoted in Andrew W. Vorzimer, Milena D. O'Hara, and Lori D. Shafton, "Buzzanca v. Buzzanca: The Ruling and Ramifications," *Journal of Assisted Reproductive Law.* Downloaded from http://www.inciid.org/ (10 April 2002).

6. Though John's attorney was present at the hearing that accepted this stipulation, he made no objection. Yet on appeal, he did argue that the surrogate is the lawful mother of Jaycee by virtue of having given birth to her. Additionally, he argued that if Pamela and her husband chose not to subsume the responsibilities of Jaycee, then the burden ought to revert to the state.

7. See *People v. Sorensen* (1968) 68 Cal. 2d 280, 284–286 [66 Cal. Rptr. 7, 437 P.2d 495, 25 A.L.R.3d 1093].

8. *Johnson v. Calvert* (1993) 5 Cal. 4th 84 [19 Cal. Rptr. 2d 494, 851 P.2d 776].

9. *In re Marriage of Buzzanca,* 1412–13. A fuller citation of the ruling of the court reads as follows:

> We disagree. Let us get right to the point: Jaycee never would have been born had not Luanne and John both agreed to have a fertilized egg implanted in a surrogate.
>
> The trial judge erred because he assumed that legal motherhood, under the relevant California statutes, could only be established in one of two ways, either by giving birth or by contributing an egg. He failed to consider the substantial and well-settled body of law holding that there are times when fatherhood can be established by conduct apart from giving birth or being genetically related to a child. The typical example is when an infertile husband consents to allowing his wife to be artificially inseminated. As our Supreme Court noted in such a situation over 30 years ago, the husband is the "lawful father" because he consented to the procreation of the child. (See *People v. Sorensen* (1968) 68 Cal. 2d 280, 284–286 [66 Cal. Rptr. 7, 437 P.2d 495, 25 A.L.R.3d 1093]).

10. From birth and throughout the years of legal proceedings, Jaycee was in the custody of her mother, Luanne. The final court rulings simply made their mother-daughter relationship legal and required John to provide child support. Presumably, this continues on into the present day. Though I have searched for updated information on Jaycee, for privacy reasons, I am not surprised that my searches have been unsuccessful.

11. Vorzimer, O'Hara, and Lori D. Shafton. Under the Act, paternity may be established in a variety of ways. In addition to blood tests, one may establish paternity by being married to a child's mother when she gives birth, or through consenting to adopt the child of one's wife. Also, if a man's wife undergoes artificial insemination (AI) with the husband's consent, the law will treat the husband as if he were the natural father of the child (*In re Marriage of Buzzanca,* 1417).

12. George J. Annas, "Assisted Reproduction: Who is the Mother?" *New England Journal of Medicine* 340:8 (25 February 1999), downloaded from Ovid (30 August 2001); Brill, 39; Hale, 24:335; Jonathan B. Pitt, "Fragmenting Procreation," *Yale Law Journal* 108:1893 (May, 1999), downloaded from LEXIS-NEXIS (30 August 2001).

13. Thomas Reich, ed., 2233.

14. Reich, 2223, 2227; See also discussion in previous chapters.

15. Jyotsna Agnihotri Gupta, "Women's Bodies: The Site for the Ongoing Conquest by Reproductive Technologies," *Issues in Reproductive and Genetic Engineering: Journal of International Feminist Analysis* 4:2 (1991): 93–107; Lakshmi Lingam, "New Reproductive Technologies in India: A Print Media Analysis," *Issues in Reproductive and Genetic Engineering* 3:1 (1990): 13–21. Both Gupta and Lingam express their concerns regarding the utilization of assisted reproductive technologies.

16. New York State Task Force on Life and the Law, *Assisted Reproductive Technologies: Analysis and Recommendations for Public Policy* (1998), 114–15.

17. Reich, ed., "Reproductive Technologies," 2233.

18. Desai, *Health and Medicine in the Hindu Tradition,* 68; Narayanan, "Hindu Ethics and Dharma," 192. There is discussion regarding the acceptability of anonymous sperm donors. While Desai makes no distinction, Narayanan indicates that the husband's sperm, or sperm from one of his family members, is preferred by "higher caste" Hindus. This same sentiment was expressed by a few of the individuals I interviewed for this study. This issue of biological connections is discussed below.

19. Mr. C, interview by author, tape recording, Loma Linda, CA, 30 July 2001; Mr. F, interview by author, tape recording, San Bernardino, CA, 1 December 2001; Ms. B and Dr. D, interview by author, tape recording, Riverside, CA, 30 July 2001.

20. The status of the embryo is of primary concern when considering the implementation of some assisted reproductive technologies, particularly IVF. "Bioethics for Clinicians: Assisted Reproductive Technologies," *Canadian Medical Association Journal* 164:11 (29 May 2001): 1589–94. Downloaded from http://gateway1.ovid.com (12 July 2001); F. Shenfield, "Current Ethical Dilemmas in Assisted Reproduction," *International Journal of Andrology* 20: Suppl. 3 (1997): 74–78. While Paul Ramsey expresses his opposition to IVF in *Fabricated Man: The Ethics of Genetic,* Kass presents his objections to IVF in the essay, "Babies by Means of In Vitro Fertilization: Unethical Experiments on the Unborn?" *New England Journal of Medicine* 285 (1971): 1174–79. Joseph Fletcher, in "The Ethics of Genetic Control: Ending Reproductive Roulette," argues for the ethical acceptability of utilizing IVF.

21. While working in a large teaching hospital on the East Coast, I once had to prepare the body of a twenty-six-week fetus that had been aborted. She had multiple deformities, and may not have survived in utero, much less through the birthing process. The entire body of the fetus fit within my hands together, but not overlapping. Another nurse entered the room in which I was preparing the body. She shook her head sideways and said, "That's just tissue." Looking up at her, I couldn't help but respond, "Well if you and I are 'just tissue,' then OK." At twenty-six weeks, a fetus is not "just tissue."

22. Ethics Committee of American Fertility Society, 34S–35S.

23. Augustine, *City of God,* xxi.10.

24. Ambrose, *On Belief in the Resurrection,* 2.113.

25. Tertullian, *A Treatise on the Soul,* xxvii.

26. *Ibid.,* xxxvii. Emphasis added.

27. W. A. Wallace, "Hylomorphism," *New Catholic Encylopedia.*

28. Aquinas, *Summa Theologica,* I.76.3.

29. As cited in Donceel, 78.

30. *Instruction,* 22.

31. *Ibid.,* 26.

32. Jennifer Gunning and Veronica English, *Human In Vitro Fertilization: A Case Study in the Regulation of Medical Innovation* (Aldershot: Bartmouth, 1993), 29; Ethics Committee of the American Fertility Society, *Ethical Considerations of New Reproductive Technologies,* 31S. In the eighth chapter, the Ethics Committee report presents a concise discussion regarding the complexities involved in the process of human development in utero. James Diamond also discusses the early process of human development in his essay, "Abortion, Animation, and Biological Hominization," *Theological Studies* 36 (June 1975): 307–12.

33. American Fertility Society, *Ethical Considerations of New Reproductive Technologies,* 32S; Diamond, 307–12.

34. Karl Rahner, *Schriften Zur Theologie* 8 (Einsiedeln, 1967), 287, as cited in Donceel, 99–100.

35. V. W. Karambelkar, *The Atharva-Veda and Ayur-Veda* (Nagpur: Majestic Printing Press, 1961), 106.

36. Ram Karan Sharma and Vaidya Bhagwan Dash, *Agnivesa's Caraka-Saṃhitā,* vol. XCIV (Varanasi: The Chowkhamba, Sanskrit Series, 1976), 391–400. It is interesting to note that in his discussion on abortion, Lipner lists the various terms used for an abortion. For example, *srāva,* or "emission," is the term used to indicate miscarriages until the fourth month of pregnancy. For miscarriages occurring in the fifth and sixth months, the term *pāta,* fall, is used. The different terms utilized are related to the developmental stage of the fetus (Lipner, "The Classical Hindu View on Abortion," 42–43).

37. Lipner's designation of "major" and "minor" is related to the apparent weight of authority and strength of evidence.

38. *Agnivesa's Caraka-Saṃhitā,* 366.

39. *Ibid.,* 372–73.

40. Lipner, "The Classical Hindu View on Abortion," 52.

41. *Ibid.,* 54.

42. *Ibid.,* 56.

43. According to the *Gautama Dharmasūtra,* "A man should disown a father who assassinates a king; sacrifices for a abortionist" (20.1). "A woman falls from her caste by carrying out an abortion" (21.9). The *Ṛg Samhitā,* a text containing some of the earliest canonical Hindu texts, refers to Viṣṇu as the "protector of the child-to-be." According to the *Atharva Veda,* abortions are amongst the most heinous of crimes. Lipner, 41–61; Narayanan, 193; Desai, 64; Jayapaul Azariah, et al., *Bioethics in India,* 54. Regarding the prohibitions against abortion, Jhingran remarks that of primary concern for these Hindu authors was the value of property, not necessarily life (89). Even so, this does not negate the argument that the fetus is an entity of value.

44. V. W. Karambelkar, *The Atharva-Veda and Ayur-Veda* (Nagpur: Majestic Printing Press, 1961), 106–107.

45. Jean-Claude Carriére, 174–177.

46. Narayanan argues that contemporary couples seek out the use of these technologies in order to fulfill their obligations to have children (192). As discussed in chapter 3, children are a priority for most Indian and Hindu traditions. Lipner comments that having children is a public duty for those in the householder stage of life. According to him, it is "unHindu" to see procreation related issues as a private concern of mother or individual family alone ("The Classical Hindu View on Abortion," 59).

47. Reich, 2234. Discussions regarding issues associated with the utilization of assisted reproductive technologies in contemporary contexts of global overpopulation, availability of healthcare, or lack thereof, and costs are immensely important. It is prudent to question whether or not it is even appropriate to use these technologies in light of other global issues. The current focus is localized to discussions in the United States and acknowledges the reality that these technologies are being widely used.

48. In the United States, a constitutional right NOT to procreate is clearly established (*Roe v. Wade,* 410 U.S. 113). *Meyer v. Nebraska,* 262 U.S. 390 (1923) established that it is a constitutional liberty for an individual to have the right to marry, set up a home, and bring up children. *Skinner v. Oklahoma,* 316 U.S. 535 (1942) established that the state has no right to interfere with an individual's procreative capacities through forced sterilization. This ruling explicitly mentions that individuals have a right to have children. This is considered a fundamental, basic liberty. Individual rights and the right to privacy regarding contraception and termination underlie the decisions established by *Griswold v. Connecticut,* 381 U.S. 479 (1965), *Eisenstadt v. Baird,* 405 U.S. 438 (1972) and *Roe v. Wade,* 410 U.S. 113 (1973). These cases suggest that there exists a right to reproduce. However, it is a negative, not a positive, right. In the *Eisenstadt v. Baird* ruling, Justice Brennan stated: "If the right of privacy means anything, it is the right of the individual, married or single, to be free of unwarranted governmental intrusion into matters so fundamentally affecting a person as the decision whether to bear or beget a child" (as cited in Richard T. Hull, *Ethical Issues New Repro Tech,* 9).

Carson Strong in his book, *Ethics in Reproductive and Perinatal Medicine: A New Framework,* reflects on the issue of the right to procreate. In his book, *Children of Choice,* J. Robertson attempts to extend the right to reproduce to include the right to utilize assisted reproductive technologies such as IVF (Princeton: Princeton University Press, 1994).

49. Fenwick, 302–6. In his essay "Medical Technologies and Ethics," Gino Papola argues that contemporary societies are schizophrenic when they allow the killing of over a million children through abortion, yet at the same time condone the use of assisted reproductive technologies. *Issues in Biomedical Ethics: Proceedings from the Festival of Life International Congress,* ed. C. J. Vas and E. J. de Souza (Delhi: Macmillian India Limited, 1990), 249.

50. de Melo-Martin, 13. de Melo-Martin juxtaposes the risks and high costs of IVF and other assisted reproductive technologies with their low rate of success and other societal needs for medical care, and cautions against an uncritical acceptance of these new technologies. According to her, the common good sometimes ought to override procreative liberties and the focus ought to be on preventing infertility and improving the overall health of members of society (66–68, 90–123). Regarding societal goods, issues relating to distribution of resources and overpopulation are also very important.

51. Jhingran, 101.

52. Creel, 6.

53. When one examines the familial relationships of the various characters within the *Mahābhārata,* a clear pattern of interconnectedness emerges. Ultimately everyone is somehow related to everyone else. Śaṃtanu fathers Bhīṣma and the latter becomes the patriarch of the Bhārata clan. Satyavatī, Śaṃtanu's second wife, is Vyāsa's mother. Upon her request, Vyāsa fathers Dhṛtarāṣṭra, Pāṇḍu, and Vidura. Through blood and marriage relationships, practically every primary character of this paradigmatic epic is related to one another. These narratives also reflect a fluidity between the realms of existence of human, divine, and animal. For example, Bhīṣma is the son of a human king and the goddess Gangā. Kuntī's and Mādrī's sons are also half human and half divine. Their mother-in-law, Satyavatī, is half divine and half fish.

54. Murthy, "Professional Ethics in Ancient Indian Medicine," 127.

55. Ronald Nakasone, "A Buddhist Response," in Regina Wentzel Wolfe and Christine E. Gudorf, eds., *Ethics and World Religions: Cross-Cultural Case Studies* (New York: Orbis, 1999), 329–30. Though Nakasone is utilizing the metaphor of ice and water to describe the interconnectedness in Buddhism, it is applicable to a similar concept within Hinduism. The principle of *pratītyasamutpāda,* or "co-dependent origination," is one of the central philosophical paradigms of Buddhism. This is not to say that Buddhism and Hinduism are very distinct religious traditions. For example, while Buddhism rejects the existence of a soul (*anātman*), the upaniṣadic understanding of *ātman* argues it is ultimately *Brahman.*

56. Louis Dumont, *Homo Hierarchius: The Caste System and Its Implications,* trans. Mark Sainsbury (Chicago: University of Chicago Press, 1970), 6–7.

57. Fenwick, 306.

58. Cahill, "Christian Ethics: Problems and Prospects," 63.

59. Nicholas Sutton argues that this emphasis on individuality is supported by free market capitalism, the dominant system in the U.S. According to him, free market capitalism is primarily concerned with the individual and "stresses self aggrandizement as a primary motivation for human activity and as the natural stimulus for human achievement." *Religious Doctrines in the Mahābhārata* (Delhi: Motilal Banarsidass Publishers, 2000), 448.

60. Sutton, 451.

61. Sutton, 448. Emphasis added.

62. Callahan, "Bioethics and Fatherhood," 99.

63. *MBh.* III.292.5–25.

64. Callahan, "Bioethics and Fatherhood," in *Sex/Machine: Readings in Culture, Gender, and Technology,* ed. Patrick D. Hopkins (Bloomington: Indiana University Press, 1998), 99. Reich, 2222.

65. *Instruction,* 27.

66. *Ibid.,* 32. Emphasis added.

67. *Ibid.,* 28.

68. Hull, 17.

69. Callahan, "Bioethics and Fatherhood," 100.

70. Ronald Munson, "Artificial Insemination: Who's Responsible?" in *Sex/Machine: Readings in Culture, Gender, and Technology,* 107–15.

71. *Instruction,* 28.

72. James Dobson, "Future of the Family." Downloaded from http://www.family.org/docstudy/newsletters/A0016707.html (26 July 2001).

73. Rosemary Radford Ruether presentes an insightful discussion on the history of the "traditional" family in the U.S. in her book, *Christianity and the Making of the Modern Family: Ruling Ideologies, Diverse Realities* (Boston: Beacon, 2000).

74. Confucius (551–480 B.C.E.) saw filiality and brotherly respect as the roots of *ren,* or moral perfection/virtue. The *Analects* records: "It is unlikely that one who has grown up as a filial son and respectful younger brother will then be inclined to defy his superiors." Thus, the passage concludes: "there has never been a case of one who is disinclined to defy his superiors stir up a rebellion" (1.2). Again, according to this text, a "student should be filial toward his parents when at home and respectful toward his elders when abroad" (1.6). Confucius believed that families made up the core of society and if the families were in order, then society would be in order (Edward Gilman Slingerland, trans. in *Readings in Classical Chinese Philosophy*).

According to the neo-Confucians, the *Great Learning* was a classic Confucian text. Chu His (1130–1200), drew on it to ground many of his teachings. Regarding the family vis à vis society, the *Great Learning* reads: "The ancients who wished to manifest their clear character to the world would first bring order to their states. Those who wished to bring order to their states would first regulate their families [. . .]." Having order within one's family, one could then be assured of order within the state. Familial order ensured societal stability (Wing-Tsit Chan, trans., *A Source Book in Chinese Philosophy,* 86).

Ancient Shinto traditions see familial ties as establishing not only the order of society, but the Japanese Islands and people as well. The *Nihongi* and *Kojiki* myths record the actions of the kamis, Izanami and Izanagi. As a couple, "they stood on the floating bridge of heaven [. . .] together they create the Japanese Island, descend and dwell on them. Then, through their daughter Amaterasu comes the imperial line and the Japanese people" (Tsunoda, Ryusaku, Wm Theordore De Bary and Donald Keene, *Sources of Japanese Traditions,* vol. 1 (New York: Columbia University Press), 15, 25.

75. Mr. A, interviewed by author, 23 July 2001, Riverside, CA.

76. My father, being one of the oldest Assamese living in southern California, is the "grandfather" of sorts to the Assamese community in the area. Individuals from as far away as West Virginia and Texas consider my parents their "grandparents." My parents' home is their home.

77. Christopher K. Chapple, "Arjuna's Argument: Family Secrets Unveiled," *Journal of Vaishnava Studies* 9:2 (Spring 2001): 23–31.

78. *Manu* IX.145–146.

79. Callahan, "Bioethics and Fatherhood," 99–100.

80. In his chapter "Artificial Insemination: Who's Responsible?" Munson argues that being a biological father is not a sufficient condition for being deemed a moral or social father. *Sex/Machine: Readings in Culture, Gender, and Technology,* ed. Patrick D.

Hopkins (Bloomington: Indiana University Press, 1998), 114. Gunning and English indicate that illegitimate children provide a clear example of how biological and social elements of fatherhood are separable (77).

81. Chaitanya, 155–56.

82. James L. Fitzgerald, "The Great Epic of India as Religious Rhetoric: A Fresh Look at the *Mahābhārata*," *Journal of the American Academy of Religion* 51:4 (December 1983): 620.

83. Recall that Dhṛtarāṣṭra is born blind and Pāṇḍu pale. Vidura means "far-sighted." Throughout the *Mahābhārata*, his advice reflects sound reason and insight. Unfortunately, his words are continually ignored by Dhṛtarāṣṭra and his one hundred sons.

84. Narayanan, 192.

85. Ms. B, interviewed by author, 30 July 2002, Riverside, CA.

86. *MBh. Udyoga Parvan*, chapters 145–46.

87. Chaitanya, 130.

88. Mr. C, interviewed by author, 30 July 2002, Loma Linda, CA.

CONCLUSION

1. Antonio T. de Nicolas, *Avatāra: The Humanization of Philosophy Through the Bhagavad Gītā* (New York: Nicolas Hays Ltd., 1976), 20.

2. *Ibid.*, 20–21.

3. Paul Ricoeur, *Figuring the Sacred: Religion, Narrative, and Imagination* (Minneapolis: Augsburg Fortress, 1995). See also *The Symbolism of Evil* (New York: Beacon), 1969; Richard Kearney, *On Stories* (New York: Routledge), 2002.

4. Warren Thomas Reich, "A New Era for Bioethics: The Search for Meaning in Moral Experience," in *Religion and Medical Ethics* (Grand Rapids: Eerdmans Pub. Co., 1996), 114.

5. Albert R. Jonsen and Stephen Toulmin, *The Abuse of Casuistry: A History of Moral Reasoning* (Berkeley: University of California Press, 1988), 5–11.

6. Eck, 80–81.

7. Mr. A, interviewed by author, 23 July 2002, Riverside, CA.

8. Mr. F, interviewed by author, 1 December 2002, San Bernardino, CA.

9. Hopkins, 119.

10. Jonsen and Toulmin, 10.

11. *Ibid.*, 293.

12. *Ibid.*, 330.

13. *Ibid.*, 272–73. For the seminal work on situation ethics see Joseph Fletcher's *Situation Ethics: The New Morality* (Philadelphia: Westminster Press, 1966).

14. Jonsen and Toulmin, 302.

15. Albert R. Jonsen, "Casuistry," in *Methods in Medical Ethics*, ed. Jeremy Sugarman and Daniel P. Sulmasy, 121.

16. David DeGrazia & Tom L. Beauchamp, "Philosophy," in *Methods in Medical Ethics*, ed. Jeremy Sugarman and Daniel P. Sulmasy, 40.

17. McKim Marriott, "Constructing an Indian Ethnosociology," in *India Through Hindu Categories*, ed. McKim Marriott (New Delhi: SAGE Publications, 1990), 3.

18. http://www.chausa.org/ (24 May 2005).

19. In my interview with Dr. E, an obstetrics-gynecology physician, I asked her when human life begins. Her answer: "Life begins when two halves meet to form a whole, which is conception [. . .]. Yes, a zygote is a human being." I then asked her if she offers abortions or not. She replied:

> I do abortions because I've been trained in it. Women have died in my hands because of septic abortions. So I perform abortions on principle. I detest it. But I do it because I'm trained better than anyone else they could go to, and I feel obligated I should give them my training. Until the point we have the perfect form of contraception. We don't have that now, so as a medical person, I feel as though I have to perform them [. . .]. Yes, I am ending life, absolutely [. . .]. Saying "it's tissue" is rationalizing. It [a fetus] is certainly a human being. I do ultrasounds in my office. I've seen the heart beating from week six. And I have performed abortions on conceptions that I have seen the heart beating in, so I know what I'm doing. I hate it. But I do it because I'd rather not have the mother die somewhere else. And if I don't do it, I can't refer my patients to somewhere else.

Dr. E's words regarding the status of fetuses, her position as a medical doctor, and abortions, reflect her concept of *dharma* and the multivalent nature of Hinduism. In keeping with her tradition, she acknowledges that a zygote is a human being. She rejects the argument, the rationalization, that fetuses are simply tissue and admits that in performing abortions she is ending life. However, her decision is grounded in her desire to preserve the sanctity of the life of a woman who could die of a septic abortion and her *dharma* as a physician (Dr. E, interviewed by author, 2 August 2002, Anaheim Hills, CA).

20. Fox, 281–98; Barbara Crossette, "Darkest Hour at U.N. For Richest Deadbeat," *The New York Times* (21 September 1998); Susan A. Cohen, "Abortion Politics and U.S. Population Aid: Coping with a Complex New Law," *International Family Planning Perspectives* 26:3 (September 2000): 137–139, 145; Frances Kissling, "Church and State at the United Nations," *USA Today* 130:2678 (November 2001); John Leo, "Cracking the U.N. Code," *U.S. News & World Report* 131:10 (17 September 2001): 70; Steven V. Roberts, "Unveiling the Face of Abortion Politics," *U.S. News & World Report* 117 (19 September 1994): 10–11.

Bibliography

Abrams, M. H. *A Glossary of Literary Terms.* 6th ed. New York: Harcourt Brace, 1993.

American Public Health Association. "9814: Preservation of Reproductive Health Care in Hospital Mergers and Affiliations with Religious Health Systems." *American Journal of Public Health* 89:3 (March 1999): 440–41.

American Public Health Association. "20003: Preserving Consumer Choice in an Era of Religious/Secular Health Industry Mergers (Position Paper)." *American Journal of Public Health* 91:3 (March 2001): 479–82.

American Radio Works. "Surrogate Motherhood: Continuing Controversy." http://www.americanradioworks.org (10 April 2002).

Annas, George J. "Assisted Reproduction: Who is the Mother?" *New England Journal of Medicine* 340:8 (25 February 1999): 656–57.

Anonymous. "Doubts Grow about India's 'Cryogenic' Infant." *Medical World News* 19:26 (25 December 1978): 11.

Appleton, Susan Frelich. "Access to Justice: 'Planned Parenthood': Adoption, Assisted Reproduction, and the New Ideal Family." *Washington University Journal of Law and Policy* 1:85 (1999).

Augustine, St. *City of God: Against the Pagans.* Translated by David S. Wiesen. Cambridge: Harvard University Press, 1968.

Azariah, Jayapaul, Hilda Azariah, and Darryl R. J. Macer, eds. *Bioethics in India: Proceedings of the International Bioethics Workshop in Madras: Bioethical Management of Biogeoresources, 16–19 Jan. 1997, University of Madras.* Christchurch: Eubios Ethics Institute, 1998.

Babb, Lawrence A. *The Divine Hierarchy: Popular Hinduism in Central India.* New York: Columbia University Press, 1975.

Barbour, Ian G. *Ethics in an Age of Technology.* New York: HarperCollins Publishers, 1993.

Barlingay, S. S. *A Modern Introduction to Indian Ethics: My Impressions of Indian Moral Problems and Concepts.* Delhi: Penman Publishers, 1998.

Baumgardner, Jennifer. "Immaculate Contraception." *The Nation,* 25 January 1999, 11–15.

Beauchamp, Tom L. and James F. Childress. *Principles of Biomedical Ethics.* 4th ed. New York: Oxford University Press, 1994.

Becker, Penny Edgell and Nancy L. Eiesland. *Contemporary American Religion: An Ethnographic Reader.* Walnut Creek: Altamira Press, 1997.

Bellandi, Deanna. "Reproductive Services Kept in CHW Deal in California." *Modern Healthcare* 31:17 (23 April 2001): 4–5, 16.

———. "Separation of Church and State." *Modern Healthcare* 31:28 (9 July 2001): 18–19.

Bellandi, Deanna and Elizabeth Thompson. "Matters of Principle." *Modern Healthcare* 30:25 (19 June 2000): 6, 14.

Bhatia, S. L. *A History of Medicine: With Special Reference to the Orient.* New Delhi: Management Committee, Office of the Medical Council of India, 1977.

Bhave, Vinoba. *Talks on the Gita.* 11th ed. Varanasi: Sarva Seva Sangh Prakashan, 1995.

Brannigan, Michael C. *Ethical Issues in Human Cloning: Cross-Disciplinary Perspectives.* New York: Seven Bridges Press, 2001.

Brill, Laura A. "When Will the Law Catch Up With Technology? Jaycee B. v. Superior Court of Orange County: An Urgent Cry for Legislation on Gestational Surrogacy." *The Catholic Lawyer* 39: 241. (Summer/Fall 1999).

Brody, Baruch. "Religion and Bioethics." In *A Companion to Bioethics,* edited by Helga Kuhse and Peter Singer, 41–48. Malden: Blackwell Publishers, 2001.

Brooks, Douglas R. "Taking Sides and Opening Doors: Authority and Integrity in the Academy's Hinduism." *Journal of the American Academy of Religion* 68:4 (December 2000): 817–29.

Cahill, Lisa Sowel. "Can Theology Have a Role in 'Public' Bioethical Discourse?" *Hastings Center Report* 20:4 (July/August 1990): 10–14.

———. "Theology and Bioethics: Should Religious Traditions Have a Public Voice?" *Journal of Medicine and Philosophy* 17:3 (June 1992): 263–72.

———. "The Bible and Christian Moral Practices." In *Christian Ethics: Problems and Prospects,* edited by Lisa Sowel Cahill and James F. Childress, 3–17. Cleveland: Pilgrim Press, 1996.

———. "Religion and Theology." In *Methods in Medical Ethics,* edited by Jeremy Sugarman and Daniel P. Sulmasy, 47–69. Washington: Georgetown University Press, 2001.

Caldwell, Sarah and Brian K. Smith. "Introduction: Who Speaks for Hinduism?" *Journal of the American Academy of Religion* 68:4 (December 2000): 705–10.

Callahan, Daniel. "Religion and the Secularization of Bioethics." *Hastings Center Report* 20:4 (July/August 1990): 2–4.

———. "Bioethics and Fatherhood." In *Sex/Machine: Readings in Culture, Gender, and Technology,* edited by Patrick D. Hopkins, 98–106. Bloomington: Indiana University Press, 1998.

Campbell, Courtney S. "Religion and Moral Meaning in Bioethics." *Hastings Center Report* 20:4 (July/August 1990): 4–10.

Campbell, Courtney S. and Joan Woolfrey. "Norms and Narratives: Religious Reflections on the Human Cloning Controversy." *Journal of Biolaw and Business* 1:3 (Spring 1998): 8–20.

Canales, Mary K. and Barbara J. Bowers. "Expanding Conceptualizations of Culturally Competent Care." *Journal of Advanced Nursing* 36:1 (October 2001): 102–11.

Carman, John and Mark Juergensmeyer, eds. *A Bibliographic Guide to the Comparative Study of Ethics.* Cambridge: Cambridge University Press, 1991.

Carrick, Paul. *Medical Ethics in Antiquity: Philosophical Perspectives on Abortion and Euthanasia.* Boston: D. Reidel Publishing Company, 1985.

Carriére, Jean-Claude. *The Mahābhārata: A Play Based Upon the Indian Classical Epic.* Translated by Peter Brook. New York: Harper & Row Publishers, 1987.

Carrillo, J. Emilio, Alexander R. Green, and Joseph R. Betancourt. "Cross-Cultural Primary Care: A Patient-Based Approach." *Annals of Internal Medicine* 130:10 (18 May 1999): 829–34.

Carter, Stephen L. *The Culture of Disbelief: How American Law and Politics Trivialize Religious Devotion.* New York: Anchor Books, 1993.

Chaitanya, Krishna. *The Mahābhārata: A Literary Study.* New Delhi: Clarion Books, 1985.

Chapple, Christopher. *Karma and Creativity.* New York: State University of New York Press, 1986.

Chapple, Christopher Key. *Nonviolence to Animals, Earth, and Self in Asian Traditions.* New York: State University of New York Press, 1993.

———. "Arjuna's Argument: Family Secrets Unveiled." *Journal of Vaishnava Studies* 9:2 (Spring 2001): 23–31.

Cohen, Cynthia B. "'Give Me Children or I Shall Die' New Reproductive Technologies and Harm to Children." *The Hastings Center Report* 26:2 (March/April 1996): 19–27.

Cohen, Jonathan R. "In God's Garden: Creation and Cloning in Jewish Thought." *The Hastings Center Report* 29:4 (July/August 1999): 7–12.

Congregation for the Doctrine of the Faith. *Instruction on Respect for Human Life in its Origin and on the Dignity of Procreation Replies to Certain Questions of the Day.* Vatican, 1987. http://www.vatican.va (20 March 2002).

Conklin, Melanie. "Blocking Women's Health Care." *The Progressive* 62 (January 1998): 23–25.

Corbie-Smith, Giselle. "The Role of Cultural Competence in Addressing Health Disparities." *SGMI Forum.* 24:10 (October 2001): 1, 7.

Coward, Harold G., Julius J. Lipner, and Katherine K. Young. *Hindu Ethics: Purity, Abortion, and Euthanasia.* New York: State University of New York Press, 1989.

Coward, Harold and Pinit Ratanakul. *A Cross-Cultural Dialogue on Health Care Ethics.* Ontario (CN): Wilfrid Laurier University Press, 1999.

Coward, Harold G. and Tejinder Sidhu. "Bioethics for Clinicians: 19. Hinduism and Sikhism." *Canadian Medical Association-JAMC.* 163:9 (31 October 2000): 1167–70.

Crawford, Cromwell S. *The Evolution of Hindu Ethical Ideas.* Asian Studies at Hawaii, series no. 28. Hawaii: University Press of Hawaii, 1984.

———. "Hindu Ethics for Modern Life." In *World Religions and Global Ethics,* edited by S. Cromwell Crawford, 5–35. New York: Paragon House, 1989.

———. *Dilemmas of Life and Death: Hindu Ethics in a North American Context.* New York: State University of New York Press, 1995.

———. "Hindu Developments in Bioethics." In *Bioethics Year book.* Vol. 5, *Theological Developments in Bioethics: 1992–1994,* edited by Andrew Lustig, 55–74. Boston: Kluwer Academic Publishers, 1997.

———. *Hindu Bioethics for the Twenty-first Century.* New York: State University of New York Press, 2003.

Creel, Austin B. *Dharma in Hindu Ethics.* Calcutta: M. K. Mukerjee Temple Press, 1977.

DeGrazia, David and Tom Beauchamp. "Philosophy." In *Methods in Medical Ethics,* edited by Jeremy Sugarman and Daniel P. Sulmasy, 31–46. Washington: Georgetown University Press, 2001.

de la Fuente Fonnest, Isabel, Finn Sondergaard, Gert Fonnest, and Agnete Vedsted-Jacobsen. "Attitudes Among Health Care Professionals on the Ethics of Assisted Reproductive Technologies and Legal Abortion." *ACTA Obstetricia et Gynecologica Scandinavica* 79:1 (January 2000): 41–53.

de Melo-Martin, Inmaculada. *Making Babies: Biomedical Technologies, Reproductive Ethics and Public Policy.* Boston: Kluwer Academic Publishers, 1998.

de Nicolas, Antonio T. "The Unity and Indivisibility of the Self (Brahman)." *Main Currents in Modern Thought* 29:4 (1973): 130–37.

———. *Avatāra: The Humanization of Philosophy Through the Bhagavad-Gītā.* New York: Nicolas Hays Ltd., 1976.

Declaration on Abortion: Sacred Congregation for the Doctrine of the Faith. Washington: Office of Publishing and Promotion Services United States Catholic Conference, 1974.

Desai, Mahadev. *The Gospel of Selfless Action or The Gita According to Gandhi.* Ahmedabad: Navajivan Publishing House, 1995.

Desai, Prakash N. *Health and Medicine in the Hindu Tradition: Continuity and Cohesion.* New York: Crossroad, 1989.

———. "Hinduism and Bioethics in India: A Tradition in Transition." In *Bioethics Year book.* Vol. 1, *Theological Developments in Bioethics: 1988–1990,* edited by Andrew Lustig, 41–60. Boston: Kluwer Academic Publishers, 1991.

Dey, Ian. *Qualitative Data Analysis: A User-Friendly Guide for Social Scientists.* New York: Routledge, 1993.

Dhand, Arti. "The Subversive Nature of Virtue in the *Mahābhārata*: A Tale about Women, Smelly Ascetics, and God." *Journal of the American Academy of Religion* 72:1 (March 2004): 33–55.

Diamond, James. "Abortion, Animation, and Biological Hominization." *Theological Studies* 36 (June 1975): 305–24.

Doniger O'Flaherty, Wendy. *Women, Androgynes, and Other Mythical Beasts.* Chicago: University of Chicago Press, 1980.

———, ed. *Karma and Rebirth in Classical Indian Traditions.* Berkeley: University of California Press, 1980.

———, trans. *The Rig Veda: An Anthology.* New York: Penguin Books, 1981.

Doniger, Wendy and Brian Smith, trans. *The Laws of Manu.* New York: Penguin Books, 1991.

Dumont, Louis. *Homo Hierarchicus: The Caste System and Its Implications.* Translated by Mark Sainsbury. Chicago: University of Chicago Press, 1970.

Dwivedi, O. P. "Dharmic Ecology." *In Hinduism and Ecology: The Intersection of Earth, Sky, and Water,* edited by Christopher Key Chapple and Mary Evelyn Tucker, 3–22. Cambridge: Harvard University Press, 2000.

Eck, Diana L. *A New Religious America: How a "Christian Country" Has Become the World's Most Religiously Diverse Nation.* New York: HarperSanFrancisco, 2001.

Ellenson, David H. "How to Draw Guidance from a Heritage: Jewish Approaches to Moral Choices." In *Contemporary Jewish Ethics and Morality: A Reader,* edited by Elliot N. Dorff and Louis E. Newman, 129–39. New York: Oxford University Press, 1995.

Elster, Nanette. "Who is the Parent in Cloning?" *Hofstra Law Review* 27:535 (Spring, 1999).

Emerson, Robert M., Rachel I. Fretz, and Linda L. Shaw. *Writing Ethnographic Fieldnotes.* Chicago: University of Chicago Press, 1995.

Emeneau, M. B. and B. A. van Nooten. "The Young Wife and her Husband's Brother: Ṛg Veda 10.40.2 and 10.85.44." *Journal of the American Oriental Society* 111:3 (1991): 481–94.

Englert, Y. "From Medically Assisted Procreation to Euthanasia: A Modern way to Deal with Ethical Dilemmas in Modern Medicine." *European Journal of Genetics in Society: An Ethical Approach to Genetics* 3 (1997): 22–26.

Ethics Committee of the American Fertility Society. "Ethical Considerations of The New Reproductive Technologies." *Fertility and Sterility* 53 (April–June, 1990), edited by Charlotte Scarader: 1S–109S.

Fadiman, Anne. *The Spirit Catches You and You Fall Down: A Hmong Child, Her American Doctors, and the Collision of Two Cultures.* New York: Farrar, Straus, and Giroux, 1997.

Farley, Margaret. "The Role of Experience in Moral Discernment." In *Christian Ethics: Problems and Prospects,* edited by Lias Sowle Cahill and James F. Childress, 134–51. Cleveland: Pilgrim Press, 1996.

Feldman, Emanuel and Joel B. Wolowelsky, eds. *Jewish Law and The New Reproductive Technologies.* Hoboken: KTAV Publishing House, 1997.

Fenwick, Lynda Beck. *Private Choices, Public Consequences: Reproductive Technology and the New Ethics of Conception, Pregnancy, and Family.* New York: Dutton, 1998.

Finke, Roger and Rodney Stark. *The Churching of America 1776–1990: Winners and Losers in Our Religious Economy.* New Brunswick: Rutgers University Press, 1992.

Fins, Joseph J. "Encountering Diversity: Medical Ethics and Pluralism." *Journal of Religion and Health* 33:1 (Spring 1994): 23–27.

Fitzgerald, James. "India's 5th Veda: The *Mahābhārata*'s Presentation of Itself." In *Essays on the Mahābhārata,* edited by Arvind Sharma, 150–70. Netherlands: E. J. Brill, 1991.

Fitzgerald, James L. "The Great Epic of India as Religious Rhetoric: A Fresh Look at the *Mahābhārata.*" *Journal of the American Academy of Religion* 51:4 (December 1983): 611–30.

Fongwa, Marie Ngetiko. "Advancing Healthcare Practices: Linking Quality with Culture." *Journal of Nursing Administration* 30:6 (June 2000): 291, 294.

Fox, Thomas C. *Sexuality and Catholicism.* New York: George Braziller, 1995.

Frankena, William K. *Ethics.* New Jersey: Prentice Hall, 1973.

Furth, Charlotte. *A Flourishing Yin: Gender in China's Medical History, 960–1665.* Berkeley: University of California Press, 1999.

Gandhi, M. K. *An Autobiography: Or the Story of My Experiments with Truth.* Translated by Mahadev Desai. Ahmedabad: Navajavan Publishing House, 1976.

Ganguli, Kisari Mohan, trans. *The Mahābhārata.* Vol. I–IV. New Delhi: Munshiram Manoharlal Publishers Pvt. Ltd., 1993.

Garcia, Sandra Anderson. "Sociocultural and Legal Implications of Creating and Sustaining Life Through Biomedical Technology." *Journal of Legal Medicine* 17:469 (December 1996).

Gbadegesin, Segun. "Bioethics and Cultural Diversity." In *A Companion to Bioethics,* edited by Helga Kuhse and Peter Singer, 24–31. Malden: Blackwell Publishers, 2001.

Gilligan, Carol. *In a Different Voice: Psychological Theory and Women's Development.* Cambridge: Harvard University Press, 1982.

Greer, Germaine. *Sex and Destiny: The Politics of Human Fertility.* New York: Harper & Row, 1984.

Griffith, Ralph T. H. *The Hymns of the Atharvaveda: Translated with Popular Commentary.* Vols. I & II. Varanais: The Chowkhamba Sanskrit Series Office, 1968.

Gunning, Jennifer and Veronica English. *Human In Vitro Fertilization: A Case Study in the Regulation of Medical Innovation.* Aldershot: Bartmouth, 1993.

Gupta, Jyotsna Agnthotri. "Women's Bodies: The Site for the Ongoing Conquest by Reproductive Technologies." *Issues in Reproductive and Genetic Engineering: Journal of International Feminist Analysis* 4:2 (1991): 93–107.

Gustafson, James M. "Styles of Religious Reflection in Medical Ethics." In *Religion and Medical Ethics: Looking Back, Looking Forward,* edited by Allen Verhey, 81–95. Grand Rapids: Eerdmans Publishing Company, 1996.

Gutmann, Amy, ed. *Multiculturalism.* Princeton: Princeton University Press, 1994.

Hale, Jerald V. "From Baby M to Jaycee B.: Fathers, Mothers, and Children in the Brave New World." *Journal of Contemporary Law and Family Studies* 24:335 (1998).

Harman, William. "Speaking About Hinduism and Speaking Against It." *Journal of the American Academy of Religion* 68:4 (December 2000): 733–40.

Harris, John and Soren Holm, eds. *The Future of Human Reproduction: Ethics, Choice, and Regulation.* Oxford: Clarendon Press, 1998.

Hartouni, Valerie. *Cultural Conceptions: On Reproductive Technologies and the Remaking of Life.* Minneapolis: University of Minnesota Press, 1997.

Hauerwas, Stanley. *A Community of Character: Toward a Constructive Christian Social Ethic.* Notre Dame: University of Notre Dame Press, 1981.

———. "How Christian Ethics Become Medical Ethics: The Case of Paul Ramsey." In *Religion and Medical Ethics: Looking Back, Looking Forward,* edited by Allen Verhey, 61–80. Grand Rapids: Eerdmans Publishing Company, 1996.

Hawley, John Stratton. "Who Speaks for Hinduism—and Who Against?" *Journal of the American Academy of Religion* 68:4 (December 2000): 711–720.

Hiltebeitel, Alf. *The Cult of Draupadi: Mythologies: From Gingee to Kuruksetra.* Chicago: University of Chicago Press, 1988.

———. *The Cult of Draupadi: On Hindu Ritual and the Goddess.* Chicago: University of Chicago Press, 1991.

———. *Rethinking India's Oral and Classical Epics: Draupadi among Rajputs, Muslims, and Dalits.* Chicago: University of Chicago Press, 1999.

Hindery, Roderick. *Comparative Ethics in Hindu and Buddhist Traditions.* Delhi: Motilal Banarisdass, 1978.

Hodge, James G. Jr. and Lawrence O. Gostin. "Legal Methods." In *Methods in Medical Ethics,* edited by Jeremy Sugarman and Daniel P. Sulmasy, 88–103. Washington: Georgetown University Press, 2001.

Holdrege, Barbara A. "Hindu Ethics." In *A Bibliographic Guide to the Comparative Study of Ethics,* edited by John Carman and Mark Juergensmeyer, 12–69. New York: Cambridge University Press, 1991.

Holland Suzanne, Karen Lebacqz, and Laurie Zoloth, eds. *The Human Embryonic Stem Cell Debate: Science, Ethics, and Public Policy.* Cambridge: MIT Press, 2001.

Holloway, Richard. *Godless Morality: Keeping Religion Out of Ethics.* Edinburgh: Canongate, 2000.

Hopkins, Thomas J. *The Religious Life of Man: The Hindu Religious Tradition.* Belmont: Wadsworth Publishing Company, 1971.

Howard, Cheryl. A., Sally Andrade, and Theresa Byrd. "The Ethical Dimensions of Cultural Competence in Border Health Care Settings." *Family and Community Health* 23:4 (January 2001): 36–49.

Hull, Richard T. *Ethical Issues in the New Reproductive Technologies.* Belmont: Wadsworth Publishing Company, 1990.

Hurwitz, Ilana. "Collaborative Reproduction: Finding the Child in the Maze of Legal Motherhood." *Connecticut Law Review* 33:127 (Fall 2000).

Irving, Dianne N. "Which Medical Ethics for the 21st Century?" http://www.lifeissues.net (28 May 2001).

Jaycee B., Petitioner, v. The Superior Court of Orange County. 42 cal. App. 4th 718, 1996. Cal. App. LEXIS 101.

Jhingran, Saral. *Aspects of Hindu Morality.* Delhi: Motilal Banarsidass Publishers, 1989.

Jones, Howard W. and Susan L. Crockin. "On Assisted Reproduction, Religion and Civil Law." *Fertility and Sterility* 73:3 (March 2000): 447–452.

Jonsen, Albert R. "American Moralism and the Origin of Bioethics in the United States." *Journal of Medicine and Philosophy* 17:3 (June 1992): 113–30.

———. "Casuistry." In *Methods in Medical Ethics,* edited by Jeremy Sugarman and Daniel P. Sulmasy, 104–25. Washington: Georgetown University Press, 2001.

Jonsen, Albert R. and Stephen Toulmin, *The Abuse of Casuistry: A History of Moral Reasoning.* Berkeley: University of California Press, 1988.

Joshi, M. C. *Hindu Religion and Ethics.* New Delhi: Aryan Books International, 1994.

Kakar, Sudhir. "Health and Medicine in the Living Traditions of Hinduism" In *Healing and Restoring: Health and Medicine in the World's Religious Traditions,* edited by Lawrence E. Sullivan, 111–26. New York: Macmillan Publishing Company, 1989.

Kane, Pandurang Vaman. *History of the Dharmasastra: Ancient and Mediaeval Religious and Civil Law.* Poona: Bhandarkar Oriental Research Institute, 1930.

Karambelkar, V. W. *The Atharva-Veda and Ayur-Veda.* Nagpur: Majestic Printing Press, 1961.

Katz, Ruth Cecily. *Arjuna in the Mahabharata: Where Krishna Is, There is Victory.* Columbia: University of South Carolina Press, 1989.

Kearney, Richard. *On Stories.* New York: Routledge, 2002.

Keyserlingk, Edward W. *Sanctity of Life or Quality of Life in the Context of Ethics, Medicine and Law.* Montreal: Law Reform Commission of Canada, 1979.

Kinsley, David R. *Hinduism: A Cultural Perspective.* Englewood Cliffs: Prentice Hall, 1993.

Kitagawa, Joseph Mitsuo. "Buddhist Medical History." In *Healing and Restoring: Health and Medicine in the World's Religious Traditions,* edited by Lawrence E. Sullivan, 9–32. New York: Macmillan Publishing Company, 1989.

Klaes, Norbert. *Conscience and Consciousness: Ethical Problems of Mahābhārata.* Bangalore: Dharmaram College, 1975.

Klostermaier, Klaus K. "The Life-Ethics of the Bhagavadgītā as Interpreted by Rāmānuja." In *Life Ethics in World Religions,* edited by Dawne C. McCance, 53–66. Atlanta: Scholars Press, 1998.

Klotzko, Arlene Judith. "Medical Miracle or Medical Mischief?" *Hastings Center Report* 28:3 (1998): 5–8.

Knipe, David M. "Hinduism and the Tradition of Ayurveda." In *Healing and Restoring: Health and Medicine in the World's Religious Traditions,* edited by Lawrence E. Sullivan, 89–110. New York: Macmillan Publishing Company, 1989.

Knoppers, Bartha M. and Sonia LeBris. "Recent Advances in Medically Assisted Conception: Legal, Ethical, and Social Issues." *American Journal of Law and Medicine* 17:329 (1991).

Kosmin, Barry A. and Seymour P. Lachman. *One Nation Under God: Religion in Contemporary American Society.* New York: Crown Trade Paperbacks, 1993.

Kuhse, Helga and Peter Singer. "What is Bioethics? A Historical Introduction." In *A Companion to Bioethics,* edited by Helga Kuhse and Peter Singer, 3–14. Malden: Blackwell Publishers, 2001.

Lammers, Stephen E. "The Marginalization of Religious Voices in Bioethics." In *Religion and Medical Ethics: Looking Back, Looking Forward,* edited by Allen Verhey, 19–43. Grand Rapids: Eerdmans Publishing Company, 1996.

Lee, Tao. "Medical Ethics in Ancient China." In *Cross Cultural Perspectives in Medical Ethics: Readings,* edited by Robert M. Veatch, 132–39. Boston: Jones and Bartlett Publishers, 1989.

Leonard, Barbara J. and Gregory A. Plotnikoff. "Awareness: The Heart of Cultural Competence." *American Association of Critical-Care Nurses* 11:1 (February 2000): 51–59.

Lingam, Lakshmi. "New Reproductive Technologies in India: A Print Media Analysis." *Issues in Reproductive and Genetic Engineering* 3:1 (1990): 13–21.

Lipner, Julius J. "The Classical Hindu View on Abortion and the Moral Status of the Unborn." In *Hindu Ethics: Purity, Abortion, and Euthanasia,* edited by Harold G. Coward, Julius J. Lipner, and Katherine K. Young, 41–70. New York: State University of New York Press, 1989.

———. "A Hindu View of Life." In *The Meaning of Life in the World Religions,* edited by Joseph Runzo and Nancy M. Martin, 111–35. Oxford: Oneworld Publications, 2000.

Locsin, Rozzano C. "Building Bridges: Affirming Culture in Health and Nursing." *Holistic Nursing Practice* 15:1 (October 2000): 1–4.

Long, Bruce J. "The Concepts of Human Action and Rebirth in the *Mahābhārata.*" In *Karma and Rebirth in Classical Indian Traditions,* edited by Wendy Doniger O'Flaherty, 38–60. Berkeley: University of California Press, 1980.

MacIntyre, Alasdair. *After Virtue.* Notre Dame: University of Notre Dame Press, 1984.

Mahoney, John. *The Making of Moral Theology: A Study of the Roman Catholic Tradition.* New York: Oxford University Press, 1987.

Malpani, A. and A. Malpani. "Simplifying Assisted Conception Techniques to Make them Universally Available—A View from India." *Human Reproduction* 7:1 (1992): 49–50.

Manickavle, V. "The Role of A Hindu Cultural Determinism in the Execution of Autonomy in the Modern Health Care System in Nepal." *Eubios Journal of Asian and International Bioethics* 10 (2000): 51–53.

Mappes, Thomas A. and David DeGrazia. *Biomedical Ethics.* 5th ed. New York: McGraw Hill, 2001.

Marriage of John A. and Luanne Buzzanca. 61 Cal. App. 4th 1410; 1998 Cal. App. LEXIS 180.

Marriott, McKim. "Constructing an Indian Ethnosociology." In *India Through Hindu Categories,* edited by McKim Marriott, 1–39. New Delhi: SAGE Publications, 1990.

Marriott, Mckim and Ronald B. Iden. "Caste Systems." *Encyclopaedia Britannica.* 15th ed. (1981), Macropaedia, Vol. 3, 982–91.

Marty, Marty E. "Religion, Theology, Church and Bioethics." *Journal of Medicine and Philosophy* 17:3 (June 1992): 273–89.

Matilal, Bimal Krishna. *Moral Dilemmas in the Mahabharata.* New Delhi: Shri Jainendra Press, 1989.

McCollum, Monica J. "Spirited Controversy." *Hospitals & Health Networks* 72:12 (20 June 1998): 56.

McDermott, Rachel Fell. "New Age Hinduism, New Age Orientalism, and the Second-Generation South Asian." *Journal of the American Academy of Religion* 68:4 (December 2000): 721–31.

McFague, Sallie. "New House Rules: Christianity, Economics and Planetary Living." *Daedalus* 130:4 (Fall 2001): 125–40.

Mellema, R. L. *Wayang Puppets: Carving, Colouring and Symbolism.* Amsterdam: Koninklijk Instituut voor de Tropen, 1954.

Miller, Barbara Stoler. "Karṇabhāra: The Trial of Karṇa." In *Essays on the Mahābhārata,* edited by Arvind Sharma, 57–67. Netherlands: E. J. Brill, 1991.

Monier-Williams, Sir Monier. *Indian Wisdom: or, Examples of the Religious, Philosophical, and Ethical Doctrines of the Hindus.* London: Luzac & Co., 1893.

———. *Sanskrit-English Dictionary.* New York: Oxford University Press, 1995.

Munson, Ronald. "Artificial Insemination: Who's Responsible?" In *Sex/Machine: Readings in Culture, Gender, and Technology,* edited by Patrick D. Hopkins, 107–15. Bloomington: Indiana University Press, 1998.

Murthy, B. Srinivasa. *The Bhagavad Gītā.* Long Beach: Long Beach Publications, 1998.

Murthy, K. R. Srikanta. "Professional Ethics in Ancient Indian Medicine." In *Cross Cultural Perspectives in Medical Ethics: Readings,* edited by Robert M. Veatch, 126–32. Boston: Jones and Bartlett Publishers, 1989.

Myser, Catherine. "How Bioethics is Being Taught: A Critical Review." In *A Companion to Bioethics,* edited by Helga Kuhse and Peter Singer, 485–500. Malden: Blackwell Publishers, 2001.

Narayanan, Vasudha. "Diglossic Hinduism: Liberation and Lentils." *Journal of the American Academy of Religion* 68:4 (December 2000): 761–79.

———. "Hindu Ethics and Dharma." In *Ethics in the World Religions,* edited by Joseph Runzo and Nancy M. Martin, 177–95. Oxford: Oneworld Publications, 2001.

New Oxford Annotated Bible. New Revised Standard Version. New York: Oxford University Press, 1991.

New York State Task Force on Life and the Law. *Assisted Reproductive Technologies: Analysis and Recommendations for Public Policy.* New York: New York State Task Force on Life and the Law, 1998.

Noonan, John T. "The Catholic Church and Abortion." *The Dublin Review* 514 (Winter 1967/68): 300–45.

Nott, S. C., ed. *Mahabharata of Vyasa Krishna Dwaipayana: Selections from the Adi Parva and the Sambha Parva.* New York: Philosophical Library, 1956.

Numbers, Ronald L. and Darrel W. Amundsen, eds. *Caring and Curing: Health and Medicine in the Western Religious Traditions.* New York: Macmillan Publishing Company, 1986.

O'Connor, Garry. *The Mahabharata: Peter Brook's Epic in the Making.* London: Hodder & Stoughton, 1988.

Olivelle, Patrick. *Upaniṣads.* New York: Oxford University Press, 1996.

Overall, Christine. "New Reproductive Technology: Some Implications for the Abortion Issue." In *Sex/Machine: Readings in Culture, Gender, and Technology,* edited by Patrick D. Hopkins, 201–14. Bloomington: Indiana University Press, 1998.

Perrett, Roy W. *Hindu Ethics: A Philosophical Study.* Honolulu: University of Hawaii Press, 1998.

Pitt, Jonathan B. "Fragmenting Procreation." *Yale Law Journal* 108:1893 (May, 1999).

Pope John Paul II. *The Gospel of Life: Evangelium Vitae.* New York: Random House, 1995.

Pope Paul VI. *Humanae Vitae.* San Francisco: Ignatius Press, 1978.

Pressfield, Steven. *The Legend of Bagger Vance: A Novel of Golf and the Game of Life.* New York: Avon Books, 1995.

Radhakrishnan. *The Hindu View of Life.* New Delhi: Indus, 1993.

Rajagopalachari, C. *Mahabharata.* Bombay: Bharatiya Vidya Bhavan, 1996.

Ramanujan, A. K. "Is there an Indian Way of Thinking?" In *India Through Hindu Categories,* edited by McKim Marriott, 41–58. New Delhi: SAGE Publications, 1990.

Reich, Warren Thomas, ed. "Reproductive Technologies." *Encyclopedia of Bioethics.* New York: Macmillan Publishing Company, 1995.

———. "A New Era for Bioethics: The Search for Meaning in Moral Experience." In *Religion and Medical Ethics: Looking Back, Looking Forward,* edited by Allen Verhey, 96–119. Grand Rapids: Eerdmans Publishing Company, 1996.

Ricoeur, Paul. *The Symbolism of Evil.* New York: Beacon, 1967.

———. *Figuring the Sacred: Religion, Narrative, and Imagination.* Minneapolis: Augsburg Fortress, 1995.

Rosen, Steven J. *Gita on the Green: The Mystical Tradition Behind Bagger Vance.* New York: Continuum, 2000.

Salimbene, Suzanne. "Cultural Competence: A Priority for Performance Improvement Action." *Journal of Nursing Care Quality* 13:3 (February 1999): 23–25.

Sarma, Deepak. "Let the Apta (Trustworthy) Hindu Speak!" *Journal of the American Academy of Religion* 68:4 (December 2000): 781–90.

Seeger, Elizabeth. *The Five Brothers: The Story of the Mahābhārata.* New York: The John Day Company, 1948.

Shah, Shalini. *The Making of Womanhood: Gender Relations in the Mahābhārata.* New Delhi: Manohar Publishers, 1995.

Shanner, Laura and Jeffery Nisker. "Bioethics for Clinicians: 26. Assisted Reproductive Technologies." *Canadian Medical Association Journal* 164:11 (29 May 2001), 1589–94.

Shannon, Thomas A. *An Introduction to Bioethics.* 3rd ed., revised and updated. New York: Paulist Press, 1997.

Sharma, Arvind. "The Puruṣārthas: An Axiological Exploration of Hinduism." *Journal of Religious Ethics* 27:2 (Summer 1999): 223–56.

———. "Who Speaks for Hinduism? A Perspective from Advaita Vedānta." *Journal of the American Academy of Religion* 68:4 (December 2000): 751–60.

———. "When it Comes to Karma." In *Ethical Issues in Human Cloning: Cross-Disciplinary Perspectives,* edited by Michael C. Brannigan, 98–99. New York: Seven Bridges Press, 2001.

———. "On Hindu, Hindustān, Hinduism and Hindutva." *NVMEN* 49:1 (2002): 1–36.

———, ed. *Essays on the Mahābhārata.* Netherlands: E. J. Brill, 1991.

Sharma, Ram Karan and Vaidya Bhagwan Dash. *Agnivesa's Caraka-Saṃhitā.* Vol. XCIV. Varanasi: The Chowkhamba, Sanskrit Series, 1976.

Shenfield, F. "Current Ethical Dilemmas in Assisted Reproduction." *International Journal of Andrology* 20: Suppl. 3 (1997): 74–78.

Sherwin, Byron L. "The Golem, Zevi Ashkenazi, and Reproductive Biotechnology." *Judaism* 44 (Summer 1995): 314–22.

Singer, Peter. "Medical Ethics." *British Medical Journal* 321:7256 (29 July 2000): 282–85.

Singh, Balbir. *Hindu Ethics: An Exposition of the Concept of Good.* Atlantic Highlands: Humanities Press, 1984.

Smith, Brian K. "Who Does, Can, and Should Speak for Hinduism?" *Journal of the American Academy of Religion* 68:4 (December 2000): 741–49.

Smith, David H. "Religion and the Roots of the Bioethics Revival." In *Religion and Medical Ethics: Looking Back, Looking Forward,* edited by Allen Verhey, 9–18. Grand Rapids: Eerdmans Publishing Company, 1996.

Smith, Mary Carroll. "Epic Parthenogenesis." In *Essays on the Mahābhārata,* edited by Arvind Sharma, 84–100. New York: E. J. Brill, 1991.

Smith, Wilfred Cantewll. *The Meaning and End of Religion.* New York: Harper & Row Publishers, 1978.

Srikanta Murthy, K. R. "Professional Ethics in Ancient Indian Medicine." In *Cross Cultural Perspectives in Medical Ethics,* edited by R. M. Veatch, 126–30. Boston: Jones and Bartlett Publishers, 1989.

Stoler Miller, Barbara. "The *Mahābhārata* as Theatre." In *Approaches to the Asian Classics,* edited by Wm. Theodore de Bary and Irene Bloom, 136–46. New York: Columbia University Press, 1990.

Stout, Jeffrey. *Ethics After Babel: The Languages of Morals and Their Discontents.* Boston: Beacon Press, 1988.

Strong, Carson. *Ethics in Reproductive and Perinatal Medicine: A New Framework.* New Haven: Yale University Press, 1997.

Sukthankar, Vishnu S. *The Adiparvan: Being the First Book of the Mahābhārata the Great Epic of India.* Poona: Bhandarkar Oriental Research Institute, 1933.

Sullivan, Bruce M. "The Religious Authority of the Mahabharata: Vyasa and Brahma in the Hindu Scriptural Tradition." *Journal of the American Academy of Religion* 62:2 (Summer 1994): 377–402.

Sulmasy, Daniel P. "Reading the Medical Ethics Lit: A Discourse on Method." In *Methods in Medical Ethics,* edited by Jeremy Sugarman and Daniel P. Sulmasy, 286–97. Washington: Georgetown University Press, 2001.

Sulmasy, Daniel P. and Jeremy Sugarman. "The Many Methods in Medical Ethics (Or, Thirteen Ways of Looking at a Blackbird)." In *Methods in Medical Ethics,* edited by Jeremy Sugarman and Daniel P. Sulmasy, 3–18. Washington D.C.: Georgetown University Press, 2001.

Sumner, L. W. and Joseph Boyle. *Philosophical Perspectives on Bioethics.* Toronto: University of Toronto Press, 1996.

Sutherland, Gail Hinich. "*Bsja* (Seed) and *Kṣetra* (Field): Male Surrogacy or Niyoga in the *Mahābhārata.*" *Contributions to Indian Sociology* (n.s.) 24:1 (1990): 77–103.

Sutton, Nicholas. *Religious Doctrines in the Mahābhārata.* Delhi: Motilal Banarsidass Publishers, 2000.

Tanne, Janice Hopkins. US Hospital Mergers Threaten Reproductive Services." *British Medical Journal* 315:7119 (22 November 1997): 1330.

Tendler, Moshe D. "Contraception and Abortion." In *Medicine and Jewish Law,* edited by Fred Rosner, 105–22. New Jersey: Jason Aronson, 1990.

Thatamanil, John J. "Managing Multiple Religoius and Scholarly Identities: An Argument for a Theological Study of Hinduism." *Journal of the American Academy of Religion* 68:4 (December 2000): 791–803.

Tiwari, Kedar Nath. *Classical Indian Ethical Thought: A Philosophical Study of Hindu, Jaina and Bauddha Morals.* Delhi: Motilal Banarsidass Publishers, 1998.

Tizzard, Juliet. "Reproductive Technology: New Ethical Dilemmas and Old Moral Prejudices." In *Abortion Law and Politics Today,* edited by Ellie Lee, 184–97. New York: St. Martin's Press, 1998.

Tubb, Gary A. "Santarasa in the *Mahābhārata.*" In *Essays on the Mahābhārata,* edited by Arvind Sharma, 171–203. Netherlands: E. J. Brill, 1991.

Turner, Leigh. "Medical Ethics in a Multicultural Society." *Journal of the Royal Society of Medicine* 94(11) (November 2001); 592–94.

van Buitenen, J. A. *The Mahābhārata: I. The Book of the Beginning.* Chicago: University of Chicago, 1973.

———. *The Bhagavadgītā in the Mahābhārata.* Chicago: University of Chicago Press, 1981.

Verhey, Allen. "Introduction." In *Religion and Medical Ethics: Looking Back, Looking Forward,* edited by Allen Verhey, 1–8. Grand Rapids: Eerdmans Publishing Company, 1996.

Vorzimer, Andrew W., Milena D. O'Hara, and Lori D. Shafton. "Buzzanca v. Buzzanca: The Ruling and Ramifications." *Journal of Assisted Reproductive Law.* 2:1 http://www.vgme.com/new2.htm (10 April 2002).

Wach, Joachim. *The Comparative Study of Religions.* New York: Columbia University Press, 1958.

Warner, R. Stephen and Judith G. Wittner. *Gatherings in Diaspora: Religious Communities and the New Immigration.* Philadelphia: Temple University Press, 1998.

Wind, James P. "What Can Religion Offer Bioethics." *Hastings Center Report* 20:4 (July/August 1990): 18–20.

Wolf, Susan M. *Feminism & Bioethics: Beyond Reproduction.* New York: Oxford University Press, 1996.

Wolfe, Regina Wentzel and Christine E. Gudorf, eds. *Ethics & World Religions: Cross-Cultural Case Studies.* Maryknoll: Orbis Books, 1999.

Woods, Julian F. *Destiny and Human Initiative in the Mahābhārata.* New York: State University of New York Press, 2001.

———. "The Doctrine of Karma in the Bhagavadgītā." *Journal of Studies in the Bhagavadgītā* 8–9 (1988–1989): 47–81.

Yashapal. "Surgery and Medicine in the Days of Gautama." *Indian Historical Quarterly* 25 (1949): 102–109.

Young, Katherine K. "Hindu Bioethics." In *Religious Methods and Resources in Bioethics,* edited by Paul F. Camenisch, 3–30. Boston: Kluwer Academic Publisher, 1994.

Zysk, Kenneth G. *Medicine in the Veda: Religious Healing in the Veda.* Delhi: Montilal Banarsidass Publishers, 1998.

Index